Consuming Fears

CONSUMING
FEARS

THE POLITICS OF
PRODUCT RISKS

Harvey M. Sapolsky

EDITOR

Basic Books, Inc., Publishers   New York

Library of Congress Cataloging-in-Publication Data

Consuming fears.

Includes bibliographical references and index.
Contents: Introduction/Harvey M. Sapolsky—
The changing politics of cigarette smoking/ Harvey M.
Sapolsky—Hearts and minds/ Janet M. Levine—[etc.]
1. Product safety.   2. Products liability.
I. Sapolsky, Harvey M.
TS175.C66   1986   363.1'9   86–47503
ISBN   0–465–01411–9

4/87

CONTENTS

CONTRIBUTORS

LINDA C. CUMMINGS, Ph.D., is Program Manager at the Massachusetts Department of Commerce and Economic Development, Boston, Massachusetts.

JANET M. LEVINE, Ph.D., is an Assistant Professor of Political Science at the College of the Holy Cross, Worcester, Massachusetts.

HARVEY M. SAPOLSKY, Ph.D., is Professor of Public Policy and Organization at Massachusetts Institute of Technology, Cambridge, Massachusetts.

MARK J. SEGAL, Ph.D., is Director of the Department of Health Care Financing, American Medical Association, Chicago, Illinois.

SANFORD L. WEINER is a Reasearch Associate at Whitaker College, Massachusetts Institute of Technology, Cambridge, Massachusetts.

PREFACE

The idea for this book originated because of my growing awareness over the last few years that much of my life was being governed by product fears. I had given up eggs and the salt shaker. I was not permitted to smoke my pipe on airplanes or in the presence of certain of my friends. And I worried but knew not what to do about the asbestos in my office ceiling and furnace room at home. Surely, there was a book in all of this.

An autobiography would not do; my experience, though no doubt fascinating, was really not unique. Some friends would not drink cola beverages for fear of caffeine. Others were haunted by the dangers of food additives and "other chemicals." Moreover, I had a group of doctoral students to tend to, all eager for dissertation topics. A while back I had prepared a paper on the politics of cigarette-smoking control for a conference on the role of science in decision making, and had been struck by how much cigarette smoking persisted despite scientific condemnation. A comparative study of product risk controversies that would analyze their dynamics seemed intriguing. Perhaps, if more were known about the growth and interaction of product fears, there would be a better understanding of the confusion that appears to exist about what is truly dangerous and what is not.

A sponsor was at hand. Officials at Philip Morris Companies Inc. had heard about my cigarette study and were curious as to whether I wished to pursue the subject. I proposed that the firm support the comparative study. Obviously Philip Morris, as a leading producer of cigarettes, beer, and packaged foods, could not be considered a disinterested observer of product risk controversies, but I thought it would be possible to arrange an independent project through the Massachusetts Institute of Technology. So it was, thanks especially to Clifford Goldsmith and James Bowling of Philip Morris, and Samuel Goldblith of MIT. Philip Morris has provided a grant to MIT for the study, but has not had nor sought a role in the conduct, management, or publication of the study. I am grateful for the opportunity this financial assistance has given the graduate students and me to do the independent research that we envisioned.

The relationship with Philip Morris will surely disturb some. There are those who assume that manipulation is likely when corporations are involved in sponsoring research potentially affecting their business interests. Protestations of one's integrity cannot be expected to convince those skeptical of it. Instead, I invite all to search for bias in this volume.

The graduate students selected their own topics and, sometimes to my consternation, set their own pace. Our practice was to assemble the case studies independently and to meet at regular intervals to compare experiences. Occasionally, we invited guests to our informal seminar who would describe other cases or critique our evolving synthesis. For their assistance and that of the many individuals interviewed for the case studies, I am most appreciative.

In the end, though, it is the editor who bears responsibility for the final product. I took the task of seeking to identify and express the central themes. My interpretations ran the gauntlet of the seminar several times. Each of the participants helped shape the final result at those sessions and in comments on the drafts. But none will want to have my views taken totally for his or hers. Their cases deserve separate attention just as their full dissertations deserve independent publication.

I am concerned about the societal distortions revealed in the comparison. The competition for attention and resources among government agencies, public interest groups, business firms, and other organizations observed in our cases often leads to misrepresentation of product risks. The inevitable outcome is that some people say everything kills so nothing is especially important, while others fear the least dangerous more than the most dangerous. Too often we either dismiss risks or are prisoners of them.

It does not seem possible to devise a policy to correct this. Competition makes too great a contribution to our economy and polity to wish to tame organizational rivalry in favor of better risk management. Each of us either gains insight into the behavior of organizations or lives in ignorance. The cynics are probably the least frustrated, for they never expected public problems to be solved in ways that satisfy the common good. Those who have other expectations expose themselves to greater hazards than that threatened by even the most hazardous product.

This work would not have been possible without the assistance of two very special friends. William Ruder, a former Assistant Secretary of Commerce, is a public affairs counselor to many senior corporate executives who value his calm, clear thinking about the way the world works. I met him while tracking one controversy and found that he was informed about them all. Our small band benefited greatly from his encouragement. In contrast, Judith Spitzer never offered encouragement. As master of the word processor, she continually pointed out the embarrassing gaps in our knowledge of grammar and our failure to keep the project on schedule. Worse still, she positively flourished while consuming the products we studied.

HARVEY M. SAPOLSKY
Belmont, Massachusetts

Consuming Fears

Chapter 1

Introduction

HARVEY M. SAPOLSKY

Americans live in fear. Our economy is in jeopardy, our nights are given over to criminals, our armed forces are ever on alert—even our consumer products can no longer be trusted. Every day, it seems, we learn that another food or common convenience has turned against us, having been identified as a health risk. The Tylenol madness aside, there is hardly an item on the supermarket shelf that is not thought to pose a danger of some sort.

The dangers are not trivial. Frequently used products have been linked to a multitude of diseases that kill or disable. Coffee may cause pancreatic cancer, eggs atherosclerosis, and aluminum pots Alzheimer's disease. Peanut-based products can contain aflatoxin, a powerful carcinogen; some hair dryers may release asbestos fibers that, if inhaled, can produce asbestosis, a deadly lung ailment. This morning's corn flakes may contain hazardous amounts of the pesticide EDB. Tonight's aspirin promises relief, but also the possibility of an ulcer in the not-too-distant future. We are told that our life chances depend upon how wisely we choose among the array of goods available to us. We are, it is said, the victims of what we eat, drink, and breathe, as well as of our genes.

The problem, though, is to choose wisely, because the risks for most product groups are not well defined. Simply because animals fed a steady diet of peanut butter or Red Dye no. 3 (with or without the cherries) may be found to develop tumors does not mean that humans who include those items in their diets will necessarily develop tumors. Nor does an epidemiological finding that those who take just a nip or two of schnapps each day seem immune from early heart attacks offer much comfort because there may be some confounding factor such as dietary habits or level of exercise that was unexplored in the study, but that actually provides the immunity. In most instances where products are challenged, there are counterstudies that appear to exonerate them. The debate over the validity of the various studies is usually intense and, more than occasionally, confusing.

If life is hazardous for consumers, it is hazardous for at least some producers as well. Successful products, thought to be safe as well as profitable, can suddenly stand accused of causing disease. Rarely is the link to ill health unambiguously established. Manufacturers must then decide whether to defend or abandon the tainted, but perhaps guiltless product. The special skills of advertising agencies, liability lawyers, and Washington lobbyists can, for a price, be quickly organized to defend the manufacturer's interest, but there is no guarantee that they can restore confidence in a product's safety once it is questioned. Like consumers, manufacturers must choose among risks.[1]

Finding a Perspective

The continuing cascade of consumer product controversies—by our count at least a dozen new ones are begun each year—has generated much interest and some analysis. The serious research seems to be divided into two categories: reports that analyze risk from the perspective of the individual, and reports that take a societal perspective. Neither approach quite satisfies.

Studies of individual perceptions of product risks attempt to understand why consumers fear some risks more than others.[2] Much attention is directed toward identifying the specific factors that influence the fears consumers hold. Is the risk exposure assumed voluntarily? Is the exposure thought to be controllable? Are the consequences of exposure especially dreaded? How certain are the consequences? Questionnaires allow risk perceptions to be measured and compared along these and similar dimensions. Judging by their survey reponses, people apparently have less fear of hurtling down a mountain with their feet attached to two thin boards than they have of drinking their favorite beverage, which may be laced with an additive that has some unknown potential for causing cancer in twenty or thirty years. But it is unclear how much these stated perceptions of risk actually affect behavior. Would any skier really cringe at the prospect of a beer or a soft drink in the lodge after a run? Or has it become socially expected to *express* fear of some risks, but not others? Studies of risk perceptions do not reveal very much about the mobilization against certain products by abstainers. What factors sustain the concern about products when the supposed risks are assumed voluntarily and thus can be controlled by the individual consumer?

The second category of product risk studies takes a societal perspective. Such studies concentrate on improving the *management* of risk by society.[3] Various approaches for identifying and ranking the risks of common products and activities have been proposed. Alternative schemes for regulating risks have been devised. These are essentially efforts to rationalize the often confusing and conflicting processes by which society currently deals with common risks so as to calm public fears. The problem with this approach is that the concern for risk may not be easily assuaged. What set of governmental actions can fulfill the quest for immortality or assure a risk-free society? Is it not possible that the more attention paid to risks, the more fears of exposure are increased? Certainly improvements in safety, even if achievable, provide no guarantee that consumers will feel more comfortable with the remaining risks.

The crucial limitation in both perspectives is that they ignore the fact that our political and economic lives are shaped by organizations. It is not society that regulates risks, but rather specific government agencies, each with its own legislative history, ambitions, and guiding professional values. It is not the consumer who identifies the existence of risk, but rather the news media, public interest groups, businesses, and scientific organizations—all subject to the pressures exerted by rivals and their own desire for perpetuation. Although society and individuals suffer the consequences of exposure to product risks, the risks themselves are certified, evaluated, heralded, and prescribed for by organizations whose vision is always less than that of society, and whose interests are different from those represented by the aggregate of their members' interests.

An important exception to the general failure to consider the organizational perspective on risk is Mary Douglas and Aaron Wildavsky's *Risk and Culture*, an analysis of the concern over environmental hazards.[4] Douglas and Wildavsky describe the development of a sectarian culture in America that is extremely hostile to industry, especially large corporations. Through a network of activist organizations, the members of this culture protest the existence of environmental hazards in order to undermine the political and economic power of industry. The hazards that they choose to protest are those that most implicate large corporations. Convinced of the moral purity of their cause, the leadership of these activist organizations invariably describe the environmental dangers in apolitic terms: The world as we know it will end unless this risk is eliminated. No doubt Douglas and Wildavsky would argue that this culture is at the core of the controversies that we examine here, and that product risks are merely an extension of the pollution risks challenged by this anti-industry movement.

Such a conspiratorial perspective, even one that recognizes the role organizations play in the development of product fears, gives one pause. To begin with, there is a danger of focusing too much on the strange and wonderful beliefs of a minority while ignoring the beliefs of the majority. We are, after all, interested in explaining why most Americans fear their consumer products, not why some have real or imagined grievances against particular products or producers.

The fluoridation controversy, in which many communities voted to reject the addition of fluoride compounds to the public water supply to reduce dental caries, provides an example of this problem.[5] The most frequently offered explanation for the rejection of this public health initiative was that voters, in turning down fluoridation, were expressing their alienation from big government and the mass society of post–World War II America. Because all social science commentators thought fluoridation was a rational policy, there was a need to explain its consistent rejection by the voters, and alienation is the standard sociological explanation for irrational social behavior. To be sure, alienation was obvious in the views of those who led campaigns against fluoridation. (Recall General Jack D. Ripper's concern for fluoridation's effects on his "bodily fluids" in the movie *Dr. Strangelove.*) But when the campaigns themselves are examined, one is struck by the contradictory evidence about the health consequences of fluoridation presented to the voters by those with apparently appropriate and valid scientific credentials who were marshaled on both sides of the dispute. Although most physicians and dentists supported fluoridation, in nearly every local referendum there were some who did not. Several government agencies, including the National Institutes of Health and the National Science Foundation, publicly endorsed the safety of fluoridation, but the National Nutrition Foundation, a private organization with an official-sounding name, was prominent in the fight against its adoption. Instead of being alienated, most voters were likely confused by the campaign and chose the safest course by rejecting fluoridation. The alienation of the antifluoridation leaders was largely irrelevant to the outcome.

The standard explanation also tends to ignore the counterstrategies of those the activists attack. In the fluoridation controversy, public health officials refused to debate the antifluoridationists as a matter of policy, not wishing to legitimize their opponents' standing as experts by appearing on the same public platforms. In their view, the antifluoridationists were no more than scientific quacks, unworthy of direct answer. But because voters are conditioned to expect representation by both sides in a referendum, and grow suspicious of attempts to suppress such representation, the strategy of the public health officials was self-defeating.

We share Douglas and Wildavsky's belief in the importance of examining the organizational dimension of risk controversies, but we disagree with their conclusion in *Risk and Culture* that one type of organizational culture determines the course of these controversies. It seems to us that it is the interaction of organizations that makes politics. It is the effect of this interaction in a particular set of controversies that we seek to describe.

Product risk controversies, we believe, are materially shaped by the maintenance needs of organizations, not all of which have a direct financial or policy interest in the outcomes of these controversies. No matter what their stated purpose is, organizations seek to survive and prosper. Product risks represent opportunities to some organizations and threats to others, independent of the effects on human health. The ways government agencies, professional associations, business firms, and other organizations involved in product risk controversies react to these opportunities and threats determine the dynamics of the controversies. In turn, the dynamics of these controversies significantly affect the public's understanding of health risks, an understanding that is unburdened by much independent factual knowledge.[6]

Our book will not tell anyone which risks to accept and which to avoid. We claim no special medical or technical expertise. No doubt we are as squeamish about what we consume as are the rest of today's Americans. Our intent is to explain the origins and development of product risk controversies, identify their common features, and provide a perspective on the processes by which product fears have become so much a part of our lives. Given the near panic that greets the discovery of each new risk, some solace is needed, if only that of understanding the causes of our national predicament.

Background Factors

The temptation in studying societal concerns is to search for a precipitating event, an incident that can be credited with giving rise to a set of public attitudes that become self-perpetuating. One might cite the 1953 report by

Memorial Sloan-Kettering Cancer Center investigators linking cigarette tars to cancer or the 1954 popularization of this work and some related epidemiological studies in *Reader's Digest*, the nation's best-selling magazine.[7] There is no doubt that these events profoundly affected the public's perceptions of the risks of smoking cigarettes, one of the most commonly used consumer products. Yet, it is also true that reports linking cigarettes to disease, including cancer, appeared not infrequently during the preceding half-century.[8] Apparently, the social environment has much to do with the degree of attention paid to events. We have identified four background factors that appear to have facilitated the growing public concern about the health risks of consumer products. They are (1) a change in the leading causes of death; (2) improvements in scientific methodologies; (3) an increase in the level of national affluence; and (4) a change in the population of national organizations.

HEART DISEASE, CANCER, AND LITTLE ELSE

Vital statistics make heartening reading. In 1900 the average life expectancy for Americans was 47.3 years. By 1950 the average had improved to 68.2 years; today it is 74.7, giving promise of several years of retirement for most. We now live longer, healthier lives than did our forebears.[9]

Significant improvements in life expectancy have come about in two major waves, one at the beginning of the twentieth century and another more recently. During the initial decades of the century, we learned to cope with at least some of the ills accompanying industrialization and urbanization. In 1900 the leading causes of death in the United States were infectious diseases, specifically influenza, pneumonia, and tuberculosis, which continuously culled the population and which thrived in the crowded conditions of factories and cities.[10] Due primarily to improvements in public sanitation, but also to the development of effective therapies, the infectious diseases were gradually brought under control, although not quite eliminated. By the 1930s heart disease, stroke, and cancer had replaced infectious diseases as the leading causes of death. (See figure 1.1) For males the risk of dying of heart disease nearly tripled and for females it doubled between 1920, when the rate began to accelerate significantly, and 1950, when it peaked. Worse yet, there was a parallel increase in cancer deaths, especially lung cancer, whose rate more than quadrupled.

Taken together, cardiovascular disease and cancer came to account for well over half of the nation's deaths. Not surprisingly, when the significance of the increase in chronic disease was recognized, health officials thought that they faced a problem of epidemic proportions. By the late

FIGURE 1.1

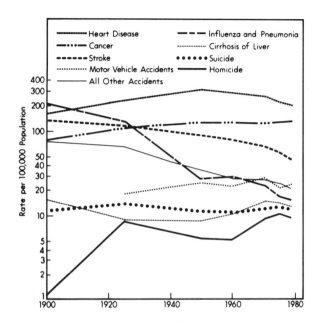

Trends in Age-Adjusted Death Rates from Selected Causes: Selected Years, 1900–78

NOTE: The selected years are 1900, 1925, 1950, 1960, 1970, 1975, and 1978. SOURCES: Department of Health and Human Services, *Healthy People: The Surgeon General's Report on Health Promotion and Disease Prevention,* 1979; National Center for Health Statistics, *Special Report on Diabetes,* vol. 43, no. 12, 1956; National Center for Health Statistics, *Vital Statistics Special Report,* vol. 43, no. 3, 1956.

1940s the puzzle over the cause of heart and cancer deaths was at the top of the scientific agenda.

Various explanations were proposed, most centering on dietary and behavioral factors. The twentieth century brought improvements in sanitation and medicine, but it also brought alterations in diet, and processed foods and additives, with unknown consequences. Per capita income and quality of housing increased, but so did the prevalence of smoking and the exposure to agricultural and industrial chemicals. The suspicion was that hidden in the good news was the bad.

Important new gains in longevity for Americans began in the 1950s. Recent improvements in health status have been across a broad front. We have been getting healthier and healthier. Infant and maternal death rates have declined. So have accidental deaths, including the most common form of all, those related to motor vehicles. Even some types of cancers have decreased—stomach and liver, for example. But given its importance in the overall death rates, the more than 20 percent reduction in cardiovascular deaths over the last two decades is most significant.

The fact that heart disease and stroke are declining gives little comfort to the many who are still prematurely stricken. The questions for science then become: What has caused the unexpected and continuing decline in cardiovascular deaths? and how can it be encouraged? Some investigators believe the decline is due to the adoption of preventive measures such as changes in diet, increased exercise, and quitting cigarette smoking. Others attribute the decrease to improvements in medical and surgical therapies. Still others argue that control of hypertension is the cause. Unresolved, the debate draws increased attention.[11]

The quest to understand cancer is at least as intense as that for cardio-vascular disease. Here too the speculation about links to diet and behavior remains strong.[12] The identification of potentially hazardous products raises doubts about the safety of other man-made products. Once human beings ignorantly caused death with dirty water and hands. The fear is that humans are at fault again.

ONE IN A BILLION

Somewhere amidst the hundreds of thousands of deaths occurring each year lies the answer to the real causes of changing death rates. Different scientific disciplines approach the same problem differently. Epidemiology seeks insights from the experience of large populations. Pathology looks at the results in individual cases. Biology uses experiments to understand fundamental processes within living systems. But all depend on precise measurement.

Precision is hardest for the epidemiologists because they must often recreate human experience through fragmented records or faulty memories. Vital statistics are maintained in different ways in different jurisdictions—variations in definitions and completeness occur frequently. When public surveys are undertaken, it is discovered that people have difficulty in recalling accurately products and quantities consumed. But public health record systems have improved gradually with the recognition that medical histories might hold clues as to the causes of diseases. Moreover, epidemiologists have become skilled at utilizing established institutions to enhance the completeness and reliability of their data. For example, leading postwar epidemiological studies that linked cigarette smoking to lung cancer were ingenious in their use of available resources. E. C. Hammond mobilized the volunteer network of the American Cancer Society to collect his data; Richard Doll decided to study British physicians because of the likelihood that they would be cooperative and responsible respondents.[13]

The improvement in experimental techniques is even more impressive. Increased support for research has permitted the development and maintenance of large colonies of specially bred animals for laboratory experiments. Data processing advances allow easy manipulation of vast quantities of research information. And progress in the technology of scientific instrumentation has made routine the identification of one part per billion in chemical analyses—the equivalent of measuring one second in a period of thirty-three years.[14] All this has meant that during the years since World War II there has been a substantial increase in the capability of science to ferret out health risks, the small as well as the large.

Advances in detection capabilities help in the constant search for potential hazards in consumer products. What was once considered safe and commonplace can become viewed as dangerous when instruments are sensitive enough to detect minute quantities of potentially harmful elements. Lead additives for gasoline were developed in the 1920s as the solution to the persistent knocking problems of high-compression automobile engines. Serious health effects were soon noticed in those working closely with the additives, arousing fears for the safety of the public. In 1924 an accident in a New Jersey processing plant killed five workers and hospitalized thirty-five others due to lead poisoning. That same year, New York City imposed a temporary ban on the manufacture, sale, and use of leaded gasolines. Despite these events, a 1925 survey by the staff of the Surgeon General and a panel of expert consultants failed to find a clear public risk associated with leaded gasoline.[15] Manufacturing safety was improved, and leaded gasoline became the national standard. Only with the precise measurement in the 1970s of the dispersion of lead by-products of combustion into the atmosphere was the risk better defined. Engines were required to be redesigned in order to eliminate the use of leaded gasoline and have been sputtering ever since.[16] The hazard of lead, fully revealed, takes precedence over automobile performance.

The line of defense against the dangers of everyday living was thin a half-century ago. There was little else besides a federal poison squad—a group of young volunteers to sample foods—and a handful of industrial test laboratories. Today an army of investigators ponder what we eat, drink, or use. The federal agencies include the Food and Drug Administration, the National Institutes of Health, the Environmental Protection

Agency, the Consumer Products Safety Commission, and a half-dozen others with similar responsibilities.[17] State governments duplicate many of the federal activities, although on a less lavish scale. Hundreds of private laboratories stand ready to contract with governments and firms for product safety tests. Many millions of animals are sacrificed each year in the United States in an unending quest for improvements in human health.

What can be measured will be measured. The law often mandates it. The curiosity of scientists encourages it. And the possibility of a liability suit makes it unwise not to.

IF YOU HAVE YOUR HEALTH, YOU HAVE EVERYTHING

Aaron Wildavsky has reminded us that richer is healthier.[18] Affluent societies are healthier than are poverty-stricken ones. Wealthy people tend to be healthier than poor people. America grew richer during the twentieth century and, as we have seen, its people came to live longer, healthier lives. When per capita income increases, diet, education, and access to medical care—all factors related to good health—generally improve as well. Within a society the groups that lag in income lag in health status too.

But the rich worry more about their health. When bread is not an issue, jam is; when basic needs are met, there are other things to fret about. Although many may try, good health cannot be purchased. It matters not to the rich that as a class they are healthier, for eventually we all must die. The great desire to avoid this fate is understandable, especially when most or all other desires are fulfillable. After all, as the cliché goes, when you have your health, you have everything.

There is another way to view the effect of affluence on attitudes toward health. Joseph Schumpeter, an Austrian-educated economist who taught at Harvard, predicted in 1942 that capitalist societies (the only affluent societies, in his scheme) would be transformed by their own success.[19] Only these societies, he argued, could afford to create a large number of highly educated young people who would strive to rationalize all aspects of life, including the entrepreneurial underpinnings of capitalism. Later social theorists have built upon his insight to argue that this group of educated dissidents constitute a new political class whose interests are antagonistic toward business because they find employment in the staffs of social service, regulatory, and other agencies which depend on public sector expansion.[20]

One does not have to accept completely the "new class" argument to recognize that there are political implications in the recent rapid growth in the medical, legal, and government service professions. And physicians, lawyers, and policy analysts need not gain personally from restrictions on corporate behavior to be concerned about the health consequences of products. These professionals are probably most aware of products that pose health threats and most knowledgeable about procedures to control these products. They are identical in terms of education and income with those segments of the population that are most interested in environmental preservation, physical fitness, and nutrition.[21] They heed the product labels that they cause to be written. In essence, they constitute a market for bad news about products, a market that, because of its affluence and position, wields influence over both the producers of consumer goods and politicians.

NADER'S INNOVATION

Joseph Schumpeter studied entrepreneurial behavior because he believed that he saw in it the engine of economic progress. Entrepreneurs, he argued, accepted the risks of innovation in the hope of having one day the mansion on the hill, the fortune of a Ford, a Woolworth, or a Rockefeller. The success of one entrepreneur encourages others to follow. Soon there is a herd, copying and refining the innovation until it is commonplace and vulnerable to another innovation promoted by another entrepreneur. Another herd of copiers and refiners follows. Economic progress, it seemed to Schumpeter, was the sum of these successive waves of "creative destruction."

But, as Schumpeter also envisioned, not all empires in capitalist societies need be economic. Depending upon social conditions, empires can be built in nearly every field. Consider the legacies of bureaucratic entrepreneurs such as J. Edgar Hoover, Robert Moses, and Hyman Rickover. These men saw opportunities for change in government where others did not and, although they did not necessarily create personal fortunes, they left behind impressive organizational monuments—the Federal Bureau of Investigation, the New York state parkway system, the Navy's nuclear propulsion program—in testimony to their willingness to undertake the risks of innovation.

Surely, one of the most important political innovations in recent years has been the formation of public interest groups, reform organizations that claim a disinterested, but analytical approach to public policy issues. As the federal government expanded during the twentieth century, various interests organized on a national scale to influence its policies.[22] The obstacles to organization have not been great enough to prevent business people, trade unionists, and professionals of nearly every description to form associations and to gain effective Washington representation.[23] But not until Ralph Nader outmaneuvered the admittedly inept General Motors Corporation in the early 1960s on the automobile safety issue did the nation discover political influence was also available to those who did not bother or were initially unable to assemble an actual membership base for their activities.

Nader recognized that a constituency existed for his ideas and that the news media would mobilize it for him when it was needed. The civil rights movement had trained Americans to appreciate the necessity of public protests to obtain morally desirable ends. Years of affluence had created a generation of educated youth who sought public-spirited commitments to replace the materialistic goals their parents had so compromisingly pursued. It was Nader's genius to appeal to this generation by attacking the failings of established institutions, using a mixture of moral protest and policy analysis. With these techniques of advocacy research, he attacked corporations and government agencies in particular. Moral protest was necessary to demonstrate commitment, but the claim of factual evidence was also required to satisfy the prevailing levels of sophistication and education. The David versus Goliath image evoked by Nader's initial battle with General Motors served his cause well because it provided the news media with an easily understandable format for presenting the many complex policy disputes Nader's actions involved. That battle, through a legal settlement, also helped finance a network of public interest organizations that Nader founded.[24]

Dozens followed Nader's example, some of whom he trained, others learning effective strategies on their own in the antiwar, antipoverty, or environmental conservation movements. The organizations they established drew sustenance from foundations and government grants and gained a strangely establishmentarian permanency in our political life. What the Left pioneered, the Right copied, ensuring that conservative perspectives were well represented in the burgeoning public interest movement.[25] There is now hardly a topic of political concern that has not been claimed by one or more organizations asserting to represent the public interest.

The growth in public interest groups has coincided with (and surely has contributed to) a precipitous decline in the public's confidence in government and business. Of course, vivid exposure of official deceit in Vietnam, Watergate, and Three Mile Island were central to the erosion of confidence, as was a chronically weak economy, but the mundane targets of the public interest groups, one's beer or breakfast, made everyday experience yet another source of anxiety. Since the mid 1960s Americans have expressed increasing distrust in politicians, federal officials, and corporate executives —indeed, a substantial majority now report that they have no faith in the honesty of these representatives of business and government.[26] Instead, trust is placed in those who purport to be above interest and who seek to expose the failings of society's special interests, which in the popular perception includes government as well as business.[27] With the creditability of the certifiers and purveyors of goods in question, it is no wonder that Americans fear their consumer products.

Making Our Choices

The case studies that follow show how nurturing American society has been for product fears. They describe the origins and development of six product risk controversies, none of which has been fully resolved. The organizations involved in the controversies, like the products themselves, are familiar ones, common household names once trusted but now much less so. How their fears shape ours is an important comparative theme. It is through their promotion and suppression of risks that we learn what hazards lurk in our lives.

In any comparative study the choice of subjects is crucial to the success of the effort. We wanted our selection of cases to be representative of all product controversies, but realized that the number of potentially important variations among them would be too great. We wanted to include cases involving big hazards as well as small, but knew that we could not be certain of the true dangers posed by any product because they are continually being redefined. We thought controversies of a more recent origin could be affected by the accumulation of past ones, yet could not predict the magnitude of the impact. Like consumers, we found risks in every choice.

We selected cigarettes, dairy and meat products, salt, artificial sweeteners, tampons, and urea-formaldehyde insulation. Two of these—cigarettes and dairy products—the Surgeon General in all his recent incarnations has warned us about. Cigarettes are implicated in a number of diseases, especially heart disease and cancer. Dairy and meat products, laden with saturated fats, are thought to be linked to atherosclerosis. Both cigarette smoking and dairy and meat products are issues with relatively long histories, beginning in a serious manner in the 1940s. The controversies involving salt and artificial sweeteners, in contrast, have been with us for only the last fifteen years. Salt has been linked to hypertension, which in turn is linked to heart attacks, strokes, and kidney failure. Cyclamate and saccharin, two of the more prominent artificial sweeteners, are believed by some experts to be carcinogenic. A third sweetener, aspartame, has just reached the market, but already is suspected to be a cause of illness. Recently, with the identification of the toxic shock syndrome, one brand of tampons was withdrawn from sale and others of similar formulation were placed under suspicion. Consumers have lodged a long series of health complaints, especially respiratory ailments, against urea-formaldehyde foam. Worse still, formaldehyde, a key component of the insulation product as well as many others, is now thought to be a potential carcinogen.

These products differ significantly in risk and their precise health effects are not known. Surely, though, cigarettes must be considered to be the most hazardous of the lot. Estimates of the annual toll of premature deaths in the United States due to smoking range from 300,000 to 500,000. Some say that if serum cholesterol levels can be reduced only by 10 percent with decreased consumption of meat and dairy products, the coronary death rate would fall by one third, a savings of several hundred thousand lives each year. Gains potentially achievable by reduced sodium intake are less dramatic, but hardly trivial given the prevalence of hypertension in the American population. Perhaps tens of thousands of deaths due to diseases of the circulatory system could be avoided by the careful management of hypertension through a combination of dietary change and drugs.

At our present state of knowledge, the other products examined have to be considered minor risks. Saccharin has been linked to bladder cancer, but this form of cancer accounts for less than 11,000 deaths each year in the United States, and not all of them, or even any, may be due to the use of this artificial sweetener. Toxic shock frightens many, but very few are stricken. All of us are exposed to formaldehyde at some level because it is such a widely used chemical. Whether or not the exposure is detrimental to our health remains to be determined. Thus, the rank order of risk appears to run from cigarettes to urea-formaldehyde. It is in this order that the cases are presented.

The cigarette controversy in many ways is the precedent-setting case. Epidemiology, it is said, matured as a science in the search for the health effects of cigarette smoking. Many of the types of regulations now proposed for suspect products, health warning labels and advertising restrictions for instance, were first established for cigarettes. Attempts by industry to defuse product controversies and adjust marketing strategies to assuage health concerns are strikingly visible in the cigarette case. And yet, there are unique features of this controversy. No other product has such committed opponents as does the cigarette. And no other set of producers have weathered their travails as successfully as have the cigarette producers. Cigarettes, however, may well be at an important turning point—good fortune may be shifting from the product's defenders to the product's critics.

A central feature in all the controversies is the struggle among interested groups to control governmental agendas. In the dietary fats case, the relevant policies are the government's nutrition guidelines. Although the scientific debate over the health consequences of cholesterol continues, advocates of dietary changes to reduce cholesterol levels have enjoyed recent success in gaining governmental endorsement of their views, but not without arousing the ire of others. As Janet Levine reports, even industries that would benefit from reductions in the public's consumption of dietary fats are not anxious to have the government intervene in the issue. The analysis of this strong preference for a market decision in dietary matters reveals contrasting business strategies for dealing with the growing concern over the health risks of cholesterol.

Salt, despite evidence that its dietary use is linked to serious illness, has more often been a hapless pawn in political and scientific disputes rather than the primary issue under scrutiny. For most affected by its potential regulation, including even the salt producers, it is the classic secondary issue. Nevertheless, there are moments when the convergence of interests forces salt to center stage. In the salt case, Mark Segal explores the pressures that drive congressional committees, health and trade associations, regulatory agencies, and firms to claim a substantial stake in what would be an otherwise minor issue.

The artificial sweetener case prepared by Linda Cummings focuses on the dilemmas of a regulatory agency trying to cope with the hazards of consumer products. Three times in the last fifteen years the Food and Drug Administration has attempted to decide the fate of an artificial sweetener and three times it has provoked a storm of protest for its efforts. The agency's problem lies in the public's contradictory interest in the challenged products; for some consumers the desire is for absolute protection while for others it is for the freedom of choice. Cummings analyzes the efforts to mobilize consumers for one or the other of these positions and describes the trials of an agency having to play a politicized role of market arbitrator when its preferred role is that of neutral recorder of scientific consensus.

Sanford Weiner notes in his analysis of the tampon controversy that public health surveillance systems now have the capacity to detect risks at a prevalence of fifty cases per 240 million population. Although few in number, the identification of toxic shock victims caused near national panic. State health officials and individual researchers, not always unwillingly, were thrust into the media spotlight to offer advice as the federal government and the tampon manufacturers struggled to decide upon a course of action. Weiner examines the defensibility of the action taken under the pressures of the moment.

Organizations are primed to react to very specific types of information. For some it is reports of a new disease. For others it is the suspicion that a product is carcinogenic. As the urea-formaldehyde case illustrates, consumer complaints about the health effects of exposure to the product provoked little regulatory activity because they were insufficiently dramatic. Enterprising state officials and health activists may wish to intervene, but they need a galvanizing medical finding to gain a wide hearing. According to Sanford Weiner who also prepared this case, the chance discovery by an industry group that formaldehyde could produce cancer in laboratory animals was such a finding. Regulatory agencies and trade associations uninterested in the fate of the home insulation material or its consumers had well-established positions to defend when this cancer link was reported. The subsequent policy debate has ensnared many additional products because of formaldehyde's ubiquitous uses and promises to allow everyone to reiterate opinions about appropriate standards for the regulation of potential carcinogens.

Our research strategy was straightforward if not especially elegant. We interviewed those expected or reported to be knowledgeable about the controversies. We dug through the records and read the news accounts. We decided early on to let each case be analyzed on its own terms rather than to impose a standard format on such diverse situations. Periodic reviews of our common progress allowed identification of common themes and a sharing of insights. A concluding chapter brings together the general findings, but each case offers its own lessons as well.

Chapter 2

The Changing Politics of Cigarette Smoking

HARVEY M. SAPOLSKY

Cigarette manufacturing is surely the most resilient of businesses. At the turn of the century when cigarette smoking was first becoming popular in the United States, the Women's Christian Temperance Union and school principals who were worried about the decay of public morals (and, some say, cigar manufacturers who were worried about competition) succeeded in having fourteen states ban the production, advertisement, and sale of cigarettes. These laws proved ineffectual because cigarette smoking had already become a symbol of maturity, sensuality, and modernity for most Americans.[1] Consumption boomed. The laws were quietly repealed.

After experiencing growth for three decades, the cigarette industry was hit hard by the onset of the Great Depression. Several years of faltering demand and competitive price cutting followed. But economic recovery and war spurred consumption. Soldiers received cigarettes with their field rations for their own use or trade. Even after price cutting ceased, the cost of cigarettes remained relatively low because of the large domestic production of tobacco and moderate taxation of cigarettes. By 1953, cigarette sales were over three times what they had been in 1929. More than half of adult males and about a quarter of adult females smoked.

Then came the first of the smoking-and-health scares, the release of epidemiological studies linking cigarettes with lung cancer. Sales staggered, but were revived by filtered brands, now the mainstay of the industry. By the late 1950s, per capita consumption of cigarettes was rising again.

The second smoking and health scare came in 1964 with the publication of the Surgeon General's report that officially identified cigarette smoking as a serious health hazard. Since then there have been many market disruptions: the requirement that cigarette packages and advertisements carry a health warning, the removal of cigarette advertisements from radio and television, the restriction of smoking aboard commercial aircraft, a rising concern about the health effects of side-stream smoke, and the release of additional reports linking cigarette smoking to heart disease, stroke, emphysema, birth defects, and various forms of cancer, to mention only the most significant health risks. Millions of Americans have quit smoking.

Remarkably, the industry has not collapsed. Instead, it has prospered. Although the portion of the adult population that smokes has shrunk to about a third, cigarette sales have increased. In 1984, about 600 billion cigarettes were sold, nearly 20 percent more than the total for 1964 (see figure 2.1). The tobacco industry has met every challenge and has even converted some into benefits. The introduction of brands that appeal to women and brands low in tar and nicotine for the health-conscious have helped stem the market erosion. So too has the coming of age of the postwar baby boom generation.

Opponents of cigarettes must wonder when, if ever, the smoking problem (or as some prefer to describe it, the epidemic of smoking) will be controlled. Even the most committed among them know that cigarettes are not likely to be banned again. Cigarettes are too deeply embedded in American society, as is the memory of the social disruption and criminal activities caused by the attempt to ban alcohol during the 1920s. Moreover, as some have begun to recognize, the industry has been extremely skillful in turning regulatory challenges into economic advantages. When warning labels were demanded in 1964, the firms acquiesced after a brief struggle. (Until recently, the caution used was "The Surgeon General Has Determined That Cigarette Smoking Is Dangerous To Your Health"; now there is a quarterly rotation of warnings, each describing a specific risk of smoking or a benefit of quitting.) Some say they gave in to avoid disruptive state labeling legislation. But others think it was to gain valuable protection from lawsuits seeking damages for the death or disability of smokers. After all, a smoker who is warned knows about the risks involved in smoking and thus can be said to consent to harming his or her own health if any injury occurs.[2] When the Fairness Doctrine required antismoking advertisements on radio and television to counter cigarette ads, cigarette sales began to fall. The industry voluntarily agreed to withdraw, beginning in 1971, all radio and television advertisements for cigarettes, thereby elimi-

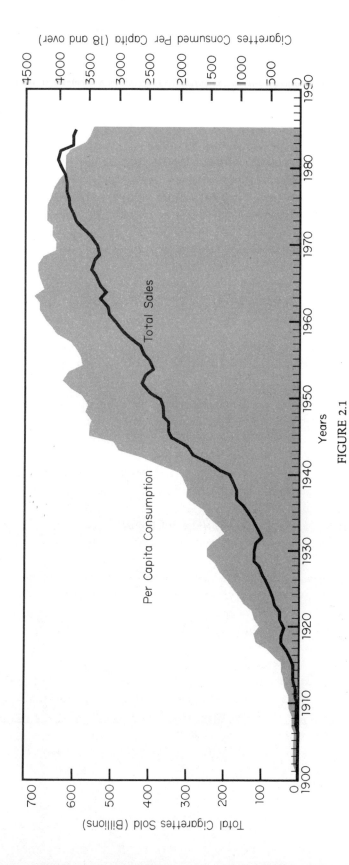

FIGURE 2.1

U.S. Cigarette Consumption, 1900–1985

Source: Economic Research Service, U.S. Department of Agriculture, from *Tobacco International* (1 April 1983): 69; and *Tobacco Outlook and Situation Report* (March 1986): table 1, p. 4.

nating any need for the counteradvertisements and much of their depressing effect on sales.[3]

And yet the industry's good fortune may not be endless. The growth in the population of potential new smokers is slowing.[4] More important, cigarette smoking is losing its allure for influential segments of that population, the social and political trend setters. What was once so fashionable is becoming unfashionable. And stagnant or declining markets are likely to strain the industry's political base. Already there is a divergence of interests developing between tobacco farmers and cigarette manufacturers and among the manufacturers themselves. As its political base weakens, the industry becomes vulnerable to attack by groups that are more numerous and powerful than its traditional opponents.

Who Smokes and Who Does Not

Although the number of Americans who smoke cigarettes has actually increased since the Surgeon General's 1964 report, the campaign against smoking has not been without effect. Kenneth Warner estimates that the per capita consumption of cigarettes would be 40 percent higher today if the well-publicized concerns about the health effects of smoking did not exist.[5] During the 1960s and 1970s, cigarette smoking appears to have been initiated by a declining percentage of an expanding population. New smokers exceeded quitters, but not by much. Today, about 55 million Americans smoke cigarettes, only a few million more than did in 1964.[6]

Of course, it is impossible to be precise about the prevalence of smoking. Estimates are based upon surveys, and people's responses are likely to be affected by the negative health connotations associated with cigarette smoking. Smokers are thought to report inaccurately about their use of cigarettes.[7]

We do know that the percent of people who identify themselves as smokers has declined since the 1960s. In 1965 nearly 42 percent of those over seventeen years of age said they were current cigarette smokers; by 1986 less than 31 percent said they were. More men than women smoke, though the gap between the sexes has apparently narrowed over the years. In 1965 just over 51 percent of the men surveyed and 33 percent of the women said they smoked. By 1986 approximately 35 percent of men and 28 percent of women said they smoked. The decline in cigarette smoking reported by adult males has been fairly steady since the mid 1960s, but the decline for adult females is more recent.[8]

The rate of smoking among teenagers has apparently declined too, although the reliability of these figures must be even more suspect than those for adults. Today less than 20 percent of teenagers admit to smoking cigarettes, whereas in the mid-1970s over 25 percent did.[9] As is the case in most industrialized nations, more girls than boys in the United States say they smoke, 19 percent for females versus 16 percent for males.[10]

Smoking seems to be related to social class. Less than a third of those in professional or business occupations questioned in a 1981 Gallup survey said they smoke cigarettes; nearly 40 percent of clerical or blue-collar workers said they did. People who had some college education were less likely to smoke than people with only high school educations. Higher-income people were less likely to smoke than lower-income people. More blacks than whites were smokers.[11]

The changing characteristics of smokers affect the industry's commercial and political opportunities. The smaller the percentage of smokers in the population, the easier it is to restrict their behavior. The more the smoking population becomes black, female, and blue collar, the less economic and political strength it represents. The ability of smokers to absorb tax and price increases will diminish, as will their power to resist direct legislative restrictions on smoking.

Perhaps most significant, cigarette smokers of every description are acquiring a negative self-image. When asked, most smokers say that they regret their habit, are embarrassed by it, and want to quit.[12] Nearly all are aware of and believe in the health danger associated with cigarette smoking even if they are somewhat vague about the specific risks involved.[13] Few are proud of smoking despite the positive advertising used to promote it. For example, a survey of teenage use of common stimulants—alcohol, tobacco, coffee, and marijuana—found that users felt guilty only about cigarette smoking.[14] Other studies report that smokers are increasingly uncomfortable about smoking in the presence of nonsmokers.[15] Smoking is now thought to be a liability in career advancement and social interaction, whereas recently the opposite was the case.[16] The more widely such negative beliefs are held among smokers, the more difficult it is to mobilize them to defend smoking. The less favorably smoking is viewed, the fewer new smokers are likely to be recruited.

The Tobacco Connection

Americans not only smoke cigarettes, they also grow tobacco, a fact of no small political importance. American farmers produce about 2 billion pounds of tobacco, over 90 percent of which is accounted for by varieties used in cigarettes and two thirds of which is destined for domestic consumption. Tobacco is our sixth most important field crop and currently generates about $2.8 billion in farm income.[17]

Tobacco's political significance stems not from its role in agriculture—tobacco accounts for only about 2 percent of gross farm income and is grown on less than 1 percent of U.S. cropland—but rather from the *characteristics* of its production.[18] Although tobacco is grown in twenty states, the bulk of the production of the two prime varieties used for cigarettes, burley and flue-cured, is concentrated in just six states: North Carolina, Kentucky, Tennessee, Virginia, South Carolina, and Georgia (listed in order of importance). Tobacco farms tend to be quite small by American standards, averaging less than 10 acres in size, and highly labor-intensive, requiring hundreds of man-hours per acre to produce a crop. For a few Southern states and many Southern farmers and farm workers, tobacco is not only important, it is crucial for their economic livelihood.[19]

The structure of burley and flue-cured tobacco farming is buttressed by a federal price-support program. When the program was instituted during the 1930s, tobacco was grown on small-scale farms that used little or no mechanical technology. Tobacco is still grown on small-scale farms with relatively little mechanical technology, primarily because of the continuation of the price-support system.[20]

The purpose of price supports is to provide a stable market for producers. Every year prior to the growing season support prices are set for each variety and grade of tobacco included in the program with the prices based on historical market relationships and an index of recent changes in factor costs. Growers unable to sell their tobacco at prices above the support price are eligible to offer their crop for a federal cash loan at the support price. Unless market prices improve, the loans are not redeemed and the government stores the tobacco for later sale. To prevent the accumulation of a large market "overhang," the government limits tobacco growing to allotment holders, adjusting the size of the allotments each growing season either in acreage or poundage to clear the market. Allotment decisions are based on the previous season's experience.[21]

Allotments are essentially federal licenses to grow tobacco. The system freezes tobacco growing in location and, at least partially, in technology. The number and distribution of the allotments reflect the situation of tobacco farming during the Depression when the basic system was established and when production was just beginning to shift to land where large farms could be assembled and technology employed efficiently. Currently there are about 520,000 allotments, with an average holding of less than 2 acres.[22] Tobacco allotments, governed by annual marketing quotas, may be sold or leased, but only within counties, not between them. The number of producing units has shrunk to under 180,000 due to leasing, but because of restrictions on intercounty allotment transfers, relatively few of the units are yet large enough to utilize advanced mechanization.[23]

Some think it is strange that the federal government would seek to provide price supports and a stable market for cigarette tobacco when it also seeks to curtail cigarette smoking. There are increasing attempts in Congress to eliminate all of the tobacco "subsidies."[24] The cost of inspecting and grading tobacco was shifted from the government to the farmers in 1981. Beginning with the 1982 crop, farmers must pay an assessment on each pound of tobacco they sell in order to finance loans made for the surplus production.[25]

Legislative challenges aside, the support program is approaching collapse. The formula for establishing the support level for tobacco, which overcompensates for inflation, has caused the price of American leaf to escalate rapidly in recent years. The strong dollar, perhaps a temporary phenomenon, has also hurt sales. Foreign buyers are turning to cheaper tobacco produced in Zimbabwe, Malaysia, Brazil, and India, among other places.[26] Once American-produced varieties accounted for over half of the world trade in tobacco; now they represent less than one fifth and are continuing to slide.[27]

American cigarette manufacturers are also shifting to foreign leaf suppliers—they now import almost a third of their needs.[28] In addition, the overall tobacco content of American cigarettes has been reduced to accommodate filters and the desire for lower tar and nicotine levels. The average cigarette today contains one third less tobacco than it did in the early 1960s.[29] Combined, these factors prevent domestic tobacco growers from sharing in the market expansion that occurred despite the Surgeon General's warnings that cigarettes are a health hazard.

A large surplus of tobacco has been accumulating despite controls intended to prevent it. In 1983 almost one half of the burley crop and one quarter of the flue-cured crop was sold for storage. Over a year's supply of these varieties is being held under the loan arrangements.[30] The more tobacco stored, the higher the assessments to growers. (The fees already exceed 15 percent of the prices that farmers receive.) Attempts to control surpluses through allotment restrictions have been self-defeating. Lower allotments raise the rents for growers who lease their acreage. They also tempt growers to produce lower-quality tobacco, further hurting the marketability of American leaf, which had commanded premium prices because of its traditionally high quality.

Several stopgap measures have been adopted. The support prices for the 1983, 1984, and 1985 crops were frozen at 1982 levels or lowered through administrative action by the Department of Agriculture. Corporate entities such as businesses, schools, churches, and utility companies, which had acquired tobacco allotments through bequests and purchases, are now required to sell them. Legislation has banned the leasing of allotments after 1987, by which time owners will have to sell their allotments, acquire tenants, or become growers themselves.[31]

Despite these measures, the continued accumulation of surpluses seemed certain unless more radical changes were made. Some growers have sought to restrict manufacturer imports of tobacco leaf through the imposition of a special tariff.[32] Others wanted to use part of the federal cigarette tax to pay for the price supports. There was also pressure to have the cigarette manufacturers buy, over several years, the entire stock of accumulated tobacco in order to reduce storage assessments and save the federal support program. But the firms are said to believe that the program can be maintained only if leaf support prices are significantly reduced and tobacco production is tightly controlled.[33]

The congressional compromise that was worked out for the 1986 deficit reduction act gives the manufacturers a direct role for the first time in setting the growing quotas in exchange for their commitment to share half the cost of maintaining the price-support program with the growers, and to buy up the existing tobacco surpluses. The purchases of the surplus stocks are to be made at discounts that are estimated to cost the government $1.1 billion. The hope is that tighter quotas and reduced price supports will eventually produce equivalent program savings. The future of the program, however, is not assumed. Many growers are unhappy with the prospect of declining income that the act holds. A few have even sided with the forces opposing smoking and urged the abolishment of the support/allotment system as a way to free tobacco growing entirely from government-mandated control.[34]

The elimination of the tobacco support program would, of course, lower tobacco prices and presumably, if passed along to the cigarette consumer, would be at least a moderate stimulus to the demand. More important, however, it would reduce the number of people in several Southern states who depend to some degree on the cigarette market. Production would shift to more efficient locations (within those states and elsewhere) and would use more efficient methods.[35] Many who now hold the more than half-million tobacco-growing allotments would no longer be involved with the crop; many thousand fewer farmers and farm workers would be needed to produce it. The interest of Southern congressmen and senators in defending tobacco and its prime method of consumption would be bound to decline. Although the cigarette industry survives even in countries where little, if any, tobacco is grown (Great Britain, for example), it does so with much less confidence in its ability to withstand political attack than does the industry in countries where there is a substantial agricultural interest in tobacco. Both opponents and proponents of cigarette smoking believe that the fate of the tobacco support program has political consequence.

The Marlboro Man, Virginia Slims, and Friends

Outwardly, the cigarette industry has the appearance of a highly successful, well-entrenched oligopoly. Profits are substantial, well over $2 billion in 1984. Return on investment exceeds the average for all U.S. manufacturing by nearly 30 percent. The business is largely recession-proof, not so surprising given that the product is a pleasurable stimulant that is habituating, if not addictive. Prices move generally upward and in unison. Huge advertising expenditures and the persistent health controversy strongly discourage entry by those who might be attracted by its high margins. And yet, tension exists among the participants.

Government helped shape the industry's current structure, just as it helped shape the structure of tobacco growing. The Justice Department won a Sherman Antitrust Act case against the American Tobacco Company in 1911. The company was the key element in the tobacco trust that James B. Duke had assembled through various predatory business practices. As a penalty, the trust was dismembered and its principal cigarette business divided among a much-reduced American Tobacco Company and three of its former subsidiaries: R. J. Reynolds Tobacco Company, Liggett & Meyers Tobacco Company, and P. Lorillard Tobacco Company.[36] These four firms and two others—Brown & Williamson Tobacco Company, an American affiliate of B.A.T. Industries (formerly

British American Tobacco Company), the severed British subsidiary of the old tobacco trust, and Philip Morris, Inc., an independent in the days of the trust—now control over 99 percent of the U.S. cigarette market. With the antitrust suit, government traded monopoly for oligopoly in the cigarette industry.[37]

The oligopoly's main mode of rivalry quickly became advertising. In 1913, R. J. Reynolds introduced Camels, a cigarette blended from burley, Turkish, and Maryland tobaccos, and heavily advertised it.[38] The other firms responded with similarly constituted cigarettes and promotional efforts. The full genius of the advertising imagination was soon brought to bear on the problem of marketing cigarettes, contributing such marvelous bits of Americana over the years as "Reach for a Lucky Instead of a Sweet," "I'd Walk a Mile for a Camel," "So-o-o-old American," "L.S./M.F.T." (Lucky Strike Means Fine Tobacco), "Call for Philip Morris," the dancing cigarette packages, the smoke ring billboard in Times Square, and the Marlboro Man.[39]

The firms have used their marketing skills to counter the various shocks that have hit the industry since World War II. Filter cigarettes were heavily promoted in the 1950s after the initial cancer scare and now account for over 90 percent of sales. The Surgeon General's 1964 report brought a proliferation of brands designed to appeal to particular market segments through variations in length, flavor, or image (Benson & Hedges, Kool, Tareyton, and Virginia Slims). More recently, cigarette firms have introduced low-tar brands (Carlton, Now, Merit, and Kent IIIs) and heralded government tar ratings in their advertising. Once smokers had a few dozen brands to choose among; they now have over 230 due to differentiation by filter, length, packaging, and tar levels.[40]

As Table 2.1 indicates, not all firms adjusted equally well to these market changes. American Tobacco, the largest manufacturer in 1953, was slow to introduce filters and, as a consequence, lost considerable market share. Lorillard and Liggett & Meyers were inept in developing new brands, paying the price in their market rankings. In contrast, Philip Morris, once the sixth largest firm, has been extremely perceptive in identifying evolving consumer preferences—and recently overtook R. J. Reynolds for the market lead. Together, Philip Morris and Reynolds control over two thirds of industry sales. Philip Morris's Marlboro brand alone accounts for over 22 percent of the American market and is the world's largest-selling cigarette.[41]

Because of production efficiencies and low advertising costs per carton sold, well-established cigarette brands have rates of return on investments

TABLE 2.1

Share of U.S. Cigarette Market (%), Selected Years

Company	1953	1963	1970	1985
Philip Morris	9.6	9.4	16.5	35.7
R. J. Reynolds	26.5	34.3	31.7	32.0
Brown & Williamson	6.6	10.5	16.7	11.8
Lorillard	7.2	10.9	8.7	8.1
American Brands	33.3	24.8	19.6	7.4
Liggett Group	16.8	9.7	6.8	5.0

SOURCE: John C. Maxwell, Jr., Furman Selz Mager Dietz & Birney Inc., New York.

of well over 30 percent. Improvements in cigarette-making machines have increased production capacity for a single unit from 180 packs (eighteen cartons) per minute in 1965 to 400 a minute today. Once a significant market share is obtained, advertising costs per carton drop considerably. A single point of market share, the industry standard for a brand's success, is currently worth more than $250 million in annual revenues and tens of millions of dollars in profits. No wonder marketing efforts exceeding $100 million have been made to introduce new brands.[42]

Much of the industry's huge cash flow, however, has been used for diversification because the firms recognize the cigarette market's potential for decline.[43] All firms have eliminated the word *tobacco* from their corporate name. RJR Nabisco (formerly R. J. Reynolds Tobacco, R. J. Reynolds, and R. J. Reynolds Industries) owns Del Monte, a major fruit and vegetable processor; Heublein, a marketer of distilled spirits and wines and the corporate parent of Kentucky Fried Chicken; and Nabisco Brands, the nation's fourth largest food-processing firm. Among the well-known brands in the Reynolds food and beverage line are Hawaiian Punch; Chun King oriental foods; Vermont Maid syrup; My-T-Fine puddings; Planters peanuts; Ritz crackers; Almost Home cookies; Smirnoff vodka; and Inglenook, Colony, and Lancer wines. Philip Morris owns Miller Brewing, the nation's second largest beer producer (Miller Highlife, Lite, and Löwenbräu brands). In 1985 the firm restructured, changed its name to Philip Morris Companies Inc., and purchased (in one of the largest nonoil transactions) General Foods, producer of Maxwell House coffee, Jello, Post cereals, among other popular labels. American Brands, formerly American Tobacco, sells crackers (Sunshine Biscuits), bourbon (Jim Beam), toiletries (Andre Jergens), insurance (Franklin Life), and office supplies (Swingline and Wilson Jones) as well as cigarettes. It recently acquired Pinkerton's, the nation's largest private security and investigation agency, and Wells Fargo, the bank transfer service. Brown & Williamson is part of BATUS, the American subsidiary of B.A.T. Industries, an international enterprise whose American holdings include the Saks Fifth Avenue and Marshall Field department stores.

The two other firms, Lorillard and Liggett & Meyers, have been acquired by larger, noncigarette based firms. Lorillard is a division of the Loews Corporation, the owner of a chain of hotels (including L'Enfant Plaza in Washington, D.C., and the Regency, the Summit, and the Drake in New York City) and CNA Finance, an insurance and consumer credit company. Loews recently purchased 25 percent of the Columbia Broadcasting System, helping the television network avoid a hostile takeover. Liggett & Meyers, after changing its name to The Liggett Group and acquiring interests in pet foods (Alpo, Vets, and Liv-A-Snaps) and distilled spirits and wine (J&B, Bombay, Grand Marnier, and Campari) was itself acquired by Grand Metropolitan, a British conglomerate active in hotel, brewery, restaurant, and gambling businesses. It now operates as a subsidiary of GrandMet U.S.A. (which, after acquiring Pearle Health Services, a franchiser of eye care centers, and Quality Care, a nursing home chain, supposedly now wishes to dispose of Liggett's cigarette business as it seeks a larger role in health care services).

As a result of this diversification, none of the corporate owners of the six major cigarette companies is much more than 40 percent dependent for its revenues on the fortunes of the domestic cigarette market. Few of the acquisitions, however, approach the profitability of the cigarette business; tobacco remains the key source of earnings for the owning firms no matter the involvement in other activities.[44] Not surprisingly, there has been some interest in expanding into the world market for cigarettes, which is still growing if only slightly. American Brands controls Gallaher, a major British cigarette manufacturer. Philip Morris and Reynolds fought recently for a share of Rothman's, a British-based firm that has important cigarette holdings in several foreign markets; Philip Morris won.[45] Reynolds has since signed agreements with the People's Republic of China for the establishment of manufacturing facilities in the world's largest cigarette market.[46] And both Philip Morris and Reynolds are seeking better access to the Japanese cigarette market, which is only now converting to free enterprise after having long been controlled by a state-owned monopoly.[47]

All this activity means the firms may begin to view the industry's profit potential differently. Already, some splits have occurred. Liggett, the firm with the smallest market share, introduced a line of low-priced generic (unbranded) cigarettes, threatening the industry's long-established pricing harmony.[48] Philip Morris and Reynolds successfully sued Brown & Williamson over the tar rating advertised for its Barclay cigarettes. Philip Morris and Reynolds claimed misrepresentation was endangering public confidence in the cigarette rating system.[49] The emphasis on tar ratings in cigarette advertising was started by American Brands when it boasted about the low-tar rating of its Carlton cigarettes, much to the consternation of the major producers.[50] Philip Morris lobbied state legislatures (unsuccessfully in most cases) seeking to block the distribution of packs of twenty-five cigarettes (the U.S. standard is twenty) pioneered by Reynolds. Reynolds itself now sees its prime growth in foods and beverages. Because of its investments in the coffee, beer, and cereal markets, Philip Morris has to worry about the maneuverings of Procter & Gamble, Budweiser, and Kellogg's as well as those of its cigarette rivals. The more diverse the firms' interests the more likely that one or another will seek quick profits in cigarettes at the expense of the industry's long-term viability.

Hard-to-Break Habits

Cigarette smoking generates revenues for governments as well as for tobacco farmers and cigarette manufacturers. The federal government's cigarette tax was raised from 8 cents to 16 cents per pack in 1982. Each state also taxes cigarettes, with rates ranging from 2 to 31 cents per pack. An additional tax of 1 to 15 cents is imposed by several hundred municipal and county governments. These excise taxes were estimated to amount to $9.3 billion in 1984 ($4.7 billion for the federal government and $4.6 billion for state and local governments).[51] Additional billions are collected through normal business and sales taxes from the growers, manufacturers, wholesalers, and retailers, and thus from the consumers of cigarettes.

The doubling of the federal tax, which had been held constant for 30 years, was a major political defeat for the industry. The need for increased federal revenues during a period of severe budget deficits overcame arguments that the tax is regressive, disproportionately burdening low-income consumers. But more important, the increase indicates that congressional delegations from tobacco-producing states no longer can protect cigarettes from the political imperatives of "taxing sin."

The consumption of certain products, cigarettes and alcohol surely among them, is strongly opposed by some people on moral grounds, aside from health concerns. Yet consumption is not much affected by carefully crafted price increases. State and foreign experiences demonstrate that the governmental temptation is to exploit the inelasticity in the demand curve for "sin" by heavily taxing the consumption of such products, in order to enhance revenues and support the product's opponents in the process. Only a minority of the population bears the tax while at least some of the rest of the population takes satisfaction in its application. Apparently there is still opportunity for this practice in the United States. In most European countries, nearly three quarters of the retail price for cigarettes is taxes; in the United States, taxes are less than half the retail price. Although the federal increase was passed as a temporary measure, it was permanently extended in 1986 amidst calls for additional increases.[52]

The limitation in taxing sin is the effect on government revenues. The federal tax increase of 8 additional cents per pack caused about a 4–5 percent decline in consumption,[53] not enough to inhibit the imposition of additional taxes, and this is an effect that wears away somewhat in time. Economists estimate that most of the impact of cigarette tax or price increases appears in the decision to smoke and not as much in the amount smoked. Teenagers, in particular, are thought to be discouraged from smoking by higher cigarette prices.[54] Faced with heavier taxation, a smoker, of course, has alternatives besides abstention or moderation. Hand rolling cigarettes is one way to reduce the cost of smoking; smoking contraband cigarettes is another.

Because of the great disparity in state cigarette taxes, it is not surprising that there is much smuggling of cigarettes. It is also no surprise that the tobacco-producing states impose the lowest tax rates. Smuggling cigarettes between the tobacco states and the high-tax states (which are concentrated in the Northeast, but which also include Florida, Illinois, and Wisconsin) is estimated to result in a revenue loss of hundreds of millions of dollars.[55] Attempts to eliminate cigarette smuggling by establishing a uniform excise tax for all jurisdictions has been blocked by the low-tax states. Instead, Congress has extended federal antiracketeering laws to cover trade in contraband cigarettes.[56] Yet criminals, organized or not, are not easily deterred from their cigarette-smuggling activities. With the difference between the price of a package of cigarettes in New Jersey or New York and the price of one in North Carolina of at least 20 cents, a single truckload of bootleg cigarettes could produce $90,000 to $100,000 in illegal profits for a smuggler.[57] Counterfeiting tax stamps and transfers between other jurisdictions permit even larger gains for smugglers.

Higher cigarette taxes forge a strange partnership. Politicians must take care that cigarette sales do not fall too much in establishing the rates. Smugglers hope that moralizers triumph in most, but not all jurisdictions. And the cigarette manufacturers advertise more heavily in the jurisdictions with the highest rates, hoping that either governments exceed their revenue expectations or that smugglers stock their brands.

The Smoking and Health Issue

Since the 1950s cigarette firms have had the difficult—many would say impossible—task of persuading the public that cigarette smoking is not harmful. Their continuing claim is that the case against smoking does not meet the strictest standards of scientific proof because the evidence linking smoking to disease is mainly statistical.[58] Initially, there was much scientific debate over the validity and meaning of the epidemiological results that identified smoking as a major factor in the development of cancer and other diseases.[59] But once the Royal College of Physicians in Britain and the Surgeon General's committee in the United States endorsed the conclusion that the risks of smoking are substantial, the smoking and health debate lost much of its scientific intensity even though the risk was not totally clarified.[60] To be sure, significant resources are still invested in studies of the health effects of smoking, but mostly because scientists see this support as an opportunity to explore a variety of other interesting questions and politicians see it as a convenient substitute for action. For all practical purposes, the smoking and health issue has become, since the mid-1960s, a protracted political struggle over the regulation of smoking.

The firms seem well situated to protect their interests. They are, after all, the central enterprises in a $30 billion industry, a source of income for hundreds of thousands of persons. Their lobbying arm, the Tobacco Institute, employs the full range of Washington insiders including former congressmen, White House aides, congressional staff members, and reporters and broadcasters. The firms hire the best available legal and public relations counsel. Through a network of detail men, distributors, and advertising agencies, they keep in close contact with state and local developments.

Executives contribute to political campaigns. And employees stand ready to write and call officials when offending legislation is contemplated.[61]

In contrast, the political opponents of smoking appear weak and divided. The two main activist organizations in the antismoking movement are Action on Smoking and Health (ASH), which concentrates on legal challenges to cigarettes before federal regulatory agencies, and Group Against Smokers' Pollution (GASP), an association of local chapters, which focuses on state and local legislative initiatives. The jurisdictional distinctions notwithstanding, ASH and GASP compete for the same limited membership and financial support. The domination of ASH by John F. Banzhaf III has been a source of antagonism between the organizations because Banzhaf has gained (and is said to seek out) journalistic recognition as the national leader of the attack on cigarette smoking.[62]

Several national disease associations, especially the big three—the American Cancer Society, the American Heart Association, and the American Lung Association—have taken official stands pointing out the health risks of cigarette smoking. However, as their critics in the antismoking movement are quick to note, the associations have been cautious in seeking restraints on smoking. For example, only recently have they hired Washington lobbyists and supported governmental efforts to combat smoking.[63] The reasons for this self-restraint are not difficult to identify. Traditionally, these organizations devote most of their resources to support medical research and training to fight a specific disease. Most funds come from public drives conducted by local affiliates. Controversial issues, like the regulation of smoking, threaten the associations because internal conflict could arise if resources are absorbed for which there are already many established claimants. The associations fear such issues could jeopardize their ability to raise funds either by reducing volunteer effort at the local level or by alienating segments of the public. Moreover, because smoking is linked to several diseases, campaigns against smoking can be seen as blurring the distinctions among the associations, destroying their unique identities and thus weakening the ability of the associations to raise funds.

Relations between the associations and the activist groups are necessarily strained. The associations are status-conferring organizations as well as charitable groups—and that encourages a strong establishment orientation. Activist groups, in contrast, require a confrontational political style to maintain support and they distrust the elitist preferences of the associations.[64]

But this description greatly underplays the strength of the antismoking movement. Support for smoking control appears at influential places in the society. Nearly every major medical organization has taken a stand against smoking. Most physicians advise abstinence. Public health and preventive medicine specialists seek a greater commitment against smoking within the profession and act as its conscience on the issue. A physician cannot hold high office within the profession and remain a public smoker. Many in the media—from Ann Landers, the popular advice columnist, to Jane Brody, the *New York Times*'s scientifically inclined nutrition editor—are sympathetic to restrictions on smoking and frequently remind their readers of dangers posed by cigarettes. Certain publications refuse tobacco advertisements and editorialize against smoking, *Reader's Digest* and *Good Housekeeping*, for example. Rarely is cigarette smoking depicted in a favorable manner on television.[65]

Opposition to smoking is a career for some and a calling for others. Thousands of health promotion specialists, many of whom make smoking cessation their main cause, have been hired by industry and schools in response to the growing interest in fitness and good health. Several Protestant denominations, the Mormons and the Seventh Day Adventists most prominent among them, are, by doctrine, opposed to the use of tobacco. The Mormon church advocates public service and many of its members are active in the campaign to regulate smoking; Seventh Day Adventist groups sponsor smoking cessation clinics.

Government also participates in the effort to control smoking.[66] Although the Office of Smoking and Health, the federal agency responsible for the management of antismoking initiatives, has been hampered by budget restrictions, it still operates an information clearinghouse used extensively by smoking-control advocates. Administration attempts to curtail regulation notwithstanding, the Federal Trade Commission and the Department of Transportation (the regulatory successor to the Civil Aeronautics Board) remain committed to policies that regulate smoking and continue to explore possible elaborations of these policies. Commissioners of public health in various states have been vocal in their condemnation of smoking. Each year, the U.S. Surgeon General—no matter who is in the White House—finds another way to reiterate the assessment that cigarettes are dangerous and gain additional publicity for the antismoking cause; most recently, it was a call for a smoke-free society by the year 2000.[67]

The problem facing the antismoking movement is not the absence of support, but rather the absence of policies, barring prohibition, that will significantly limit smoking. As mentioned previously, the addition of warning labels to cigarette packages and the elimination of radio and television advertisements for cigarettes apparently provided the industry with significant, although unintended, benefits. Moreover, despite these and other marketing handicaps, cigarettes remain a very familiar product, heavily advertised and widely consumed.[68] Further curbs along these lines, for example, requiring stronger, even gruesome warning labels or banning the street distribution of sample cigarettes, although perhaps pleasing ideologically to some proponents of the antismoking movement, may only test the ingenuity of the cigarette firms' marketing and legal staffs without causing major changes in the prevalence of smoking.[69]

In fact, it can be argued that the puritanism inherent in the antismoking movement has retarded the development of effective policies. The urge to portray cigarettes as an unmitigated evil, to condemn smokers as sinners, ignores the very real pleasures and purposes of smoking that perpetuate the practice, even in an ever more hostile environment of restrictions and threatening messages.

But after two decades of experience, the antismoking movement is gaining sophistication. Madison Avenue professionals now prepare advertisements; and scientific and public relations activities are coordinated. More importantly, the movement is adopting a new strategy with great potential for affecting cigarette consumption. This strategy involves the social isolation of the smoker, based on the recognition that smoking is chiefly a social phenomenon and can be attacked as such. The intent is to make the smoker a pariah, shunned by others and plagued by self-doubts.

One effective expression of this strategy is the demand that smokers refrain from smoking in the presence of nonsmokers. The claim is that tobacco smoke endangers the health of exposed nonsmokers. Although the medical evidence demonstrating the health effects of side-stream smoke exposure is incomplete and disputed, much of the public believes that there are important risks.[70] More and more restrictions are being placed on smoking in public locations, including government buildings, restaurants, hospitals, and auditoriums.[71]

The cigarette industry has attempted to fight the restrictions, arguing that courtesy rather than the law should govern disputes between smokers and nonsmokers. National advertising stresses the economic importance of tobacco and argues that the threat to nonsmokers has not been proved. The industry has also won several referenda on the issue of restrictions,[72] often with the support of the police, who have little taste for the complaints that they suffer from offenders when enforcing widely flouted laws.

In 1983, though, the industry lost an important referendum in San Francisco that challenged a city ordinance extending smoking restrictions to private workplaces. The introduction of mandatory restrictions into the work environment, where smoking restrictions already occur fairly frequently on a voluntary basis, threatens to curtail smoking on the clerical and manual workers who often lack the private workspace common among senior executives. The failure of many employers in San Francisco to oppose the ordinance indicates also their acceptance of claims by antismoking groups that smoking imposes significant economic costs on their business through higher insurance, medical, and cleaning expenditures.[73] This in turn may mean the further isolation of smokers in terms of work and promotion opportunities. Courts have been willing to uphold employment discrimination for smoking if on no other grounds.[74] Already dozens of other jurisdictions have followed the San Francisco example by restricting on-the-job smoking.

Another important development is the changing content of antismoking television spots directed toward teenagers. Instead of repeating the litany of health risks associated with smoking, these public service advertisements now often depict smoking as behavior that significantly reduces one's sexual attractiveness.[75] Calculated, of course, to strike terror into the hearts of young smokers, these advertisements demonstrate the growing sophistication of the antismoking movement. The very techniques that sold the cigarette habit are being used to discourage it.

Waiting to be fully tested are other strategies, some domestically developed and others imported. Product liability suits, the American way to get even (and perhaps rich as well) are again being attempted against cigarette firms. Today's social and legal climate makes such suits attractive as does the convenient designation of cigarette smoking as an addictive disease by officials at the Alcohol, Drug Abuse and Mental Health Administration. Addictive products presumably are unprotected by warning labels noting a health hazard because they remove the possibility of free choice.[76] A total advertising ban, as imposed in several foreign countries, has also been suggested, with magazines and newspapers as the specific targets on the grounds that substantial advertising by cigarette manufacturers inhibits editorial criticism of smoking.[77] Some advocate linking cigarette taxes to the cost of treating the health effects of smoking, which offers an opportunity to improve the financial base of the Medicare program while imposing a substantial penalty on smoking.[78]

A Rolling Bandwagon 時流に便乗する.

The growing social isolation of smokers and the smokers' own feelings of inadequacy create opportunities for others—businessmen, association directors, and consultants, for instance—whose task it is to identify social trends and use them for economic and political advantage. The decline of smoking is certainly one such trend. So too are the negative attitudes remaining smokers express toward their own behavior.

Consider the increased interest in preventive health efforts as a solution to the national problem of escalating health care costs. Smoking is frequently cited as the single behavior most likely to lead to chronic ill health and early death. Aware of this, many smokers claim that they wish to stop. Various programs have been established to assist them in quitting. Some utilize electric shock, others saturation smoking, and still others group therapy or nicotine chewing gum, but none can demonstrate that they achieve much success in either permanently altering behavior or reducing health care costs.[79] Yet advocacy for the expansion of preventive programs grows, especially among health care providers and health insurers who are pressed to provide options to control rising health care costs. Their willingness to ignore the evidence on prevention may not be unrelated to a need to deflect attention away from policy alternatives more threatening to the interests that they represent.[80]

Or consider the public affairs strategies of industries beset with environmental hazard problems. Many of the illnesses attributed to industrial pollution can also be attributed to or exacerbated by smoking.[81] It is not surprising that asbestos and chemical firms have joined the rising chorus against smoking. Law firms representing asbestos clients are suing the tobacco companies to involve them in the mammoth liability claims filed against the asbestos industry. Chemical firms have helped finance public interest groups with high visibility in the antismoking cause. Given the declining status of smoking, such action carries little risk and offers the possibility of some important gains.

Certainly, there are some profits to be made in attacking the vulnerabilities of smokers, as other firms have discovered. More and more products are directed toward the social fears of smokers. There are special toothpastes to brighten their stained teeth, mouthwashes to refresh their fouled breath, and room air filters to permit visits by whatever remaining friends they may have.[82] Constant reminders that "Yellow tobacco stains are U-G-L-Y" and "Bad breath is bad but smoker's breath is worse" fray the nerves of the already worried smoker. The ads probably offer effective, if unintentional reinforcement to wavering nonsmokers.

Nonsmokers themselves are an increasingly attractive market. They are offered life and health insurance discounts and smoke-free environments in which to fly, drive, dine, and vacation. The nonsmoking symbol, so offensive to some, is welcomed by many others. Converting it into a profit opportunity becomes the businessman's urge.

Cigarette smokers' problems tempt even tobacco producers. The makers of Skoal Bandits, a smokeless moist tobacco, advertise their product with the slogan "Take a pouch instead of a puff." A Texas-based firm is introducing a smokeless cigarette that offers nicotine through a plastic cigarette-like tube that is sucked rather than lit.[83]

The increasing attack on smoking emboldens those who have kept silent on the issue. More and more clergymen and editorial writers in the South now condemn smoking and their region's protection of tobacco, taking pride in their newfound courage.[84] Some school teachers and parents not only wish children to be abstainers, but also encourage them to be the proselytizing moralizers that they are so inclined to become.

Politics follows life. Enterprising politicians seek out popular causes and champion them. As nonsmoking becomes more common, so will proposals to restrict smoking further (hundreds are introduced each year in state legislatures). Discrimination against smokers will not only grow, but will carry increasingly the endorsement of government. Surely, more taxes are in store for smokers because fewer and fewer politicians will rise to defend a behavior so many others condemn.

Cigarette smoking, however, will not soon disappear in America. The pleasure it offers is too seductive to suppress; its form of consumption too convenient to supplant. Barring a successful series of liability suits, someone will always be willing to make cigarettes for sale.[85] But ostracized and heavily taxed, smokers get to rethink the decision to smoke nearly every time they light up. Cigarettes are a product falling out of fashion, falling more rapidly than either their critics or their manufacturers wish to acknowledge. Although the smoke is clearing from their world, critics of smoking will probably complain just as bitterly about any lingering fumes. Given the pressures besetting the smoker, it is unlikely that the manufacturers will be able to deflect the current market challenge as easily as they have past challenges. Changes in length, flavor, or packaging of cigarettes have their limits.

Chapter 3

Hearts and Minds: The Politics of Diet and Heart Disease

JANET M. LEVINE

On 28 May 1980, a twenty-four-page report entitled *Toward Healthful Diets* was released by the Food and Nutrition Board (FNB) in Washington, D.C.[1] The FNB is part of the National Research Council, the research arm of the National Academy of Sciences. Although it does not itself conduct primary research, the National Research Council, through special and ongoing committees in its divisions, tries to bring synthesis and clarity to scientific matters that trouble its primarily governmental clients. The gray-jacketed report by the FNB was just one of many reports released annually by the National Research Council, and by the FNB whose initial function was to prepare a statement about the micronutrient requirements of the American population (the RDAs—Recommended Dietary Allowances). Yet the report generated front-page coverage in the *New York Times* and the *Washington Post.* Both newspapers, and the *Wall Street Journal,* also felt compelled to discuss the report on their editorial pages. The report's authors became familiar figures on the television talk show circuit, ranging from the early morning short spots to an evening's coverage on the "McNeil/Lehrer Report." Two sets of congressional hearings were held. And the principal author of the report was featured in a *People* magazine story, complete with photos of him approvingly watching his wife scramble up a batch of eggs.[2]

A batch of eggs? For many, the significance of this report was directly related to what they in good conscience could enjoy at the breakfast table. The reporters who attended the briefing that accompanied the issuance of the report received a press release entitled "Research Council Group Worries About Diet Panaceas." The chairman of the FNB, accompanied by another of the principal authors of the report, did explain that their intent was to resolve some important issues regarding the American diet and in the process calm the mounting fears of Americans about the foods they put on their plates. The message that the reporters took back to their composing rooms is reflected in the page-one headline that appeared the following day in the *New York Times:* "Panel Reports Healthy Americans Need Not Cut Intake of Cholesterol: Nutrition Board Challenges Notion That Such Dietary Change Could Prevent Dietary Heart Disease."[3] Americans sat down to their morning breakfast of high-fiber cereal, low-fat milk, and decaffeinated coffee and opened their newspapers to find that bacon and eggs with buttered toast and coffee and cream might have been quite all right.

The FNB was challenging what had become conventional wisdom: that it is prudent for Americans to reduce their consumption of saturated fats and cholesterol. Saturated fat and cholesterol reduction, the cessation of smoking and the control of hypertension and obesity comprise a group of risk factors for heart disease that Americans can understand and, if desired, control in an effort to prevent or delay heart problems. The FNB, while trying to reassure Americans about the foods they eat, was questioning one of the accepted weapons in the fight against heart disease—dietary change.

Reaction was swift among scientists and policymakers associated with the diet–heart disease issue. Although some individual scientists and several groups (including the American Medical Association) endorsed the report as well reasoned, many within government and science disagreed strongly with the report's conclusions. The firm but modulated statement from the national headquarters of the American Heart Association restated its belief in the necessity of dietary modification to help prevent heart disease. More emphatic members of the Chicago branch of the Heart Association held a press conference to express their outrage at the FNB report. The tone of the conference was set by the first sentence of the prepared statement: "The Chicago Heart Association believes a great disservice has been done to the public by the Food and Nutrition Board of the National Research Council."[4]

Professional debate about the FNB report centered on what was acceptable evidence, how one evaluated such evidence, and who should be involved in such an evaluation. The fifteen-member FNB (primarily nutritionists and biochemists and one or two social scientists) did not feel it necessary to include a cardiologist or an epidemiologist in its ranks or among the report's prerelease evaluators. And it is around FNB evaluation of the epidemiological evidence (which it claims can only point the direction for scientific research) and the clinical trials (which it deemed inconclusive) that the scientific dispute centered.[5]

Gradually, the controversy over the report shifted from reporter-guided public alarm and scientific dispute to questions of process and propriety. The procedures of the academy were questioned as it was revealed that the initial outside review (which was not followed by an optional upper-level National Academy of Sciences review) was conducted by at least one person whose own work was significantly cited in the report. And more explosively (though, in the end, perhaps less profoundly), the industry connections of several board members were revealed in the press. Along with one member who was acknowledged to be employed by industry, several of the FNB members either consulted for or received research money from industry groups, such as the American Egg Board and Dart-Kraft Inc. In true tabloid fashion this was trumpeted to the *New York Daily News* readers: "Food Biz Linked to Diet Report."[6]

The affected industries reacted. Commodity groups representing beef, dairy, and egg interests were quick to see the value in the FNB document. To the dismay of the FNB, the Belles of the National Cattlemen's Association gave them a citation. More direct attempts by the dairy and meat organizations to reach the public included synopses of the report as front-page items in the newsletters sent to nutrition professionals, press releases supporting the FNB sent to food editors and other interested reporters, and articles for opinion pages in newspapers and major journals supporting the report and calling for a reconsideration of an earlier publication released by the U.S. Departments of Agriculture and Health and Human Services (USDA/HHS). Those industries that benefited from support of the diet–heart disease link—the polyunsaturated oils and margarine manufacturers along with egg and meat substitute producers—maintained a discreet silence.

Science and Policy

Coronary heart disease remains, in many ways, a puzzle for research scientists and physicians. The origins of the disease(s) are theoretical; no one has yet been able to demonstrate what causes damage to the arteries and sometimes to the muscles of the heart. What is known is that atherosclerosis (thickening, narrowing, and hardening of blood vessels) is the cause of angina pectoris and most heart attacks. Partial blockage of the arteries, reducing the amount of blood and oxygen the heart receives, can lead to intermittent chest pain, especially when the individual exercises. Heart attacks occur when a portion of the heart muscle is deprived of oxygen. The process of atherosclerosis, by narrowing the arterial passageways and changing the characteristics of the inner lining of the arterial walls from smooth, elastic cells to rough, uneven surfaces, is a major cause of heart attacks.[7]

The diet–heart disease hypothesis postulates that there is a positive relationship between the level of cholesterol in the blood (serum cholesterol) and the development of atherosclerosis and coronary heart disease. It also postulates that the amount of cholesterol (dietary cholesterol) and saturated fats we eat affects the level of serum cholesterol. Thus, the hypothesis concludes, if we reduce the amount of dietary cholesterol and saturated fats in the American diet, the incidence of atherosclerosis and heart disease will decrease.[8]

The debate that was aired when the FNB report became public encapsulates many of the scientific issues in the diet–heart disease controversy. The evidence never speaks for itself, and in the diet–heart disease area there are many sources of evidence and many sources of evaluation. Research ranges from epidemiological research at the national and subnational levels, to animal studies (on rabbits, baboons, monkeys, chickens, swine, and turkeys), to human clinical trials (on those with genetic predisposition to high serum cholesterol levels, and on average populations in institutional settings and in normal settings). Researchers include nutritionists, biochemists, physician-cardiologists, physician-epidemiologists, and epidemiologists. The breadth of evidence combined with the varied backgrounds of the scientists evaluating it ensures debate not only over what is acceptable evidence, but also over *who* should be selecting and interpreting the evidence.

In some ways the diet–heart disease hypothesis can be seen as very attractive for policymakers and the public. It offers a solution—if only a partial solution—to a disease that accounts for more American deaths than any other. People who have organized to fight heart disease can see some results for their money-raising and other efforts. A government, burdened by health care costs, can turn to prevention as a means of decreasing future costs. And the public, menaced by the specter of heart attacks that cut short lives, can become actively involved in dietary practices that help reduce their risk of the disease. However, viewed from another perspective, one could anticipate public resistance to the recommended diet changes.

The proponents of the diet–heart disease link urge people to change their diets. They want Americans to turn from items high in cholesterol and saturated fats (eggs, marbled red meat, high-fat dairy products) to low-cholesterol, low-fat, or polyunsaturated products (egg substitutes, vegetables, margarines, oils, fish, and chicken). The diet switch—known as the prudent diet—recommended by the diet–heart disease proponents argues that Americans should forswear their traditional foods and venture into the unknown territory of grains, vegetables, and lean meats. (This "new" diet probably resembles the traditional diet of a hundred years ago.) The foods we are being asked to limit or forgo have none of the stigma of forbidden pleasures. Indeed, they are associated with protein, calcium, and energy—the very properties of foods that are good for you. And it is not what has been added to the foods that is being condemned. Artificial ingredients are not the issue, rather it is the natural components of the products themselves. One might expect some public skepticism about the necessity of making such changes.

By separating foods into more healthy and less healthy groups, the diet–heart disease hypothesis has split the food industry into those able to take advantage of the labels "low fat" and "low cholesterol" and those farm commodity producers who have sought to rebut the scientific evidence. Along with efforts of voluntary health agencies, government, and consumer groups, the extent of industry involvement remains very important for understanding how the views of competing scientists were transmitted to a concerned public.

The reaction to the FNB report gives one indication of the extent to which the press and perhaps the public has accepted the link between diet and heart disease. And, to some degree, Americans have already changed their diets during the post–World War II era. We are eating less butter, more margarine, fewer eggs, less milk (and of milk consumed, a higher percentage is low-fat milk), less red meat (consumption began to dip in 1977), more cheese, more chicken and turkey, and less grains and apples.[9] (See figures 3.1–3.4.) This somewhat murky picture of decreases in some areas of cholesterol and saturated fats (such as the switch to margarine, low-fat milk, and chicken) and increases in other areas of highly saturated fats (more cheese) becomes even cloudier when one attempts to understand the reason for the changes. The major confounding factor is economic. Many substitutes, such as margarine and chicken, are less expensive than butter and red meats. Additionally, changes in life-style have made the leisurely family breakfast of two eggs and bacon an anachronism. Although not all Americans have succumbed to the continental breakfast of a roll and butter or jam, we have turned to quicker, more easily prepared breakfasts that pour out of a container.[10]

There is some evidence that Americans are aware of the diet–heart disease hypothesis and are involved in or interested in changing their behavior. Surveys indicate people believe that diet is associated with health; cholesterol is one of the key identifiable substances to be avoided.[11] The joint Food and Drug Administration/Department of Agriculture/Fed-

FIGURE 3.1

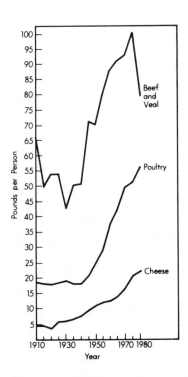

Beef and Veal, Poultry, and Cheese Consumption

NOTE: Reprinted from Letitia Brewster and Michael F. Jacobson, *The Changing American Diet*, which is available from the Center for Science in the Public Interest, 1501 16th Street N.W., Washington, D.C. 20036, copyright 1978; additional data from USDA, *Food Consumption, Prices and Expenditures, 1960-1980* (Washington, D.C.: Government Printing Office, 1981).

FIGURE 3.2

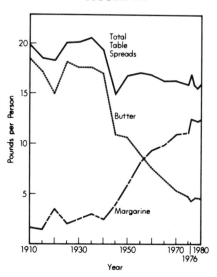

Butter and Margarine Consumption

NOTE: Reprinted from Letitia Brewster and Michael F. Jacobson, *The Changing American Diet,* which is available from the Center for Science in the Public Interest, 1501 16th Street N.W., Washington, D.C. 20036, copyright 1978; additional data from USDA, *Food Consumption, Prices and Expenditures, 1960-1980* (Washington, D.C.: Government Printing Office, 1981).

eral Trade Commission hearings on food labeling in the mid-1970s identified amounts of cholesterol and saturated fats as one of several important pieces of information that the public wanted in food labels.[12] And in the marketplace, consumers continue to buy higher-priced margarine and oil (such as Fleischmann's and Mazola) instead of the less-polyunsaturated (and thus less associated with disease prevention) lower-priced margarines and oils.

The diet–heart disease dispute will be described in this chapter in three chronological periods: 1950–76, 1976–80, and 1980 to the present. The relative activity of governmental and nongovernmental groups in each period will be explained by looking at the internal and external pressures on the organizations involved. During 1950–76, most of those motivated to act on the diet–heart disease relationship were scientists and the polyunsaturated margarine and oil manufacturers. Neither group galvanized government attention; the scientists were unable to do so, the manufacturers were uninterested in doing so. The inability of the scientists to take their case to the government or to the public can be attributed to the internal constraints on the organizations with which the scientists worked. Con-

FIGURE 3.3

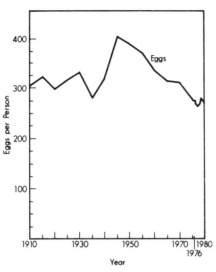

Egg Consumption

NOTE: Reprinted from Letitia Brewster and Michael F. Jacobson, *The Changing American Diet,* which is available from the Center for Science in the Public Interest, 1501 16th Street N.W., Washington, D.C. 20036, copyright 1978; additional data from USDA, *Food Consumption, Prices and Expenditures, 1960-1980* (Washington, D.C.: Government Printing Office, 1981).

trary to what one might expect, the polyunsaturated oil and margarine manufacturers were anxious to have as little governmental involvement as possible. They sought to keep the regulatory activities of the Food and Drug Administration (FDA) and the Federal Trade Commission (FTC) to a manageable level. These manufacturers chose the marketing option and brought the message of the diet–heart disease link to the public through their advertising. Besides this FDA-FTC regulatory interest, other agencies and branches of the government expressed little interest in the diet–heart disease link. This disinterest also suited the farm commodity producers; the dairy, meat, and egg producers had firm relationships with the Congress and the USDA, which ensured farmers' favored position among legislators and regulators. A balance of governmental inactivity and manufacturer activity prevailed.

The pattern of scientific ineffectiveness and governmental inactivity was drastically shaken during the 1976–80 period, when a serendipitous interaction of forces in Congress and the executive branch led to unprecedented concern and activity on the diet–heart disease issue. This, in turn, generated a response from a hitherto uninvolved sector of the industry: the

FIGURE 3.4

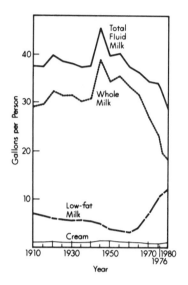

Milk Consumption

NOTE: Reprinted from Letitia Brewster and Michael F. Jacobson, *The Changing American Diet,* which is available from the Center for Science in the Public Interest, 1501 16th Street N.W., Washington, D.C. 20036, copyright 1978; additional data from USDA, *Food Consumption, Prices and Expenditures, 1960-1980* (Washington, D.C.: Government Printing Office, 1981).

farm commodity producers. The politically powerful beef and dairy inter-ests worked quickly to dissuade government officials from involvement in the diet–heart disease issue.

As the presidency changed hands and the traditional farm commodity interests reasserted themselves, the new forces that had generated the activity on the diet–heart disease issue were swept out of power. The diet–heart disease proponents were unable to leave behind an infrastruc-ture that could survive in their absence, but they did leave the legacy of a government statement on diet and health. For the involved government agencies, the public interest and health groups, and the food producers, a resurgence of agricultural political clout could not sweep away their under-standing of this new potential.

1950–76: The Quiet Balance

SCIENCE, SCIENTISTS, AND THEIR ORGANIZATIONS

Scientific interest in the diet–heart disease link began in the early 1900s when Russian experimenters linked cholesterol consumption to serum cholesterol in rabbits. Research interest continued on a low level until after World War II when significant new research took place. Several researchers noticed two striking things about the European population that had survived the war years: in many areas of Europe the population suffered deprivations of meat, butter, and eggs during the war, and these same populations showed a decline in the incidence of cardiovascular disease during the same period. Although many scientists have subsequently criticized these studies, their importance lies not in the quality of the evidence provided, but in the galvanizing effect they had on scientists looking for some manipulable variable to use against a disease that was on the increase.[13]

The impetus to study the impact of dietary cholesterol and saturated versus polyunsaturated fats on diet and heart disease continues, although the attitudes of scientists about the significance of diet in the atherosclerotic process became relatively fixed by the mid-1960s. Although hundreds of scientists participated in research on the issue, a smaller group of about thirty scientists form the core of the debate (taking either positive or negative stances). The positions of the scientists conform to some degree to their disciplinary identity—heart doctor, physician, or nutritionist. These identities are represented by several major organizations: the American Heart Association, the American Medical Association, the American Society for Clinical Nutrition, the American Institute of Nutrition, and the Food and Nutrition Board of the National Research Council.

The American Heart Association (AHA) has demonstrated the longest and most consistent commitment to the diet–heart disease hypothesis. Professional reports and statements have been the dominant manifestations of their commitment. Although individual members of the AHA have urged additional activities, the AHA has been unable to translate its professional-level activity into major mass-level commitments—either in public education campaigns or in government lobbying. Confronted both by the limitations set by scientific consensus building and by local control over program implementation, the AHA dietary-change advocates have been unable to extend their influence much beyond statements by the Epidemiology and Arteriosclerosis Councils.

The AHA was formed in 1924 as a professional association for physicians. From the mid-1920s to 1948 it continued as a professional society; its primary mission was to foster the study of the heart patient. It became chartered as a voluntary health agency in 1948. The primary motivating force for its movement from a professional to a voluntary health association was the desire to acquire funds for research. (Since then, the AHA nationally has always spent more than 50 percent of its operating budget on research.)

From its inception onward, most of the AHA's energies have been devoted to generating knowledge and interest in heart disease. Efforts to enhance knowledge about heart disease center on expanding support for research, along with programs designed to attract young physicians to heart research. The AHA also works to inform the medical community about current findings on heart disease. As early as 1961 the AHA issued a statement declaring that individuals should moderate high intakes of cholesterol and saturated fats.[14] This was not the first statement on the issue; a group of noted scientists produced the first such report in 1959.[15] The authors of the 1959 report were among the nucleus of AHA members involved with the production of the 1961 and subsequent AHA reports on diet and heart disease.

Professional reports and education, one of the major forms of activity of the AHA, remained its primary focus for diet and heart disease. The AHA cookbook, featuring recipes low in cholesterol and saturated fats,[16] was not accompanied by an active program to persuade the public to change its eating habits, however. Involvement in a federally sponsored hypertension detection, education, and follow-up program was the AHA's only serious foray into public education. A similar project for cholesterol and saturated fats was not considered.

The structure of the AHA has traditionally left the power over statements on scientific issues to scientists in the executive committees of the national council, while power over implementing programs has been vested in the state or regional offices. Even if there were a strong consensus in the scientific councils serving the national headquarters on the need for a public education program, the staff would then have to convince the many individual chapters of the association to act. In these chapters the demands of other existing programs, the difficulties of switching from professional to public education, the continuing pressure to link public relations campaigns with fund-raising efforts, and the reluctance of volunteers to become involved in a potentially controversial area, would probably provide serious resistance to an attempt at program proselytization by the national office. It is quite possible, however, that this professional orientation and concomitant low activity in the public area suits the needs of the scientific arm of the AHA as well.

Local lay control over AHA programs is counterbalanced by centralized professional control over scientific statements and reports. Through a hierarchical system of scientific councils, scientists with particular expertise are permitted to dominate the activities of a specific council. The review procedures for reports written by any of the executive committees of these councils are designed to accentuate consensus building. The products of any council are tempered by this review process which required individual council statements to be reviewed by significant members of other councils, in addition to an upper-level review committee.

Within the AHA the strongest proponents of the diet–heart disease link are found in the Epidemiology Council, followed by the Arteriosclerosis Council. Scientists who adhere to what they describe as the public health point of view dominate in the executive committees of these councils. They argue that the strength of all the various types of epidemiological, animal, and human clinical evidence is persuasive enough for them to conclude that large segments of American society are at risk. Rather than wait until they can identify the specific individuals at highest risk, which today is not technologically feasible, they argue that we should be making prescriptions for society as a whole. Those at risk will be protected and the low-risk people will not be harmed. Many scientists whose interests would lead them to be members of the Epidemiology and Arteriosclerosis Councils but who disagree with the position of these councils on the diet–heart disease issue have chosen instead to leave the AHA. Either as individuals or as members of like-minded organizations, these scientists continue to question the AHA position in articles and editorial pieces that appear in major medical journals.

Other dissenters in different fields (such as cardiology and surgery) remain within the AHA and continue to question the importance of diet for heart disease prevention. Professional norms require them to defer to the opinions of the experts in the diet–heart disease field. The existence of doubters within the AHA weakens the impetus for any programs that go further than the regularly issued professional statements. There are many claims on resources of the AHA. Resistance to new claims on resources, which a major public education campaign would entail, is only strengthened by the lack of scientific unanimity on the merits of the diet–heart disease link.

The same internal constraints on the ability of the AHA to take a major role in public education campaigns for dietary change also contribute to its lack of participation in government lobbying. The AHA has never perceived itself as a strong lobbying organization, although representatives do appear at congressional hearings testifying for the increased funding of the National Heart, Lung, and Blood Institute (NHLBI) of the National Institutes of Health (NIH) and offering scientific statements on heart disease issues (such as diet and heart disease). Until recently, however, this was the extent of AHA involvement in legislative activity. The Washington AHA office, opened in 1981, has a strong antismoking focus. The AHA does not organize its local chapters for political pressure through constituencies.

Many of the same physicians who belong to the AHA also belong to the American Medical Association (AMA). But because the AMA includes the whole array of medical disciplines, the issue of diet and heart disease diminishes in importance relative to general concerns of the medical profession such as reimbursement and the physician-patient relationship.

The AMA has issued some statements about diet and health.[17] The most daring of these (which occurred, it was reported, because some advocates from the AHA were on the AMA Nutrition Committee) emphasized the necessity of screening for heart disease, diet change as decided by the physician, and continued physician supervision.[18] The ongoing position of the AMA is that heart disease is a medical problem; people should not treat themselves. The AMA reports on diet and heart disease were geared to the health professional, to assist them in patient treatment. Their common theme is that people should watch their diets to avoid obesity. In this light, control of fat intake is said to help patients avoid becoming overweight and thus should be pursued under a doctor's guidance.

The link to the physician is the key in the view of the AMA. Guided by this medical model, the AMA has never considered adopting the public health orientation of the AHA. This same medical model led the AMA in the late 1960s to lobby the FDA to change labeling regulations so that patients who needed to know the fat and cholesterol content of food would be able to do so.[19] This lobbying effort represents the extent of the AMA's pro–diet change activities: despite this demonstration of lobbying skills, the AMA apparently lacks the motivation to become involved in congressional and regulatory lobbying on the diet–heart disease issue.

Nutritionists are even more divided over the diet–heart disease issue than physicians. Of course, one problem stems from the definition of a nutritionist. Some physicians consider themselves nutritionists; other experts have degrees in nutrition, biochemistry, chemistry, and nutrition education; still others are registered dieticians. With this profusion of experts comes a whole range of organizations—the American Dietetic Association, the Society for Nutrition Education, the Institute of Food Technologists, the American Oil Chemists Society, the American Society for Clinical Nutrition, and the American Institute for Nutrition. Conflict among nutritionists over the diet–heart disease issue coupled with a preoccupation with discovering the important properties of food has led to organizational avoidance of the diet–heart disease issue. The first interests of the various associations were in the furtherance of their particular subprofession and, as public and private health care benefits expanded, gaining access to these funds for their practitioners.

One organization, however, was by its very nature expected to make policy recommendations on issues of nutrition. The Food and Nutrition Board of the National Research Council was formed just before World War II to see to the nutritional well-being of the country.[20] Spurred by the wartime draft, which revealed many potential draftees with physical disabilities linked to nutritional deficiencies, the FNB began to release its Recommended Dietary Allowances (which it continues to update).[21] In addition, the FNB set up several committees to review other nutrition-related problems, such as food safety and additives. In the leadership vacuum among nutrition groups, the FNB became a source of public policy recommendations. By virtue of its association with the National Research Council, it was a logical resource to which government agencies would turn. Its stature within the nutrition community grew while most other nutrition organizations remained silent.

This did not mean that the conflict within the profession was absent in the FNB. The one early statement the FNB was able to issue on diet and heart disease was made jointly with the AMA in 1964; it supported the previously described medical model. Although asked to produce a general diet and disease statement in the early 1970s, the composition of the FNB at the time made any consensus impossible. It was the board's visibility on the broad range of nutrition issues that made scientists in the nutrition profession and in the FNB grow accustomed to public acceptance of the FNB as the primary source of nutritional wisdom.

Scientists provided research, information, and some exhortations between 1950 and 1976, but most organizations were either unable or unwilling to make public statements, or were opposed to populationwide dietary change. The organization most committed to public change (the AHA) also experienced internal constraints on publicly advocating dietary change. A core of scientists and reports was identified as useful to those attempting to generate change or policy. The impetus had to come from outside the organizations of scientists.

THE FEDERAL GOVERNMENT: NATIONALLY INACTIVE

National Institutes of Health   The National Institutes of Health, research arm of the Public Health Service division of the Department of Health and Human Services, is the champion of basic research scientists. In their world of laboratory experiments, expenditures for human clinical trials seem a questionable drain on research funds. At the same time, the NIH scientists view themselves as the keepers of the facts. One policymaker at NIH described its role as the source of a sort of "Good Housekeeping Seal" on important health issues. As a consequence, its leadership resists making statements on scientific issues when even a hint of controversy remains. Because the diet–heart disease issue is controversial, the reasoned response from the NIH would be to study the question more fully. In this way, it could eventually provide the scientific community with additional information with which to formulate an opinion, and the NIH could appear sensitive to important issues while delaying any commitment. And herein lay the problem: among the core of scientists disputing the diet–heart disease issue there was a consensus that the best way to develop information on this issue at this time (the mid-to-late 1960s) was through a large long-term human clinical trial. Such a trial is the very type of research that basic scientists at NIH resist funding. Therefore the solution to the diet–heart disease controversy—delay by seeking more research—engendered its own conflict over the type of research that should be funded.

This conflict was expressed in the debate over whether the National Heart, Lung and Blood Institute (NHLBI is the institute within the NIH's organization with responsibility for heart disease) should support a large-scale diet–heart disease trial. The NHLBI had supported (and continues to support) the Framingham Study,[22] an important source of data linking high serum cholesterol with atherosclerosis. The NHLBI funded the Intersociety Commission on Heart Disease Resources (the ICHDR) to study the feasibility of a large-scale clinical trial on the link between diet and heart disease. The ICHDR was to determine whether diets in noninstitutionalized populations could be changed enough to have an impact on serum cholesterol. In 1968 the ICHDR reported that it was feasible to do such a study (in other words, that people would comply with the diet regimen).[23] The commission recommended that a large-scale diet–heart disease trial be initiated and, in addition, that the general public be urged to cut their consumption of saturated fats and cholesterol.

Advocates of the diet–heart disease relationship pushed for the trial, viewing it as the piece of evidence that would galvanize the rest of the scientific community and the public. The NIH commissioned a study group, which, using staff calculations on the numbers of participants necessary for the trial and the cost of the trial, concluded that the diet trial was not feasible.[24] This conclusion met with support at the NIH and the trial was scuttled.

To pacify the diet–heart disease proponents several smaller trials were subsequently initiated. The Multiple Risk Factor Intervention Trial (MRFIT) looked at three factors: smoking, hypertension, and diet.[25] It attempted to change the behavior of a test group and determine over time any differences in heart disease incidence and mortality found in the test group versus a control group. The design of the trial was such that researchers will not be able to determine the individual impact of the three factors. The Lipid Research Clinics (LRC) were developed to test whether a decrease in serum cholesterol would in the long run result in lowered heart disease incidence and mortality.[26] Both diet and drugs were used in the LRC trial, which was begun in 1973 and ended in 1984 (the MRFIT started in 1972 and concluded in 1981).

These trials to some degree satisfied scientists who wanted more data. Then NIH was confronted with those who wanted NIH not only to make statements, but also to become involved in education and prevention. The call for such activity was made possible by 1972 legislation that mandated NHLBI to provide disease prevention and education.[27] Although there was some pressure from scientists and from the Center for Science in the Public Interest (CSPI, a public interest group) for the NHLBI to become involved in the diet–heart disease issue, the heart institute chose to devote its energies to the area of hypertension detection and control.

As described by NHLBI officials, this was the least costly choice. Hypertension had the interest of HEW secretary Elliot Richardson, as well as that of Mary Lasker (philanthropist and long-time advocate of public health through Democrats in Congress), and her congressional friends. From the institute's perspective, hypertension intervention was preferable to smoking or diet intervention because there was enough scientific evidence to warrant it, because the interventions were fairly straightforward (drug therapy was being developed), and because there were no long-established groups making competing efforts. Moreover, there was no *political* opposition to hypertension intervention. Smoking, according to the calculations of NHLBI officials, had the necessary scientific evidence for intervention, but control would be difficult—how can people be made to stop smoking?

Agency competition for lead position in any effort would be fierce, and the political opposition would be very strong in the case of smoking. Diet change fared worst in their calculations. Not all scientific evidence was in yet (especially with several institute-supported trials outstanding). Intervention was problematic—changing diets is difficult and available drugs had side effects. And the political opposition would be overwhelming.

The outspoken debate among some scientists coupled with the belief that some facts were still lacking convinced leaders at the NHLBI that advocating diet change would only hurt the credibility of the institute. Fortunately for them, most outside sources of pressure, in Congress or interest groups, were either disinterested or agreed with their evaluation. Little funding was provided for education or prevention programs. The CSPI did continue to call for more action on diet from NHLBI, but to no avail. The NHLBI officials were uncomfortable dealing with groups not among their traditional sources of support. The CSPI activists did not try to develop the symbiotic relationship with which NHLBI officials were comfortable. The CSPI could not be counted on as a friend, only as a critic. As they made policy decisions, NHLBI officials were less concerned with the priorities of a group that rejected the time-honored customs of interest group and bureaucracy give-and-take.

Congress   Between 1950 and 1976 no one in Congress manifested interest in the issue of diet and heart disease nor was there an obvious organizational niche where proponents of the diet–heart disease hypothesis could gather. Congress did continue to support the research efforts of the NIH. The NHLBI grew rapidly, dwarfed only by the "War on Cancer" funds that poured into the National Cancer Institute.[28]

Congressional agriculture committees continued their support of farming research and commodity support programs. The initial 1930s commitment to farm supports became ritualized in the four-year farm bill cycle. Food stamp programs were originally a means of disposing of surplus foods. They remained in the USDA and thus under agriculture committees' purview. There were no initiatives from either the House or Senate committees on the issue of diet and heart disease. Congress did develop interest in one aspect of nutrition, the issue of "access to nutrition" (food). During the late 1960s Congress rediscovered the poor and learned that they sometimes did not have enough to eat.

Congressional interest in hunger and poverty was piqued by Senate hearings held in 1967.[29] A 1968 television documentary called "Hunger in America" led the Senate to create the Senate Select Committee on Nutrition and Human Need (SSC) the same year.[30] Chaired by Senator George

McGovern (D., S.D.) and including at different times some of the more influential senators in the health and agriculture committees (such as Senators Hubert Humphrey, Robert Dole, Charles Percy, and Edward Kennedy), the early years of the committee (1968–75) focused on the broad areas of family food assistance programs and nutrition programs for children and the elderly.[31]

The growth of federal food and nutrition programs coincided with the growth of consumer interest groups, many of which formed around the food program issue. The most notable and long-lived of these are the Community Nutrition Institute and the Food Research Action Committee. But there was little interest in diet and disease issues among these groups. For some, the thought of telling the poor what to eat bordered on the paternalism that they wished to avoid. And because they focused on the disadvantaged, they tended to ignore the diet–heart disease issue, which was the scourge of white, middle-aged, middle-class males. Broader consumer groups, such as the Consumer Federation, concentrated on economic issues. And the CSPI, although it ignited some sparks on the diet–heart disease issue and offered some diet information material, was unable to light any congressional fires, just as it was unable to build a fire at NHLBI. Thus, even though scientists stood in the wings ready to testify about the diet–heart disease issue, Congress was uninterested.

Department of Agriculture The Department of Agriculture has traditionally represented the interests of food producers.[32] The USDA's program, which emphasized research and extension services, was expanded during the Great Depression to include the management of price-support schemes. Promotion of agricultural interests continued, as the responsibilities of the food programs were added in the late 1960s and early 1970s. Before the food programs, USDA nutritional activities centered on determining the nutritional content of foods and distributing meal planning information. The "Basic Seven" (and later the "Basic Four") food groups were developed by the USDA to help consumers in planning meals. The guides emphasized the nutritional values of foods and the need for moderation. However, the USDA did not consider utilizing the diet–heart disease recommendations of the American Heart Association in its meal planning. It looked to the Food and Nutrition Board for nutrient allowances and then to its own nutritionists for meal plan guidance.

The Regulators: The FDA and the FTC The Food and Drug Administration and the Federal Trade Commission have regulatory control over food labeling and food advertising, respectively. During the 1950–76 period, both agencies were generally cautious about the diet–heart disease issue.

In 1959 the FDA prohibited any labeling claim that linked cholesterol or fats with heart disease.[33] Whether prompted by the early advertising campaigns of some of the polyunsaturated oil and margarine companies (which is the opinion of some members of the food industry) or prompted by fears of future label claims, this regulation remained in force until the early 1970s. In 1964, physicians, concerned about the inability of their patients on restricted diets to find product information on cholesterol and fats, requested the FDA to permit labeling statements. The FDA did publish a proposal to permit a factual declaration of cholesterol and fat content of foods in 1965, but subsequently withdrew it for further study.[34] The regulatory logjam was broken in 1969 with the publication of the *White House Conference Report on Food, Nutrition and Health*.[35] Officials at the FDA clearly felt that the labeling recommendations in this report were more significant than the early AHA or AMA statements, and they date their activity to that White House conference report. A final regulation was published in 1973. The label that listed fatty acid and cholesterol content was required to also include a statement to the effect that the fat and cholesterol information was available for patients whose doctors recommended that they be on a cholesterol- and fat-restricted diet.[36] According to this regulation (which is still in force), no claims can be made regarding the product's ability to reduce serum cholesterol.

The FDA views itself as a scientific organization. It has the largest food- and nutrition-related intramural research program in the government (employing several hundred researchers). As part of a research organization in the area of food and nutrition, with regulatory responsibilities concerning food safety and quality, the people who guide its policies may view its regulatory pronouncements as the necessary imprimatur on food research applications (parallel with NIH's authority over research findings). This view may contribute to its conservative stances (which recall the NHLBI's unwillingness to support populationwide dietary change).

Congressional oversight of the FDA is divided. Authorizing power is vested in the health committees but fiscal control rests in the agriculture subcommittees of the appropriations committees. This odd split results from the origin of the FDA as part of the USDA. Although FDA has long been part of the Department of Health and Human Services, the role of the agriculture subcommittees illustrates the unwillingness of the farm lobbies to relinquish fiscal control over a food regulatory agency. It is apparent that the FDA has a large number of industry forces to contend with. Often the decision that causes the least reaction is the decision to do nothing; accepting discontent with the status quo may be less worrisome to the FDA than provoking industry responses.

The FTC and FDA have an interagency agreement in their regulation of labeling and advertising. In the 1960s and early 1970s the capacity of the FTC to react systematically to breaches in food advertising regulations was limited. Critics of the FTC point out that during the 1960s the agency rarely fully performed its regulatory functions.[37]

Poor resource allocation was not the only impediment that hampered the FTC's efforts to enforce advertising regulations. Until the mid-1970s the major regulatory weapon the FTC had at its disposal was the "cease and desist order." This enforcement procedure begins with a complaint and may pass through many levels of appeal within the agency and in the courts. As students of the FTC point out, the nature of advertising (with the relatively short time span of any advertising campaign), the small degree of FTC punitive powers (simply "cease and desist orders"), and the potential for prolonging the FTC review through appeals, offers little incentive to heed the agency.[38]

During the early 1970s, the FTC staff developed a new procedure that seemed to promise more power to the FTC's enforcement capacity. The innovation was the Trade Rule Regulation (TRR), which created industry-wide standards that go beyond case-by-case consideration of advertising to the establishment of specific standards for what is permissible and required in the advertisements of an industry. The FTC staff proposed a TRR for nutrition advertising in November 1974. Although the scope of the food TRR was broader than the fat and cholesterol issue, it included a significant section on fatty acid and cholesterol advertising. The staff held extensive public hearings (required by legislation) that continued throughout the 1970s. What is significant to note now is that the slim authority that the FTC once held over industry advertising through its "cease and desist" proceedings disappeared soon after the announcement of the food TRR. "Cease and desist" orders accomplished just that—most FTC food-advertising regulation was suspended until the hearing process was completed (in December 1982). The FTC was effectively out of the business of regulating food advertising.

THE FOOD INDUSTRY

A broad range of food interests is affected by the diet–heart disease issue. Of the food producers, ranchers and dairy and egg farmers are particularly vulnerable. Industries that produce farm commodity substitutes are also directly affected: these are the manufacturers of margarine and polyunsaturated oils, as well as artificial eggs or bacon. And those who manufacture products that contain significant amounts of butter or eggs are also potentially concerned. The reaction to the diet–heart disease issue by any of these industries was determined by how they viewed the potential of the scientific ideas. For example, producers of corn oil or other substances with advantageous polyunsaturate ratings chose to champion the diet–heart disease link. They had the organizational and research tools that facilitated product development and marketing with a diet and health emphasis. They chose, therefore, the most comfortable arena in which to pursue the diet–heart disease issue: the marketplace.

Although all three (meat, dairy, and egg) commodity groups could view themselves as threatened during this period, it was the egg producers who reacted in the most vociferous, if not successful, fashion. The dairy and meat industries were not particularly alarmed by the research findings and AHA recommendations. Their long-standing research network, their comfortable relationship with the USDA, and the fact that, unlike the consumption of eggs, their total product consumption was not decreasing (in the case of the dairy industry, surplus was being absorbed by government storage programs) persuaded them that they had a more secure hold on the marketplace.

Polyunsaturated Margarine and Oils: Feeding the Fire   By the mid-1950s margarine consumption surpassed that of butter and vegetable shortening consumption exceeded that of lard. This market momentum accelerated during the subsequent decades. At first, the switch could be attributed to economics and technology. Freed in 1950 from onerous federal taxes and restrictions on the use of yellow coloring, margarine could become competitive with butter.[39] It was less expensive than butter, and the inconvenience of having to color the pallid margarine after purchase was removed. Margarine was becoming mainstream. The corn oil and cottonseed oil used in margarine were by-products of cornstarch and cotton products. Before the twentieth century corn oil was used only for soap; as technology allowed the use of these residuals as edible oils, the public was educated to find them an attractive alternative to lard.

Although the initial breakthrough into the American kitchen was made without any reference to nutrition or health, some alert executives in these industries recognized the marketing potential in presenting the product not only as a cheaper substitute but as a healthier alternative. And, as competition in the polyunsaturate field increased, this approach was a means of distinguishing one brand from another until others followed suit.

Mazola corn oil was developed by CPC/Best Foods in 1911. The by-product of cornstarch, it entered into the oils market when most cooks used hard fats such as lard and suet. The early advertising centered around teaching people how to use the product. The company's awareness of medically related advertising began in the 1920s when corn syrup (one of their products) was used for infant formula. Although ads that implied that corn oil was nutritious were introduced in the 1920s, it was not until the 1940s that CPC personnel began experimenting with ads presenting Mazola as healthy. The essential fatty acids were discovered in the 1940s —some Mazola ads of those years touted the product as a "rich source of essential fatty acids." The producers of Mazola oil were able to capitalize on free publicity when *McCall's* magazine covered a new obesity diet that used corn oil. Then, when research linking fat and cholesterol to heart disease in the 1950s used corn oil as the polyunsaturate ingredient, CPC selected the diet–heart disease link as their marketing theme.

Mazola's producers decided on a strategy that proved quite effective. They would establish legitimacy with physicians through literature, medical advertising, and attendance at medical conventions, although Mazola would never be presented as a pharmaceutical to either physicians or consumers. Consumer ads would always show the product as a food and always offered nutrition information.

Mazola's marketing activities from 1956 on reflected this strategy. The company prepared a review of diet–heart disease literature for the 1956 AMA convention. And the theme was presented to the public in 1957. Ads telling the public to "Listen to Your Heart" appeared in *Life* magazine discussing the impact of diet on the chance of a heart attack. The early success of their diet–heart disease advertising inspired CPC to develop it further.

The physicians were never forgotten. Nutrition reviews for physicians were updated every two to three years. Current scientific findings were presented in Mazola's graphically pleasing medical ads. They developed audiovisual materials for nutrition education, and CPC staff became familiar figures at medical conventions. Reputable scientists sought out CPC to help popularize the prudent diet. And CPC published several short diet advice books as well as a "risk handbook" for physicians developed by the AHA.[40]

Although CPC staff felt that physicians were the key to the hearts of some consumers, they also wanted to reach consumers directly. Early consumer advertisements included clippings from newspaper articles describing how scientific research had indicated that consumption of polyunsaturates would lower an individual's risk of heart attacks, though this practice stopped after the 1959 FDA labeling regulations. The CPC staff interpreted the regulations to mean that the company could not directly link polyunsaturates to preventing heart disease—but it could describe the polyunsaturated nature of the product without mentioning *why* people should care about polyunsaturates. Nevertheless, consumers got the message—although Mazola cost more than other oils, its sales and market share continued to rise.

Of course, the public was also being educated through other advertisements in the polyunsaturated oils market by Standard Brands (producers of Fleischmann's) and other margarine manufacturers. When the political restraints on margarine were lifted in 1950 Standard Brands margarine became an important product for the company. Alerted to the new scientific evidence linking the ratio of polyunsaturated/saturated (P/S) fats in the diet to serum cholesterol (the higher the P/S ratio the lower the serum cholesterol), Standard Brands measured the P/S ratio of margarines in the marketplace. In 1953 they discovered that this ratio was equal to or worse than that of butter. The Standard Brands technical staff were able to overcome the problem of hydrogenation, which was the source of margarine's poor P/S ratio.

Fleischmann's corn oil margarine was introduced in 1956. It differed from other margarines in two distinct ways: (1) the amount of hydrogenated vegetable oil was reduced to less than half of the oil in the product, and (2) corn oil was used (most margarines used cottonseed oil). This premium margarine was featured in successive advertising campaigns that emphasized the diet–heart disease link and the beneficial health qualities of the margarine.

Like CPC, Standard Brands also set up booths at medical conventions. Initial business would come from educated doctors who would recommend the product to their patients, then word of mouth and consumer advertising would continue the education. The advertising had a consistent theme —Fleischmann's is an important part of a prudent diet to limit the risk of heart disease. Scientific studies were cited in the consumer ads, and a cookbook was developed for consumers. The success of this "educate the consumer" approach can be seen in the current ads. It is no longer necessary to state that dietary change can lower cholesterol. Now ads merely say "low saturated fat, low cholesterol, 100 percent corn oil"; they need go no further.

Dairy Industry: Brains and Might   The dairy industry has, of the three farm commodities considered, the most protected product. The federal price-support program for dairy products guarantees farmers that their surplus milk will be purchased, thus protecting them from the competitive impact of margarine gains over butter.[41] Dairy products are also more amenable to change to accommodate low-fat diets. The rising popularity of low-fat milk is the best example of the capacity for product development. Along with its well-established links to the Department of Agriculture and congressional supporters, the dairy industry has developed an effective relationship with nutrition educators. The industry supports dairy nutrition education and research through the National Dairy Council, generic marketing is handled by the American Dairy Association.

The National Dairy Council continues to be the largest private supplier of nutrition materials to children in the United States. Emphasizing moderation in eating and selection from the "Basic Four" food groups (developed by the USDA), the Dairy Council distributes materials through their thirty-three affiliates staffed by 300 nutritionists. Their school materials have a reputation for technical quality and accepted content. In this manner the Dairy Council stresses the qualities of food, the need to combat obesity and the need for variety, and nutritional principles widely accepted in the 1960s and 1970s. Dairy products make up one of the "Basic Four" food groups, and as one dairy official commented about the nutrition education program, "The industry benefits because people eat better. When people eat better they eat dairy. We feel we have a dairy food for everyone."[42] The Dairy Council creates rapport with nutrition professionals by distributing nearly 100,000 copies of its bimonthly newsletter free of charge. Accompanying articles on nutrition are current research items on the positive properties of dairy products.

The dairy industry is well organized to promote its products and to make modifications to meet consumer demand. It felt no need to respond precipitously when diets high in saturated fats were questioned. Although the price-support system ensures a base price for dairy goods and a guaranteed market, these price supports must be protected by the dairy industry's lobby. Indeed, this is the chief focus of its well-financed political efforts.

Meat Industry: Fat and Complacent   The debate over the link between diet and heart disease did not really seem to touch the meat industry during the 1950–1976 period. The *Meat Board Reports (MBR)*, the industry newsletter published by the National Livestock and Meat Board (known as the Meat Board), did acknowledge attacks on dietary fats by proponents of the diet–heart disease link at the 1969 White House Conference on Food, Nutrition and Health; at the 1974 National Nutrition Conference sponsored by the Senate Select Committee; and at the 1974 World Food Conference. But several characteristics of the *MBR*'s presentation may have muted its impact.[43] It appears that the editors were not sure how seriously to take the diet and nutrition threat. Not all the conferences mentioned focused on the diet–heart disease link, as *MBR* stated. Criticism of meat producers for their inefficient use of resources (animal protein is more costly to acquire than vegetable protein) seemed to dominate most of the reports of *MBR* editors. And finally, when they discussed the diet–heart disease link, the editors of *MBR* either dismissed the evidence ("Trouble is, some say facts are known . . . fat's the problem. But that is not a matter of fact, at all") or they cited new studies that contradicted the diet–heart disease link.[44]

While the National Cattlemen's Association tended the Department of Agriculture and congressional relationships, the National Livestock and Meat Board concentrated on research and communications. The Meat Board has funded research on meat products since its inception in 1922, primarily funding research geared to investigate the positive qualities of meat products. Food editors across the country receive information from the Meat Board. The urge to promote industrywide advertising led to the creation of the Beef Industry Council, the Lamb Industry Group, and the Pork Industry Group in the 1960s.

The meat industry grew during the years 1950–76. Ups and downs in meat consumption could be attributed to the well-known, but uncontrollable production cycles within the industry itself. And though the popularity of vegetarianism and the rise of diet–heart disease proponents were noted with some dismay, they did not shake the dominant position meat played in the American diet.

National Commission on Egg Nutrition   Eggs are the single most concentrated form of dietary cholesterol. With the upsurge in breakfast cereals and sandwich meats, eggs are easy to replace in meals. Eggs are not protected by agricultural price supports. Egg producers belong to regional cooperatives, which have had difficulty working together on the national level. The diet–heart disease link hit the ill-prepared egg industry hard.

The National Commission on Egg Nutrition (NCEN) was established in 1971 to combat anticholesterol attacks on eggs. Organized by the American Poultry Hatchery Federation, NCEN's membership eventually included a representative from five egg industry associations. It was the federation's claim that the egg industry was losing "several million dollars per week due to anti-cholesterol attacks on eggs and . . . 'it is no wonder the egg industry under this dire [economic] stress, created a National Commission on Egg Nutrition.' "[45] The NCEN members consulted with nutritionists who assured them that they had a case to be made. They proceeded to develop the pamphlet "Eggs, Your Diet and Your Heart" outlining the case for eggs. A series of advertisements coincided, echoing the message of the pamphlet and advertising its availability. Various eye-catching cartoon-illustrated advertisements sounded a consistent theme, with such state-ments as "There is absolutely no scientific evidence that eating eggs in any way increases the risk of heart disease."[46] The case that NCEN made soon became a federal case.

The American Heart Association moved outside its normal bounds of activity and filed a complaint about the NCEN ads with the Federal Trade Commission. The FTC initiated hearings in 1974 on the nature of the claims and listened to appeals on their findings. In the end, NCEN was ordered to cease making claims that deny a relationship between choles-terol and heart disease.[47]

The costs that other members of the food industry considered simply part of their operating costs were nearly the death of the egg producers. Unprepared for the cost of pursuing the FTC case through the legal system, the egg producers had lost more than just their case. The NCEN's budget was drained, and for a while the egg producers seemed to lose heart or at least the capacity to organize against what they saw as a serious threat to their industry.

It was during the period following the 1975 collapse of NCEN that the industry leadership turned to Congress for assistance in creating a "check-off" system whereby, under the supervision of the USDA, an organization for egg promotion would be funded by egg farmers who paid a certain amount per unit of eggs sold. After congressional approval, a desperate egg-producer community overcame its aversion to government interfer-ence and discovered national harmony. They voted to fund the American Egg Board with a 5 cent check-off.[48]

1976–80: Activity

Before 1976, little legislative or regulatory attention was given to the diet–heart disease issue. As we have seen, the two groups most involved in the issue—the scientists and the margarine and vegetable oil manufac-turers—were either unable or unwilling to press the case for government involvement. The self-reinforcing networks of congressional, bureaucratic, and interest group relationships surrounding agricultural and health care had ongoing priorities that would have been threatened by the espousal of the diet–heart disease link. Indeed, the dietary changes proposed by advocates of the diet–heart disease link do threaten the American farmer:

they would alter consumption patterns of products that have enjoyed security and have been traditionally protected by legislation and regulation. These dietary changes might also raise questions about research-funding priorities in the health field.

Between 1976 and 1980, specific congressional interest in the diet–heart disease link developed, as did bureaucratic motivation to act on this issue. Strategically placed participants in Congress and the bureaucracy buttressed growing interest in the diet–heart disease link. The issue was propelled onto the agenda of the scientists within government. The momentum was well under way by the time the complacent agricultural interests became aware of the danger.

DIETARY GOALS: SETTING THE PACE

The motivating force for nutrition concerns in Congress was the Senate Select Committee on Nutrition and Human Needs. The SSC was also called the "McGovern committee" after its chairman, Senator George McGovern. By 1976 the SSC (in existence since 1968) had established its dominance over the federal food programs. Beginning in 1974 the SSC staff sought to widen the scope of the committee's interest by sponsoring a National Nutrition Conference.[49] By 1976, the SSC staff, which was undergoing a major change, had also been approached by an official in the National Cancer Institute who asked for a forum to present his views on diet and cancer. The SSC staff had been sensitized to the diet–disease issue earlier by the 1974 National Nutrition Conference that included some discussion of diet and disease. There was also the continuing problem of a select committee that needs to justify its existence annually to Congress. With these combined motivations, the SSC held a series of hearings in 1976 and early 1977 titled "Diet and Killer Diseases."[50]

The scientific debate over diet and heart disease finally had a foot in the congressional door. The hearings, which focused on diet and chronic diseases, included substantive testimony on diet and cardiovascular disease. Staff members of the SSC felt that the results of these hearings should be summarized in a short booklet that would propose dietary goals for the nation. Early in 1977, the Senate again contemplated the future of the SSC. Concerned that dissolution of the committee would halt the publication of the report—or as some critics argue, trying to breathe new life into a dying committee—staff members rushed to complete the report. *Dietary Goals for the United States* was released on 4 February 1977.[51]

There were six dietary goals presented on a single page. On the facing page, seven suggestions for changes in food selection and preparation were listed. For those concerned with the diet–heart disease issue and the products affected by it, three of the six goals and four of the seven suggested changes in food selection were directly relevant. Americans were advised to decrease total fat consumption from 40 to 30 percent of energy intake, to decrease saturated fat consumption so that it accounted for 10 percent of total energy intake and was balanced by polyunsaturated and monosaturated fat intake, and to reduce cholesterol consumption to 300 mg a day. These goals meant that Americans would have to change their diet. Suggestions for food selection changes included decreasing consumption of meat and increasing consumption of poultry and fish; cutting down consumption of foods high in fat and partially substituting polyunsaturated fats for saturated fats; substituting nonfat milk for whole milk; and decreasing consumption of butterfat, eggs, and other high-cholesterol sources.[52]

Dietary Goals did not save the SSC from extinction (which occurred in late December 1977).[53] The report was, however, a victory for the advocates of diet change and a shock to the food producers. Dairy and egg producers protested the report and advocated changes in its content, but the most concerted response came from the meat producers. The complacency of the meat producers evaporated. Through the National Cattlemen's Association and the Meat Board, they quickly moved to refute the scientific arguments about meat, urged the SSC to hold another hearing about meat, and informed their senators of their concerns.

They were successful. After discussions and negotiations with Meat Board staff, the SSC agreed to hold another day of hearings on meat in April 1977.[54] In December 1977 the SSC released the second edition of *Dietary Goals.*[55] There were several important changes. In prefatory remarks senators staked out safer ground—Senators Charles Percy (R., Ill.), Richard Schweiker (R., Pa.), and Edward Zorinsky (D., Neb.) expressed reservations about the second report and Senator Robert Dole (R., Kans.) stated he was pleased that the recommendation to "eat less meat was deleted." The language of the goals and food selection recommendations was changed. The most significant alteration was the advice about meat. It now read, "Decrease consumption of animal fat, and choose meat, poultry and fish which will reduce saturated fat intake."[56] Other recommendations were modified to indicate that young children should have whole milk and that cholesterol reductions could be amended for "pre-menopausal women, young children, and the elderly."[57]

Nick Mottern, the SSC staff assistant who wrote the first edition of *Dietary Goals,* resigned over the change in language in meat consumption.

He described the second edition of *Dietary Goals* as a victory for the meat industry.[58] The meat industry had limited success, however. The efforts of the cattlemen could not stop the wide influence of *Dietary Goals* throughout government; their experience could only prepare them for the next round.

CONGRESSIONAL PRESSURE AND THE AGENCIES' RESPONSE:
DIETARY GUIDELINES

The newfound congressional attention centered on the issue of nutrition research at NIH and USDA. The senators saw inadequate attention to nutrition research in the NIH, which led to a provision in the 1977 Agriculture Act naming the USDA as the lead agency for human nutrition research. The jurisdictional war that this action sparked ensured that NIH revised its accounting system for types of research funded and increased allocations for nutrition research. The USDA, only too happy to acquire additional responsibility and appropriations, organized the Human Nutrition Centers to focus this new foray into nutrition research. The Senate continued to exert pressure on the NIH through the Senate Agriculture Subcommittee on Nutrition. Additional pressure was provided by the Agriculture Subcommittee on Domestic Marketing, Consumer Relations and Nutrition, led by Congressman Frederick Richmond (D., N.Y.). The Richmond committee sponsored hearings on the role of the federal government in nutrition research and education. It was a constant reminder to the agencies that the Congress was watching.[59]

Probably this congressional interest alone would have sparked little agency response. The committees most aggressively questioning the lack of interest in the diet–disease issue were those with authority over agriculture. Officials at the NIH had to be polite and prepared to be questioned severely in public, but maintained their first priority to keep their own authorizing and appropriations committees happy. The USDA had orders to create a nutrition program, but simply having research programs in progress would keep the congressmen happy. The agencies' response to congressional initiative was amplified by the professional interest stimulated by *Dietary Goals*, coupled with changing organizational goals and incentives in the USDA and HHS.

The Professional Imperative Dietary Goals stirred the professional community: it was written by a nonprofessional. Although some outside consultants were used, the rush to complete the report and the enthusiasm of its sponsors led to what many professionals felt was an overstatement of the prescriptions, if not of the case itself. The professional response went beyond the reactions of individual scientists and groups oriented to making statements. The president of the American Society for Clinical Nutrition (ASCN) asked one of the chief opponents of the diet–heart disease link to chair a panel of distinguished scientists to review the evidence linking diet and chronic diseases. Released in May 1979, the ASCN report evaluated the evidence relating cholesterol and fat consumption to heart disease.[60] Its review articles were accepted by many in the scientific community as a valuable reference.

Government scientists also felt compelled to respond to *Dietary Goals.* In fact, for the two DHHS agencies that considered themselves the authoritative source of scientific knowledge (NIH) and food regulation (FDA), *Dietary Goals* was particularly galling. *Dietary Goals* disputed these agencies' contention that a statement or regulations at that time would be too precipitous and then went on to usurp their roles. From the NIH and FDA perspective, the goals *had* to be addressed, the only question was how.

Scientists at the USDA also wanted a review of *Dietary Goals.* The USDA's responsibility for the food guides and the federal food programs compelled staff members to consider a semiofficial recommendation for dietary change. The automatic reaction of the scientists at USDA was to turn to the Food and Nutrition Board for an evaluation of *Dietary Goals,* but this was forestalled by individuals in USDA and the FNB's Consumer Liaison Group. They felt that the FNB's membership at the time was too outspokenly opposed to dietary change for that agency to independently evaluate *Dietary Goals,* and a contract authorizing FNB review of *Dietary Goals* was canceled.

Instead, USDA and DHHS agreed to form a nutrition coordinating committee to review the evidence and make their own dietary recommendations. It took several years and at least a dozen drafts before *Dietary Guidelines* was released in February 1980.[61] The intense activity the guidelines generated at the two agencies gives a measure of the organizational change that was occurring.

USDA: Ignoring the Sacred Cow   The changes in the Department of Agriculture during the Carter administration transformed the staid bastion of food producers into an advocate for food consumers. With the appointment of Carol Tucker Foreman as assistant secretary of agriculture responsible for the Food and Nutrition Service (in charge of food programs), a new chapter in the department's history was opened. Not only was she the first female assistant secretary in the department, she was the former head of the Consumer Federation of America. Foreman's orientation was geared as much to those who purchase food as to those who sell it. This activist orientation at the assistant secretary level generated staff interest in consumer problems. Dietary guidelines were given high priority. Although many of USDA's permanent nutrition staff were concerned about the radical departure represented by *Dietary Goals,* the new leadership was anxious to discover how many of the goals were well grounded and could be presented to the public and implemented in the food programs. This met with the approval of USDA Secretary Robert Bergland whose own brush with heart disease had exposed him to the high cost of cholesterol screening and led him to conclude that alternative approaches should be explored. Important personnel were inserted into pivotal roles in the reorganized department: a nutrition coordinator became an assistant to the secretary, and a respected scientist convinced of the diet–heart disease link became head of the newly organized Human Nutrition Centers.

The new interests of the USDA were greeted with dismay by many of the traditional units within the department and by the commodity representatives who had always thought of the department as a source of support. The efforts of the mainstream USDA, upset at the loss of laboratories, programs, and personnel to the Human Nutrition Centers, attempted to thwart the new nutrition program. Space was guarded jealously and cooperation withheld. This response only confirmed the opinions of the new power holders that the best strategy was to avoid involving the tradition-minded units in the development of the guidelines.

The policy of ignoring the traditional producer-oriented staff meant that those having closest contacts with commodity representatives were not included in discussions of the guidelines—and they were unable to protect commodity interests in these discussions. From the perspective of the beef, dairy, or egg farmer, the Department of Agriculture had ears only for the consumer.

The new leadership in the USDA became identified with the *Dietary Guidelines.* They urged bureaucracy-bound DHHS participants to read drafts, make concessions, and reach conclusions. When the *Guidelines* were completed, the USDA pushed publication and initiated reviews to determine how the *Guidelines* could be used in the federal food programs. In the process they incurred the wrath of the representatives of farm commodity interests who felt betrayed.

Health and Human Services: The Sum of its Parts   The Department of Health and Human Services Secretary Joseph Califano was primarily interested in the elimination of smoking; other prevention programs were of less interest to him. The existence of an Office of Health Promotion and Disease Prevention and a departmentwide nutrition coordinator carries less weight in an agency with strongholds of entrenched, legislated programs such as those of the NIH and FDA. The Surgeon General could issue a report on life-style changes and important diseases,[62] the nutrition coordinator could review the efforts on nutrition in the agency, and the Office of Health Promotion could publish pamphlets on prevention activities, all without significantly altering the activities of the agencies with jurisdictional control over nutrition research and regulation.

These efforts may have an important public effect. The Surgeon General's report became part of the burgeoning record in favor of dietary change. Advocates of such change could point to the Surgeon General—whose capacity to give advice had been enhanced by the 1964 smoking warning—as a source of legitimacy. And prevention-oriented pamphlets may have brought some insight to the public. These departmentwide promotional efforts were not useful in swaying the subsidiary agencies of the DHHS from their course.

Although the scientists at NIH and FDA were provoked by the SSC's *Dietary Goals,* their perceptions of their own organizational goals and interests led them to slow down the writing process and resist proclamatory statements. The NIH officials were anxious to await the completion of agency trials on diet and heart disease and FDA officials were trying to preserve the future regulation of cholesterol and fats for the FDA.

WAVING THE RED FLAG: THE REPORT AND THE REACTIONS

The efforts of the USDA were rewarded with the publication of *Nutrition and Your Health: Dietary Guidelines for Americans* on 4 February 1980.[63] To underline the importance the USDA placed on the report, Secretary Robert Bergland accompanied Assistant Secretary Carol Tucker Foreman and Director of the Human Nutrition Centers Dr. Mark Hegsted to the press briefing. Representing the Department of Health and Human Services were Surgeon General Dr. Julius B. Richmond and Deputy Assistant Secretary for Disease Prevention and Health Promotion Dr. Michael McGinnis. Esther Peterson, special assistant to the president for consumer affairs, also attended the press conference. It was a banner day.

The only banner the farmers saw was guideline number 3: "Avoid too much fat, saturated fat, and cholesterol."[64] Here was the Department of Agriculture aligning itself with the turncoat George McGovern, who had headed the SSC. The success that the USDA achieved in publishing the report was matched by their failure to explain the report to the commodity producers.

The pressure on the USDA began immediately after the publication of the *Guidelines.* It was a presidential election year and the farmers' vote was important. Farmers poured into the offices of officials at the USDA. And, as one official later confided, it was a relief to many at the USDA that

President Carter's defeat was so resounding that it could not be attributed solely to the dissatisfaction of farmers.

The momentum of outrage against the *Guidelines* rose after the publication of *Toward Healthful Diets* by the Food and Nutrition Board. Here was the authoritative counterpoint to the *Guidelines.* Food producers could demand revision, senators could demand explanations, and the press could have a field day.

The FNB members, upset at the Senate Select Committee usurpation of what it saw as its right to set food policy, did not let the cancellation of the USDA contract stop its consideration of *Dietary Goals.* Encouraged by National Academy of Sciences President Philip Handler, who was convinced that activist scientists working with consumer groups were hurting Americans by arousing unjustifiable fears of consumer products, the FNB chose to review the report itself. Unlike the earlier attempt to review the diet–disease link, when the different positions of the members created a stalemate, the members now on the board either were strongly against the diet–heart disease link or were uninvolved with the controversy. Although critics in the scientific community pointed to the lack of a cardiologist or an epidemiologist on the panel, their criticism was seen as an effort to impose a different point of view on the panel. It angered many when the FNB presented the report as a scientific consensus, when, in view of the ongoing scientific war, it was merely another salvo by the antidietary change advocates.

Scientists seem unwilling or unable to explain their internecine disputes to the public. And scientists and consumers who supported the diet–heart disease link seemed unable to mobilize support for the *Guidelines* or protection for those who had written it. Although a petition supporting the *Guidelines* was sent to the investigating congressional committees from many of the consumer and professional societies, and scientists were available to testify at the hearings, their inability to rouse the constituents showed these groups to be a poor second to the farm commodity interests. Telegrams and letters did not pour in to congressmen requesting them to support *Dietary Guidelines,* and consumers and scientists did not crowd the halls of the USDA or DHHS to support their publications.

Two congressional hearings were held. Congressman Richmond's hearing was designed to discover how the FNB could give such misguided advice.[65] The hearings held by Senator Thomas Eagleton's (D. Mo.) Agriculture Appropriations Subcommittee placed the USDA/DHHS *Dietary Guidelines* under similar antagonistic scrutiny.[66]

The USDA officials were certainly made to feel uncomfortable. They agreed to appoint another scientific committee to study *Dietary Guidelines.*

And a one-sentence proviso was added to the explanatory text in *Dietary Guidelines:* "There is a controversy about what recommendations are for healthy Americans."[67] However, the USDA was not forced to halt distribution of the pamphlet. And, as the Carter administration began its swan song, officials at the USDA continued to plan the implementation of *Dietary Guidelines.*

Having produced *Dietary Guidelines,* officials at the NIH and FDA were content to withdraw from the dietary advice arena. Not so the change activists at the USDA. Despite the strong negative reaction by the food commodity producers, USDA officials continued some attempts to apply the recommendations of the *Dietary Guidelines* in the programs under their control, though implementation was truncated with the loss of the presidential election and the upcoming change of administration. *Ideas for Better Eating,* a consumer-oriented booklet with menus based on *Dietary Guidelines,* was published.[68] Food program implementation was begun: the WIC (Women, Infants, and Children) program allowed fewer eggs in the diet, and the School Lunch program began to cut the percentage of fat in ground meat and offered low-fat milk as an alternative to whole milk at the school lunch counter.

The margarine and oil producers quietly watched the ensuing fray. Although they are quick to use positive evidence in their advertising, these firms avoided the forefront in the fight against opponents of the diet–heart disease link. In this instance, they were concerned that the debate over the FNB report might confuse their consumers. Standard Brands reverted to their earlier practice of publicizing the diet–heart disease link in ads for Fleischmann's margarine. They reprinted an article from the *New York Times* about a new study that underscored the positive aspects of a low-cholesterol diet. (The title of the *Times* article was "Life-Saving Benefits of Low-Cholesterol Diet Affirmed in Rigorous Study.") The ad introduced the reprint in display type: "Fleischmann's Margarine Wants You to Know . . ." and ended with "Fleischmann's Margarine 0 Cholesterol."[69]

1980s: The Good New Days

In 1980 the advocates of diet change in the Senate lost George McGovern; he was soundly beaten in a bid for reelection. Though the Moral Majority worked hard to oppose his reelection, many in the nutrition field attribute his defeat to the outrage of cattle ranchers in his home state of South

Dakota. They began to organize against him soon after the release of *Dietary Goals.* McGovern's loss left Congressman Richmond as the only other strong voice in Congress for nutrition change. Most felt his voice was not nearly as strong or consistent as McGovern's; he subsequently resigned from the Congress in an unrelated scandal.

The stripped Congress was soon compounded by a dismantled USDA. The new Reagan administration appointed former National Cattlemen's Association and American Meat Institute officers to the top positions in the USDA. These opponents of *Dietary Goals* and *Dietary Guidelines* had no great affection for the Carter administration changes in the USDA. Old forces in the department began to reclaim power. The Human Nutrition Centers and other programs disappeared in a significant reorganization. Not only was nutrition submerged organizationally, but nutrition staffs were sent from Washington to offices in the Maryland and Virginia suburbs. And they soon suffered deep personnel cuts through the governmentwide reductions. Nutrition and consumer advocates had indeed lost favor.[70]

Traditional USDA antagonism to *Dietary Goals* and *Dietary Guidelines* quickly resurfaced. No longer would *Dietary Guidelines* be available free to the consumer. Also evident was an unwillingness to commit USDA resources to future publication of the document; that would be left up to the Government Printing Office or the DHHS.[71] The new USDA officials also tried to prevent publication of *Food 2,* a related diet advice publication that had been drafted in the Carter administration.[72] To accommodate a Carter administration USDA commitment to review *Dietary Guidelines,* the Reagan administration replaced the original membership of the review committee with one composed primarily of scientists opposed to the diet–heart disease link.[73]

The response at the DHHS did not approach the thorough housecleaning at the USDA. Although unwilling to disown *Dietary Guidelines,* the DHHS did revert to its pattern of limited involvement in the diet–heart disease issue. The Office of Health Promotion and Disease Prevention continued to distribute *Dietary Guidelines* for no charge and became its quiet champion. From the wide array of proposals pushed by the earlier FDA/USDA/FTC labeling effort, the FDA began to promote voluntary salt labeling,[74] but cholesterol labeling changes were written with little official hope that they would take effect until after 1987 at the earliest.[75]

Until March 1984 and the release of the results of the Lipid Research Clinic's Coronary Primary Prevention Trial, the NHLBI also remained quiet.[76] The results of this trial forged another link in the diet–heart disease chain: reduction in the level of serum cholesterol was associated with reduction in the incidence of heart disease. The following December, the

NIH sponsored a consensus conference, in which experts were asked to assemble and evalute the evidence supporting the diet–heart hypothesis.

The conference's emphatic report established elevated serum cholesterol as a cause of heart disease; anyone with significantly elevated blood cholesterol should be treated with diet and drug therapy. Stating that most Americans have undesirably high serum cholesterol levels, the report recommended that all Americans over the age of two years follow the prudent diet developed by the American Heart Association. Among other recommendations, NHLBI was urged to begin a National Cholesterol Education Program to alert professionals and the public to the problem of elevated serum cholesterol.[77]

Ironically, as government activity on diet and heart disease waned in the early 1980s, the interest of the consumer groups in the issue grew. Spurred on by *Dietary Guidelines* and a 1982 National Academy of Sciences report linking dietary change and cancer prevention[78] the ranks of the Washington-based diet forces swelled. The Center for Science in the Public Interest made a commitment in 1983 to campaign against excess consumption of fats in the American diet.[79] The CSPI was joined by a new food-oriented public interest group called Public Voice, explicitly formed to consider issues of diet and health. And organizations that once concentrated solely on federal food programs expanded their interests to include the diet–heart disease issue. They persisted in their attempts to rejuvenate the issues of food labeling, government dietary advice, and altered consumer consumption patterns. The public education efforts of the consumer groups were joined by the American Heart Association. After learning the results of the 1984 NHLBI trial and the consensus conference, the AHA began to promote dietary change more actively in a series of television commercials and other public education activities and materials.

Reagan's return of government allegiance to the farming interests has only partially reassured the farm representatives. Now alert to the potential for negative government action and spurred by the development of new substitute products (such as artificial cheese), the farm interests are expanding into the nongovernmental marketing arena. Meat, dairy, and egg organizations are paying greater attention to new product development and marketing.

The "Incredible Edible Egg" promotional effort has been joined by advertisements claiming that "Beef Gives Strength" and "Milk's Got More." Following the earlier example of the egg industry, the dairy industry sought congressional approval for an assessment program for dairy farmers. The National Dairy Promotion and Research Board, created in 1983, allocated over $60 million for advertising during 1984.[80] In 1985, the beef and pork industries promoted the passage of similar legislation.[81] The agricultural marketing arena is becoming quite crowded.

The marketing strategies of the three farm commodity producers were set by 1984, as they attempted to reclaim the mantle of health that had been captured by the marketing efforts of the margarine and polyunsaturated oil producers. The dairy association now supplements its advertising with health claims linking the high calcium content of milk to the prevention of osteoporosis.[82] Advising cooks to "throw out every other yolk" when using eggs, and reassuring them that not everyone needs to alter diet, the egg industry is trying to adapt their product to the prudent diet and to find a way to deal with scientific findings about the nature of eggs.[83]

Under the auspices of a broad-based diet and health coordinating committee, meat-producers agreed upon a strategy that promotes meat as a part of the prudent diet. The problem, they argue, is not meat consumption per se, but the *amount* of meat consumed. They recalculated the amount of meat that Americans consumed in 1984 and found it was 4 ounces per serving, rather that the often-cited 6 or 7.5 ounces. Meat producers claim that this 4-ounce serving can be well integrated into a prudent diet; therefore Americans can continue to enjoy meat dishes. This means "we no longer have to fight with the Heart Association, Cancer Society, or other groups who recommend a lower fat or cholesterol level." In 1985 this extensive promotional and research effort was financed by $5.6 million from the National Livestock and Meat Board.[84]

The food commodity producers are competing with continued efforts of the polyunsaturated oils and margarine manufacturers. According to one industry analyst, the introduction of sunflower oils has intensified the promotion of the diet–heart disease link comparable to what was undertaken by Fleischmann's at its zenith in the 1970s.

Conclusion

Many important issues never become the objects of public policy. Government agencies face many more potential policy issues than they have capacity to consider. These internal constraints are compounded by external pressures on government units to choose certain issues for action while avoiding others. Many issues do not survive.

The politics of diet and heart disease provides an example of such constraints on governmental policymaking. During the 1950–76 period, the internal dynamics of the potentially involved governmental agencies minimized the possibility for major government activity on the diet–heart disease issue. External pressures favoring the status quo dominated. Scientists and professionals, the most committed proponents of dietary change, lacked the organizational motivation and capacity to bring the case to the government. And the polyunsaturated oils and margarine manufacturers, the industries most likely to benefit from government policies to effect diet change, did not pressure government agencies and Congress for action. Instead, they chose to influence the American diet directly through advertising.

Several salient characteristics of the diet–heart disease issue help explain its pattern of activity. This is a scientific issue with competing scientific viewpoints and groups. It is also an economic issue with rival economic interests. And it is a behavioral issue whose endpoint is individual change.

Scientific controversy over diet and heart disease has split the professional community. Most observers would conclude that a majority of the involved professionals agree on the prudent diet, yet active opposition continues to generate scientific articles and public interest. Officials at the two government agencies with the closest ties to the scientific community —NIH and FDA—felt the full impact of the controversy. They were unwilling to tarnish their agencies' images by taking a position on a yet-unresolved issue. Research funding offered a respectable alternative to what might be precipitous statements.

As a scientific issue, diet and heart disease is more likely to evoke interest among professions actually involved with nutrition and heart disease. Consumer interest groups were, until the early 1980s, more interested in economic issues. As has been shown, although many of these professional groups were enthusiastic about the diet–heart disease issue, the internal constraints placed upon their reaction to a professionally divisive issue hobbled their response. Many of these organizations (such as the American Heart Association) also had a limited range of responses to issues. Unused to aggressive lobbying or public education campaigns, they responded in traditional fashion with professional reports. Thus a major potential source of outside pressure on the government was neutralized.

The economics of dietary change threatens farmers as the polyunsaturated oils and margarine manufacturers gain new markets. Diet and heart disease arouses two sets of competing economic interests. And yet, only rarely have these interests clashed in the governmental arena. Instead, as the farm interests clung to their government alliances and supports, the polyunsaturated oils and margarine manufacturers chose not to compete in the governmental arena.

Congressional and bureaucratic belief in the importance of farm interests was reinforced by the network of relationships that existed between the farm groups and the government. Before 1976 there was no need for commodity groups to oppose federal involvement in dietary change because no great movement to involve the government occurred. When, in 1976–80, the Carter government did become involved, the organized political reaction of the farming community served to remind Congress and bureaucrats alike of their traditional interests.

Where were the polyunsaturated oils and margarine manufacturers? Instead of pressuring to maintain government involvement, they took advantage of the third characteristic of the diet–heart disease issue. As a behavioral issue, the ultimate goals are individual attitudes about food and health and the resulting food choices. Government intervention is unnecessary to bring about such changes. Although this strategy was employed by voluntary health and consumer groups, the major supplier of public information has been the polyunsaturated oils and margarine manufacturers. Rather than call government attention to potential health hazards in foods that might in the long run backfire on their own products, these producers chose to pursue the diet–heart disease issue in the marketplace, the arena they knew best.

Just as the government has learned about the political costs attached to activity in the diet–heart disease issue, farm commodity producers have learned of the economic costs of minimal attention to the marketing arena. As the commodity groups move into marketing, it remains to be seen whether they will spur polyunsaturated oils and margarine manufacturers beyond protective marketing and on to pressuring the government for actions.

Events in 1984–85 indicated that, in addition to individual industry response to the farm commodity marketing challenge, the margarine and vegetable oil industries participated in a larger effort by the food-processing industry to force the FDA and the FTC to permit health claims in food labeling and advertising. The health claims issue was focused in October 1984 by Kellogg's collaboration with the National Cancer Institute in the development of advertising material for its high-fiber breakfast cereal All-Bran.[85] Kellogg, emboldened by its association with the Cancer Institute, was willing to initiate its marketing campaign without clearance from the two regulatory agencies. Its competitors, and other food processors anxious to promote food items with health claims, were not so bold. They sought FTC and FDA approval.

Influenced by the antiregulation orientation of the Reagan administration, the FTC rejected its own staff-proposed Food Trade Rule Regulation in 1982.[86] Therefore, there are no industrywide guidelines for health claims in advertising. And, Kellogg's advertising efforts, linking high-fiber diets with cancer prevention, have been applauded by the FTC.

The FDA is still reluctant to approve the Kellogg's cereal marketing scheme or to create broad-based health claims guidelines for food packages. In addition to food industry pressure, the FDA is under pressure to issue guidelines by consumer groups who fear that without clear government guidelines the public will be flooded with conflicting or partial information.

The FDA is also being pressured by the scientific community. More and more scientists believe that Americans should be concerned about and limit the amount of fat, saturated fat, and cholesterol they eat. This consensus is being presented under government auspices. The American Heart Association's prudent diet was recommended by the 1984 NIH consensus conference. Even the recommendations of the USDA advisory committee identified as antagonistic to *Dietary Guidelines* has resulted in another edition of the *Dietary Guidelines* (issued in September 1985) with only minor changes in the recommendations. Americans are still advised to limit their consumption of saturated fats and cholesterol.[87] A NHLBI-organized National Cholesterol Education Program was inaugurated in November 1985. The coordinating committee of the program, represented by many public health and government groups (including the AMA and the FDA) began its efforts by urging the public to "know your cholesterol count."[88] Although it does not directly advocate dietary change, by fostering awareness of serum cholesterol levels the program will make many more people aware of their need to control their serum cholesterol levels, perhaps leading to diet change.

The persistent reluctance of government agencies to become involved in the diet-heart disease issue has been abetted by the availability of the alternative marketing arena. Industry groups and others whose well-being or purpose is hurt by government inactivity can choose to direct their efforts to the public, circumventing the government. Thus they generate no additional pressure for government involvement. The lack of government involvement ensures that the public is provided with interpretations of scientific evidence that suit the market needs of the industry. Without consistent government activity the accuracy of public information on health prevention issues becomes dependent upon the serendipitous interaction of scientific findings and private marketing needs.

Chapter 4

The Politics of Salt: The Sodium–Hypertension Issue

MARK J. SEGAL

Common table salt, one of life's simple pleasures, has been condemned as potentially harmful to the health of consumers.* Sodium is the alleged culprit. Its intake has been linked to hypertension—high blood pressure—in a number of studies. Indeed, scientific consensus about the link between sodium and hypertension has been reported. As a result, several groups have called for the food industry to label and reduce the sodium content of foods. Nonhypertensives, as well as those suffering from or susceptible to high blood pressure, are exhorted to moderate their salt intake. These varied efforts have accelerated since the late 1970s, as has media coverage of the issue. Not surprisingly, the federal government has become involved. Several sodium labeling bills have been introduced in Congress. The Food and Drug Administration (FDA) has organized a campaign to increase public awareness of the links between sodium and hypertension and to pressure the food industry to label and reduce sodium content in processed foods. Most recently, the FDA issued regulations that will make sodium labeling mandatory for a significant fraction of processed foods.

*The research and major writing for this chapter was completed prior to the author's employment at the American Medical Association. The views expressed in this chapter are those of the author and do not necessarily represent the official policy or position of the American Medical Association.

Why this upsurge in concern with such a familiar food product? The link with high blood pressure is central. Hypertension affects an estimated 57.7 million people in the United States and is particularly prevalent among black Americans.[1] One government source claims that the annual cost of hypertension is $8 billion.[2] Although such estimates are uncertain and often prepared for political purposes, the prevention and treatment of hypertension are considered important components of a disease prevention strategy by many public health officials.

For example, over the past decade, the National High Blood Pressure Education Program, a major cooperative effort of the federal government and numerous private groups, has sought to inform physicians and the public of the need to treat hypertension.[3] This effort, with extensive media coverage, has apparently contributed to a broader public awareness of hypertension as a health threat.

Approximately 90 percent of hypertensives have essential hypertension —elevated blood pressure of unknown cause. High blood pressure is considered a significant risk factor for cardiovascular disease, kidney disease, and stroke.[4] Sodium, an essential nutrient, is considered one of several factors in the development of essential hypertension. Salt—sodium chloride—is 40 percent sodium and 60 percent chloride and is the major source of dietary sodium. Average daily sodium intake has been estimated as 3.9–4.7 grams per person, which is equivalent to 10–12 grams of sodium chloride.[5] The Food and Nutrition Board (FNB) of the National Academy of Sciences considers 1.1–3.3 grams of sodium to be "safe and adequate."[6] Salt is a key component in food processing and widely used in the home. Beyond its role as a relatively inexpensive flavor enhancer, salt is a preservative, a stabilizer, and a binder. Foods with relatively high sodium contents include processed cheese, cured meats, frozen entrees, and canned vegetables. Other important sources of dietary sodium are drinking water, certain medications, baking soda and powder, and monosodium glutamate.[7]

By the early 1980s, opinion polls showed increasingly negative attitudes toward salt. In one study, 95 percent of the consumers surveyed agreed with the statement that "eating too much salt can contribute to high blood pressure."[8] In a 1980 Gallup poll, 25 percent of meal planners cited salt as an ingredient with which they were concerned, up from 17 percent in 1979, and 13 percent in 1977. A 1982 government survey, conducted in the midst of aggressive public and private antisalt activities, found that 40 percent of respondents were using food package ingredient lists to avoid salt, up from 14 percent in 1978.[9]

Public aversion to sodium is particularly interesting because salt has long been considered a valuable commodity. Until modern times, salt was quite expensive, and in various places taxes on salt contributed to popular re-volts.[10] Attempts to modify public attitudes toward salt typify the rising public anxiety about consumer products. Growing public interest in nutri-tion intersects with product worries and with regulatory efforts regarding health and safety.

Any effort to change salt intake patterns quickly leads to the salt shaker. The fact that ultimate control over salt use rests with the individual con-sumer imposes serious limits on both regulatory efforts and pressures aimed at the food industry. Significant reductions in sodium consumption require fundamental modifications in consumer behavior. Achieving such changes is likely to be far more difficult than simply pressuring industry or government.

This chapter traces salt's emergence as a dietary villain. The picture that develops is one of complex interactions among science, government, and industry; these interactions influence mass attitudes and sometimes mass behavior. Scientific developments pressure the government to act. These attempts to force government action, and the government responses them-selves elicit industry efforts in both the political sphere and the market-place. Thus food and salt companies protect themselves by fighting gov-ernment regulations; at the same time, these firms are able to take advantage of rising consumer interest in low-salt products.

A de facto public policy emerges out of this often confusing process. Clarity will be served by a brief review of one small part of the issue, the issue of salt in baby foods, before proceeding to the larger sodium case.

Round One: Salt in Baby Foods

Since the 1960s, the level of salt in baby foods has caused concern. The resulting series of actions exemplify the dynamics of the sodium issue, in which scientific findings relevant to human health led to actions by gov-ernment and industry.

During the 1960s, Dr. Lewis K. Dahl, a specialist in the links between sodium and hypertension at Brookhaven National Laboratory in Upton, New York, attacked what he viewed as excessive levels of salt in commer-cial infant foods. Dahl asserted that consumption of excess sodium would predispose infants to later hypertension. The amount of salt added to processed baby foods seems to have been determined largely by a desire to appeal to the palate of the parent rather than the baby. Dahl's willingness to make policy-relevant recommendations on the basis of his research results was a critical link between the world of science and that of public action. He found a receptive audience in the nascent consumer movement, including Ralph Nader and his associates, and raised the concerns of parents and pediatricians.[11]

The issue moved through a series of scientific and policy reviews. Expanding public attention was both cause and outgrowth of these enquiries. The salt in baby foods was discussed at the 1969 White House Conference on Food, Nutrition, and Health. One conference panel worried that infants would consume too little sodium and was skeptical of the research linking infant sodium intake to hypertension, cautioning against hasty changes, "lest in seeking to avoid one ill we precipitate another."[12] However, another panel did call for a reduction in the amount of salt in commercial baby foods.

Following the conference, an ad hoc committee of the Food and Nutrition Board of the National Academy of Sciences convened to review the ingredients of baby food for the FDA. Senator George McGovern (D., S.D.) had suggested such a study in Senate hearings. The FNB's committee, headed by Dr. Lloyd S. Filer, Jr., a professor of pediatrics involved in the nutrition activities of the American Academy of Pediatrics, found the evidence linking infant salt intake to later hypertension ambiguous.[13] Nevertheless, because infant salt intake was several times greater than the minimum infant requirement, the committee recommended that the maximum level of salt added to commercial baby food be .25 percent of the product. One of the industry scientists involved in the review noted that although he disagreed with the specific recommendation, he was comfortable with the general findings because he felt that the baby food companies had been sufficiently involved in the report's development.

The FDA, with regulatory responsibility for the safety of most processed foods, responded to the heightened concern. In 1970, a meeting was held at the agency with representatives of the three major manufacturers of baby food—Gerber Products Co., H. J. Heinz Co., and Beech-Nut Nutrition Corp. According to one food industry participant, all parties sought a voluntary solution to the problem of sodium in baby foods. The firms agreed to conform to the FNB guidelines, in part because they saw a threat of FDA regulation if they did not act.

Parents are especially concerned about the safety of the food they purchase for their babies. Thus, the rapid acquiescence of a relatively small industry to FDA pressures reflects, to an exaggerated degree, the food industry's sensitivity to the effects of adverse publicity on its products' reputations. With no product differentiation benefits to be gained from the initial removal of sodium, and an industry aversion to advertising based upon negative issues, the first sodium removal was accomplished in a quiet manner. Subsequent market pressures produced equally swift reductions in sodium content, but with quite a bit more fanfare.

In January 1977, Beech-Nut, the smallest of the three major baby food manufacturers, announced the removal of added salt from all its baby foods. The impetus for this action was the decline in baby food sales as the baby boom faded. Industry "confusion" followed. Gerber, with a 70 percent share of the baby food market, reacted immediately to the challenge, removing added salt from half of its varieties. But this partial response was insufficient to meet Beech-Nut's competitive challenge. In October 1977, Gerber announced the removal of added salt from all its baby foods. H. J. Heinz, the other major producer, soon followed suit.[14]

The baby food companies waged a vigorous advertising war. Industry studies show mothers' concern with salt in baby food peaking during the month Beech-Nut made its move, but declining substantially by early 1978.[15] The "NO SALT ADDED" labels introduced during the product reformulation were gradually deemphasized over the years. Executives at Beech-Nut's competitors believe its strategy was unfortunate for the industry. They feel that the use of salt content labeling brought the wholesomeness of baby food into question, threatening industry sales without really benefiting Beech-Nut in the long run.

A scientific basis for action was sought by both industry and its critics. Medical and scientific organizations played a public role, providing justification and pressure for the initial move to reduce sodium, at the same time urging caution when public opinion and marketing pressure appeared to outweigh scientific concerns. Because of the seriousness of the issue, the baby food manufacturers funded research on the Dahl hypothesis.

The industry's contacts with prominent scientists reflect a strong desire to be involved with research in an area central to industry concerns. For example, Dr. Robert Stewart, director of research at Gerber and member of the Academy of Pediatrics Technical Advisory Group, wrote the final version of a 1974 academy report on sodium and hypertension. The study took a moderate view, emphasizing that only a minority of children were at risk of developing hypertension, but advising that salt content guidelines be devised for food processors.[16]

Both industry and nonindustry scientists were skeptical of the second, market-driven sodium reduction. A 1979 Academy of Pediatrics report noted that infant salt intake had decreased, but questioned "why prepared infant foods were singled out . . . for special emphasis when it is the introduction of the adult type diet which accounts for most of the salt intake in infancy." Dr. Filer, head of the FNB committee, has similarly written that the "scientific rationale [of the 1977 total removal of sodium] remains unclear."[17]

The on-again, off-again nature of the sodium issue is apparent in the baby food case. Regulatory and medical concerns with salt in baby food appear to have been assuaged by the initial reduction of salt in 1970, blunting further expansion of the issue. The competitive maneuverings of 1977 heightened public attention to the salt in baby food yet again. But once all three firms had removed the salt from their products, the advantages of focusing marketing strategies on salt slackened. The diminishing public concern with the salt content of baby foods can be linked to the reduced advertising emphasis on salt, particularly given the rise in awareness following Beech-Nut's initial move, but the direction of causality is unclear. Each burst of activity provided a context for subsequent actions, but, as a discrete issue, sodium was remarkably susceptible to declining public, industry, and government attention.

Besides signaling the first significant public actions caused by the reported relationship between sodium and hypertension, the baby food case is a simple version of a process of issue development which became increasingly complex as more and more firms, private organizations, and government agencies became involved in attempts to limit the consumption of sodium by Americans. This process translates health-related scientific findings into medical practice, organizational action, and public policy.

Sodium and Hypertension

In order to understand the course of sodium's establishment as a highly visible public health threat, the scientific issues linking sodium to hypertension, and hypertension to ill health, require review. Sodium was connected to hypertension as early as 1904.[18] During the 1940s, the "Rice-Fruit Diet" developed by Dr. Walter Kempner provided widely accepted results indicating that low-salt diets could significantly reduce blood pressure in individuals with severe hypertension.[19] These findings have since been challenged on the grounds of inadequate controls and because of the drastic salt reduction required. In the 1950s and 1960s, Dahl and others studied the links between hypertension and sodium through animal models. Salt-sensitive and salt-resistant strains of rats were bred, which suggested a genetic factor in sodium-related hypertension.[20]

Epidemiological studies, reported in the 1960s and 1970s, found that populations with very low salt intakes had minimal incidence of hypertension and that the risk of hypertension in these groups did not increase with age.[21] These studies have also been criticized because of measurement uncertainties and insufficient controls for body weight and other variables. Intrapopulation studies, the Framingham Study for instance, have generally failed to demonstrate correlations between sodium intake and hypertension.[22] Clinical studies, particularly in recent years, have reported sodium reduction as useful in treating hypertension, although results of these studies are mixed and criticized methodologically.[23] A widely accepted synthesis of this evidence posits that an unknown fraction of the population is susceptible to the hypertensive effects of sodium ingestion. As with hypertension generally, there is a strong genetic component to this population of susceptible individuals, who are, for the most part, unidentifiable prior to the onset of hypertension.[24] Hence, public health measures that seek to reduce the risk of hypertension for this salt-sensitive population will target a large portion of the population for whom such efforts will have no probable benefit. The sum of this evidence has been used to suggest an important and perhaps causal connection between sodium and hypertension. Corollaries of such a relationship suggest that reduction of sodium can both prevent and treat hypertension.

Some scientists manifest extreme skepticism regarding current evidence and reject dietary modification within what they see as feasible ranges.[25] In addition to sodium, other causal factors, such as potassium/sodium balance, obesity, and calcium intake have been suggested.[26] Alternative hypotheses weaken the case for the connection between sodium intake and hypertension and the appropriateness of sodium reduction as a preventive or therapeutic tool. Thus, these hypotheses are enthusiastically cited by opponents of sodium reduction and labeling.

Until the late 1970s, the links between sodium and hypertension, especially regarding treatment, were overshadowed by the development of antihypertensive drugs over the last several decades. The effectiveness of these therapeutics reduced the need to rely on sodium reduction in the treatment of high blood pressure. More recent studies have fundamentally altered the nature of the hypertension problem, however, by suggesting that drug treatment also benefits mild or borderline hypertensives.[27] Thus, the number of Americans labeled as hypertensive has been increased from 35 million to 58 million, approximately one quarter of the population.

Drug treatment of one fourth of our population is a daunting prospect. Antihypertensive medications are often costly, with unpleasant or dangerous side effects. The absolute risks from mild hypertension are lower than those at more elevated pressure levels. Not surprisingly, some have suggested an increased role for dietary management of high blood pressure.[28] Although the research supporting dietary treatment has been subject to much criticism, uncertainty regarding its efficacy is balanced by its lower costs and risks.

Goals, Guidelines, and Agenda Forcing

Just as it is important to understand the scientific basis of concern with sodium, so too is it essential to understand how and why these scientific concerns were injected in the public policy process. The federal government has assumed increased responsibility for protecting the public health and consumer rights since the 1960s. Sodium control involves questions of hypertension prevention and treatment, nutrition labeling, advertising regulation, and food safety review. Responsibility for these issues is dispersed throughout the federal bureaucracy. In a few cases, sodium is isolated as a problem, but most often it is joined with related issues on an agency's agenda.

A useful starting point is the 1969 White House Conference on Food and Nutrition, which heralded a public policy shift from malnutrition to the risks of overconsumption. The issue of sodium consumption was considered by the panel on adult chronic diseases, which included Dr. Dahl as a member.[29] Labeling of sodium content, which would make low-sodium diets more practical, as well as the reduction of sodium in processed foods were suggested. Discussion was not extensive, and was much briefer than that accorded dietary fats.

One of the primary federal options regarding sodium was the labeling of the mineral's content in foods. After the White House conference, the Bureau of Foods of the FDA, historically the lead agency on issues of nutrition labeling, established regulations governing the labeling of the nutrients in processed foods.[30] These regulations took effect in 1975. Nutrition labeling is voluntary unless nutrition claims are made or nutrients are added to the product. Sodium was not a part of the original labeling format, although it can be added voluntarily.

During the Carter administration, a general review of food labeling was begun by the FDA, the U.S. Department of Agriculture (USDA), and the Federal Trade Commission (FTC). In 1979, this review culminated in a voluminous *Federal Register* document. Included was a tentative proposal for regulations requiring the addition of sodium and potassium information in labels.[31] The FDA announced that it would also request legislation granting authority to require labeling of sodium and potassium "on the basis of public health significance" (similar proposals were made for sugar, fatty acids, and cholesterol). The sodium proposal was seen by FDA officials as the result of an emerging consensus on the links between sodium and hypertension, typified by the statements of groups such as the American Medical Association, the American Heart Association, and the National Academy of Sciences.

Sentiment within the Bureau of Foods was against a blanket sodium labeling requirement. Strains on agency compliance capabilities were anticipated, and labeling of many foods was not seen as relevant to the needs of either hypertensive consumers or the general population. In addition, the discussion of sodium was buried in a massive and general food labeling document, much to the distress of some bureau officials, who wanted public health matters kept separate from other labeling issues.

Sodium also was part of the food safety issue. Viewed in this light, a more regulatory approach to sodium, with restrictions on sodium use in food products, joined sodium labeling as a federal policy option. Following the ban on cyclamate sweeteners in 1969, the FDA instituted a comprehensive review of food additives given Generally Recognized As Safe (GRAS) status under the Food Additives Amendments of 1958.[32] This status exempted a whole host of additives from having to prove safety under the new food laws. Sodium chloride—table salt—was one of the GRAS substances reviewed by a select committee of the Federation of American Societies for Experimental Biology (FASEB), under contract to the FDA. In its report, the panel called for the removal of salt from the GRAS list, for guidelines to restrict the use of salt in processed foods, and for labeling of the sodium content in foods.[33] Implementation of these recommendations, particularly the first two, would have entailed significant regulatory burdens for the FDA.[34] Setting regulatory standards for a flavoring element, given the importance of product flavor to the food industry, is a far more complex endeavor than the regulation of preservatives, for which technical standards can be developed. The GRAS report, delivered in 1979, was not binding on the FDA, and the agency did not publicly respond to it until 1982.

As the various policy approaches to diet and health concerns were considered by policymakers, the development and dissemination of information on these issues, including sodium, was a natural and often deliberate by-product. For example, an important outgrowth of the new government focus on nutrition was a series of hearings, titled "Diet and Killer Diseases," begun in 1976 by the Senate Select Committee on Nutrition and Human Needs, headed by Senator George McGovern (D., S.D.). Experts testified about the links between dietary patterns and the risk of developing chronic "killer diseases." Sodium was discussed, but major concern lay with the diet–heart disease hypothesis, and with cancer.[35]

The topics raised in the hearings were discussed in a 1977 staff report, *Dietary Goals for the United States,* popularly known as the "McGovern Report."[36] Recommendations were made regarding appropriate levels of consumption for sugar, fiber, fats, cholesterol, and sodium. The volume was controversial, especially regarding fats and cholesterol. The meat and egg industries were particularly aggrieved, and supplemental hearings dealt with their problems. Although the Salt Institute and the National Food Processors Association (representing the canning industry) lobbied for changes in the report's sodium goal, its economic implications were relatively minor, and there were no hearings for sodium.

The revisions in the second edition of the *Goals* dealt with political pressures generated by the first. The original salt goal of 3 grams per day was raised to 5 grams per day, which was said to be more appropriate for the general population. Five grams of salt still represented a significant reduction from the estimated daily intake of 10–12 grams.

Food labeling hearings were begun in 1978 by the Nutrition Subcommittee of the Senate Agriculture Committee.[37] Sodium was a topic, although not a major one. Industry opposition centered on technical and cost issues, and industry representatives cited the AMA on the point that sodium reduction was not needed for the general public. Eventually two bills, one each for the FDA and the USDA, were introduced in the Senate to modify the food labeling laws, and to require mandatory nutrition labeling including sodium.[38] As part of the legislative compromise, sodium and cholesterol labeling were made optional at the discretion of the secretaries of health and human services and agriculture. A bill was close at hand when the 1980 election intervened. Senator McGovern lost his seat, and the Republicans gained control of the Senate.

During the Carter administration, executive branch concern with prevention and health promotion had increased. *Healthy People: The Surgeon General's Report on Health Promotion and Disease Prevention,* issued in 1979, was a key manifestation of this interest. It stated that, although the role of sodium in hypertension is "not yet completely understood," dietary salt restriction could be helpful in lessening the need for antihypertensive medication in some people. Significantly, it also asserted that "Americans would probably be healthier, as a whole, if they consumed . . . less salt."[39] This recommendation, again buried in a wide-ranging document, provides a basis for marketing claims that "the Surgeon General calls for Americans to reduce salt intake." A follow-up report, *Promoting Health/Preventing Disease,* issued in 1980, contains specific quantitative targets and suggestions for implementation of the goals proclaimed in *Healthy People.* Noting uncertainties in the relationship between sodium and hypertension, it proposed that average adult daily sodium intake should be reduced from 4–10 grams in 1979 to 3–6 grams by 1990.[40]

Dietary Goals generated controversy within and outside government. In the absence of an official set of goals, the Senate report was seen by many as de facto policy. Hence, there were pressures to formulate an official response. The result was *Dietary Guidelines for Americans,* published jointly by USDA and the Department of Health and Human Services in 1980.[41] Guideline 6 suggested that people "avoid too much sodium."

The development of the *Guidelines* reflected the controversies surrounding the appropriateness of nutritional goals for the nation. With fat and cholesterol intake the key issues, the goals were to serve the often conflicting needs of various parts of the government. The FDA did not want numbers included that could serve as the basis for regulations. Scientific dispute, particularly in the National Institutes of Health, arose over the degree to which sodium was in fact a problem. Some scientists were concerned that precise numbers could not be supported by the data, and felt strongly that official recommendations should be closely tied to the evidence. The final product is a consensus document, with no quantitative recommendations. The report stresses the need for dietary balance, instead of focusing on particular elements of the diet.

The McGovern goals stimulated much of the subsequent attention on salt as a health concern for the general public. Agencies within the government, as well as the American Medical Association, the American Heart Association, and various nutrition groups wanted to place their responses to the goals on the record.[42] Their motives are chiefly based on a desire to maintain jurisdiction, and each organization seeks recommendations in accord with its basic organizational premises.

For example, in 1900, the Food and Nutrition Board of the National Academy of Sciences issued *Toward Healthful Diets,* a response to the past decade's burgeoning dietary recommendations. Although controversial because it made no call for reduced saturated fat and cholesterol intake, it did make a quantitative recommendation for reducing U.S. sodium consumption, which was viewed as excessive, particularly for people at risk of hypertension.[43] Finding 3–8 grams of salt (1.2–3.2 grams of sodium) "adequate but safe," the board's recommendation was strong, particularly given the equivocal evidence reviewed. In a 1979 report, the board had been less sanguine about the desirability or ease of general sodium reduction. One former participant in federal nutrition policy during this period suggests that the board was "tougher on salt [in the 1980 report] because they had to go after something, and salt seemed to be the easier target."[44] This notion of salt as "the safer target" is a recurring one.

Medical and scientific groups appropriate spheres of expertise as their own. There is an understandable reluctance to abdicate authority by failing to respond to changing interests. If the public and the government are concerned with links between diet and disease, then groups concerned with either diet or disease are under pressure to address the relationships between the two. Their response, it appears, builds a framework for subsequent action, even for a consistently secondary issue like sodium. One wonders if the vaunted consensus on the role of sodium in hypertension is less a matter of new evidence than it is a reflection of the fact that so many groups felt the need to go on record about the various dietary practices linked to disease. As with the shift in medical approaches to hypertension, indicating a need for nondrug therapies, the increasing interest in diet and its role in disease created a new environment in which sodium was suddenly quite relevant.

Serendipity and Salt: Sodium Is Singled Out

In 1981, a significant departure from previous government approaches occurred. Sodium was singled out. Why this rapid shift took place is difficult to answer precisely, but it is clear that a decade's worth of agenda building reached fruition. A series of "policy accelerators," to some extent matters of chance, heightened action and awareness for an issue that had been steadily advancing for some time.

By 1980, after five years of internal policy development, the FDA had announced that it would request legislative authority to require sodium labeling; no action on the GRAS status of sodium was publicly discussed. One FDA official has suggested that neither Joseph Califano nor Patricia Harris, secretaries of health and human services during the Carter administration, had any particular interest in sodium labeling.[45] However, interest in sodium at the commissioner's level had reached the point where a speech announcing a major policy initiative, seeking food industry efforts to lower salt content, was to be given in the fall of 1977 by Commissioner Jere Goyan. Because of a schedule change the speech was never given. Such are the vagaries of the policy process. In 1981, the Reagan administration arrived, committed to deregulation and "voluntarism." Regulatory approaches to sodium, including mandatory labeling, did not seem a likely administration approach. Nevertheless, the new secretary of health and human services, Richard Schweiker, was publicly committed to preventive health strategies.

Like the FDA, interested members of Congress and their staffs had concluded that labeling, rather than mandatory sodium restrictions, was the most viable federal approach to the potential health threat posed by salt. In the House, a mandatory sodium labeling bill was introduced by Congressman Neil Smith (D., Iowa), in January 1981. Smith, it is said, was prompted by articles in his local paper and by letters received from Iowa physicians.[46] The American Medical Association's legislative staff members in Washington had provided him with a draft bill; the AMA's support of the proposed legislation followed from a 1979 House of Delegates resolution.[47] Smith had no cosponsors, and observers felt that his bill was not going anywhere.

Congressman Albert Gore (D., Tenn.) also became involved with sodium. Gore chaired the House Investigations and Oversight Subcommittee of the Committee on Science and Technology. This subcommittee, with no legislative authority, serves the desires of its members for the discussion of visible issues.[48] In addition, the Democratic members were interested in scoring partisan points against the new administration. In 1981, the subcommittee's new staff director, Thomas Grumbly, was looking for a provocative topic. Grumbly had been at both the USDA and FDA under Carter, and had worked on nutrition labeling. Thus, sodium was a natural subject for Grumbly, and for Gore, who had a long-standing interest in food and drug issues. Sodium was seen as involving a diet–health link so well established that agency action could be demanded. At the same time, the focus on labeling rather than the mandatory reduction of sodium in processed foods was a good approach politically, involving free market issues of information and choice. Grumbly was contacted by the Center for Science in the Public Interest (CSPI), an activist group that was putting together a sodium petition to the FDA. Interest in salt and hypertension had reached the stage where congressional incentives made it a likely topic for legislative scrutiny. Media interest and organizational activity were powerful catalysts for action.

Hearings, with a standard format, were held in April.[49] The conclusion was that with a scientific consensus on the links between sodium and hypertension, and the widespread prevalence of hypertension, sodium labeling was needed. Dr. John Laragh was the token dissenter. Laragh, a scientist who enjoys a measure of flamboyance in his public appearances, was highly critical of the arguments for the general population to reduce its salt intake.

Several important actions resulted. First, both the FDA and the USDA were forced to develop testimony detailing current or proposed actions on sodium. The FDA presentation reflected most of what Bureau of Foods officials had sought for some time, although the FDA was now stressing voluntary industry cooperation. The FDA has a tradition of mixing "voluntary" approaches with its regulatory mandate, as illustrated by the baby food events.[50] This testimony was reviewed by the newly appointed FDA commissioner, Dr. Arthur Hull Hayes, a hypertension specialist with a strong interest in sodium and hypertension. Congressional pressure was the impetus for the FDA to announce a formal sodium program.[51] A tangible program was essential because the agency sought to forestall both mandatory labeling and congressional harassment. Similar pressures stimulated USDA efforts in sodium labeling and reduction, although the FDA actions were far more visible.

According to congressional staff members, Gore assumed the lead on sodium labeling legislation. A new bill, H.R. 4031, was introduced in June 1981, now cosponsored by Congressmen Smith, Gore, Henry Waxman (D., Calif.), chairman of the Health and the Environment Subcommittee, and forty-five other members of the House. It was a politically motivated modification of the previous bills, exempting firms with less than $50,000 in annual sales and foods with less than 35 milligrams of sodium per serving. Legislative hearings were held at the end of September.[52]

COALITION BUILDING

The proposed legislation had an effect similar to that of the McGovern Report. It provided a focus for organizational position taking on the sodium issue. Groups in favor of action on sodium now had an incentive to organize coalitions to shape the bill. Such single-issue ad hoc coalitions are common in contemporary national politics.[53] Typically, one organization with a particular interest in a piece of legislation takes the initiative in organizing other groups, many of which have only limited interest in the issue. The lead group on the sodium bill, at least initially, was the Center for Science in the Public Interest.

Founded in 1971 by four Nader associates, CSPI had become a vocal critic of processed foods and the food industry. The group gave sodium a higher priority than had any other health group and pushed for limits on sodium in processed food. It wanted sodium to be treated as a food additive and emphasized the preventive effects of sodium reduction.[54] The CSPI began to concentrate on food issues as part of a 1977 reorganization. An internal review, also in 1977, led to the conclusion that fats, sugar, and salt were three major nutrition policy issues for which the evidence was sufficient for the organization to seek public action.

The center's public involvement with sodium began in 1978, when it sponsored a petition to the FDA calling for sodium labeling and regulations. The document was signed by hypertension experts, representatives of major health organizations, and fifty members of Congress. Such petitions cannot be dismissed as frivolous. Beyond their publicity value, agencies must respond and these responses can become grounds for legal action, although agency receptivity to such pressures can vary between administrations.[55]

The executive director of CSPI, Michael Jacobson, had decided to make sodium a household word. Salt was seen as less difficult to remove from food than fats, cholesterol, or sugar. In 1980, another CSPI petition circulated among health professionals and medical students. It was submitted to the FDA in early March 1981, with 5,796 signatures.

The CSPI maintained a steady correspondence with the FDA and others on the sodium issue. Letters to the FDA disputed estimates of naturally occurring sodium used in the 1979 FASEB report on the GRAS status of salt. Similarly, CSPI took issue with estimates of hypertension prevalence and the number of sodium sensitives in the population, preferring the highest estimates in its public statements.[56] The Reagan administration was seen by CSPI as less responsive to petitions than was its predecessor, so the center focused on press contacts, lobbying, and interactions with other groups.

Many industry scientists view CSPI with derision. The group was not invited to testify at the legislative hearings held in September 1981, even though they did testify at the June hearings held by Congressman Gore. According to one source close to CSPI, the bill's backers wanted the legislation to appear "mainstream."

The CSPI is a staff-led organization. Although it claims some 35,000 members, its board of directors is self-perpetuating, rather than elected by the membership.[57] Such a structure is common in public interest organizations, and can be contrasted with those of other groups, Common Cause, for example, which depend on large numbers of members for financial support, and have elected boards of directors.[58] The CSPI also concentrates on a rather narrow range of issues, as is typical of staff-led public interest groups. These factors minimize the internal and external constraints upon the group's activities, and allow it to take stronger positions than can many groups, such as professional associations or voluntary health organizations. Groups like CSPI rely heavily on links with the news media in order to exert pressure on decisionmakers.

The CSPI's satisfaction with its organizational emphasis on salt can be contrasted with the fate of an earlier activist group, called Salt Alert. Begun in 1976 by a Vermont couple, Salt Alert attempted to promote support for sodium education and reduction efforts, but was unable to generate sufficient interest to keep the effort afloat.[59] Salt Alert's genesis lay in an excessively salty meal in a local restaurant. This gastronomic misadventure led one of the founders, a scientist, to review the evidence linking sodium to hypertension.

Several prominent scientists joined the group's board, and attempts were made to involve the National Heart, Lung, and Blood Institute and the FDA in a program to educate the public and industry on the sodium "facts." Most of these efforts took place in 1977. Government interest was limited; the group's founders believe that fats and cholesterol overshadowed sodium within these agencies. Contact was made with CSPI, which was not yet working on sodium, and Salt Alert may have helped make CSPI aware of the issue. Salt Alert was actually able to get some money from the Salt Institute, of all places, but was unable to generate enough funding to get a proposed conference off the ground. The group disbanded in 1980.

A more mainstream organization involved with the issue was the American Heart Association (AHA), which has a long-standing interest in hypertension and in nutrition issues related to heart disease. Most of the group's nutrition efforts have centered on issues of fats, cholesterol, and overweight. However, since 1978, the AHA's diet statement has recommended a reduction in sodium intake.[60] The purpose for this change is hypertension prevention in susceptible individuals, and the lowering of average blood pressure levels.

The AHA's Nutrition Committee has primary jurisdiction for actions on sodium and hypertension and, according to one AHA official, has been considering a "specific [sodium] proposal" for some time, although internal debate impeded this effort.[61] Even if a position emerges from this committee, scientific and policymaking functions are dispersed throughout a large array of other committees and councils, all with veto power. Thus the association needs a near consensus for any recommendation to clear its way to the board.

Much of the disagreement on the sodium–hypertension relationship is over the adequacy of the available epidemiological evidence. There is an antiepidemiology inclination within elements of the association. Basic scientists say, "Give science a chance to find the real cause." Yet epidemiologists often feel that there is a basis for action before disease mechanisms are elucidated. Illustrating the dispute, a former AHA officer characterized epidemiologists as a "very potent force . . . which is voluble and political. They don't keep to the bounds of the evidence."

A related debate concerns the degree to which sodium reduction should be considered as either a component of treatment for identified hypertensive individuals or a general preventive measure. As one AHA paper stated, "the question of whether an effort should be made to reduce the intake of sodium for the general public is an unsettled matter."[62] Although taking a "cautious" approach to the specific relationship of sodium to hypertension, the AHA's stance was one of strong support for sodium labeling, including its preventive aspects, and some concern that the FDA's voluntary approach would not succeed.

Although not a part of the formal coalition supporting the labeling bill, American Medical Association representatives continued to work with congressional staff. But, having endorsed labeling legislation, the AMA was approached by the FDA about supporting the voluntary program. According to an AMA official, the response was, "If you can get a voluntary program to work, good." The AMA's desire to work alone engendered a measure of hostility from some coalition members, some of whom felt that from the first attempt to put together a coalition, the AMA was either neutral or subtly sabotaging the legislation. The AMA was very concerned with other legislation and the food industry was, according to one coalition member, "beating" them over their support for mandatory labeling. The AMA staff members counter that they supported the bill, although perhaps without a full commitment of resources. As one remarked, "You can only pull out the stops so often."

Industry opposition to the sodium labeling bill, H.R. 4031, accelerated during the fall and winter of 1981–82. It concentrated on a few key Demo-

trials, particularly those with major food firms in their districts.[63] As hostil
ity intensified, the AMA equivocated, saying it could support a substitute
bill which would have given the food industry a chance for voluntary
compliance. This shift was interpreted by some observers as a signal that
subcommittee moderates and industry could successfully oppose Waxman.
In March 1982, the AMA held a Washington conference on sodium labeling, known as Salt III (a 1978 AMA meeting on the subject had been dubbed
Salt II). Bringing together regulators, industry representatives, and physicians, the meeting addressed "practical" approaches to labeling issues.

A shift in AMA attitudes toward sodium labeling can be observed. The
AMA came out against FDA regulations proposed in 1982, in which nutrition labeling would trigger sodium labeling. This stance reversed an earlier
AMA position favoring such a regulation, as well as the previous support
of more sweeping legislation.[64] Yet this shift must be seen within the
context of a stable set of organizational attitudes. From its first sodium
resolution in 1977, "moderation" and cost-effectiveness were recurrent
themes. The suggested level of prudent sodium intake was actually equivalent to one estimate of current consumption.[65] The "healthy" population
is distinguished from those suffering from or at risk of hypertension, and
medical management overshadows prevention. Descriptive labels, such as
"low sodium," are seen as irrelevant for patients under a physician's care,
and potentially "misleading." The AMA officials repeatedly profess concern over "scare tactics" and "extreme" recommendations based upon
inadequate knowledge.

The AMA's shifting stance may be attributed to three principal factors.
First, the association had little interest in sodium labeling as a symbolic
issue related to general consumption of sodium, or to food industry behavior. Second, the AMA was uneasy with the tenor of the FDA labeling
proposal, which was seen as unnecessarily restrictive and costly. The intensity of Hayes's attacks on sodium was reminiscent of the "immoderate
. . . scare tactics" embodied in the McGovern Report. Finally, sodium
labeling had a "regulatory" taint at a time when the AMA was pushing
vigorously for legislation to eliminate Federal Trade Commission jurisdiction over state-regulated professions, including physicians.

Both the AMA and the AHA took conservative scientific positions on
sodium's relationship to hypertension. Yet their public approaches to the
sodium issue differed substantially. The AMA was constrained by its dual
roles as scientific organization and politically active professional association. The American Heart Association, although under some of the same
constraints, had wider public latitude.

A STAR (BUT NO LEGISLATION) IS BORN

Subcommittee mark-up sessions for the sodium labeling bill (H.R. 4031) were scheduled and postponed as it became impossible to put together a winning coalition behind labeling legislation. Although the labeling bill was finished for the 97th Congress, it was reintroduced in the 98th (1983–84) and 99th (1985–86) Congresses. Gore did well for himself and for the visibility of sodium's links to hypertension. He was featured in a 1982 *Time* cover story on sodium appearing during the week Salt III was held, as well as in a number of newspaper and magazine articles which used sodium labeling as a springboard for more general discussion of sodium and hypertension. His position became that of the watchdog over FDA efforts on sodium, without the responsibility for a bill facing uncertain implementation. By 1984 Gore's abilities on this and other issues helped him win a seat in the Senate where he submitted yet another version of the sodium labeling bill, with Congressman Smith doing the honors in the House.

From the start, the labeling legislation was cast in pro/anti regulatory terms. In this sense, its opponents controlled the issue. This context was apparent to interested House aides during early efforts to develop a Senate version of the bill. Industry opposition meshed with the antiregulatory mood sweeping Congress. The FDA voluntary program enabled opposition to the mandatory labeling bill to be clearly distinguished from any attitude toward sodium, its regulation, or its links to hypertension.

Supporters of the Smith-Gore bill reported surprise at the intensity of industry opposition. But sodium labeling symbolized a wider food industry agenda, containing such issues as nutrition labeling and food safety. Although specific segments of industry had serious problems with sodium content or its labeling, more general industry concerns predominated. Finally, the conservative mood in Washington, and perhaps the AMA's seemingly ambiguous stance, made concerted opposition to the labeling bill appear more likely to succeed.

Because the House faced many important legislative issues, such as the interminable budget debate and the Clean Air Act revisions, time available for sodium labeling was limited. It seems clear that relatively minor and discrete issues like sodium are more likely to fall victim to legislative "overload" than to cause it.

CARROT AND STICK: THE FDA'S "VOLUNTARY" EFFORT

As is frequently the case in health issues, regulatory agencies—mainly the FDA—provided fertile ground for the progress of the sodium issue. Two related themes animated FDA efforts. First, "reasonable reductions"

In the sodium content of foods were sought. Second, consumers should be able to make "informed judgments about the salt which they consume." These themes transcend traditional regulatory efforts and entail a desire to heighten popular awareness of sodium as a possible health hazard. As Commissioner Hayes stated at a food industry meeting, there is a "huge, untapped market for low sodium foods. . . . As the public becomes better educated about the role that reduced sodium can play in controlling blood pressure, there will be an increased demand for low sodium foods."[66]

The "five point plan" unveiled at the 1981 Gore Hearings set out the agency's new approach:

1. The FDA would work with industry on *voluntary* reduction of sodium in processed foods.
2. New rules requiring sodium content declaration as part of nutrition labeling would be proposed. Terms such as "low sodium" and "reduced sodium" would be defined.
3. *Legislative options* for sodium labeling would be considered.
4. The FDA would work with governmental agencies, private organizations, and industry "to help consumers make the most effective use of the new labeling, and to *raise consumer awareness of the effects of sodium on health.*"
5. Existing programs would be used to monitor changes in sodium consumption. (Emphasis added.)[67]

The FDA action on sodium labeling was sold to Secretary of Health and Human Services Schweiker as a "preventive health measure, as distinguished from the Agency's major food labeling initiatives."[68] This approach appealed to the secretary's concern with prevention, while minimizing the regulatory onus of the proposal. The plan was also used as the FDA's response to the CSPI petitions. A decision was made to separate sodium from cholesterol, sugar, and other labeling issues, because salt labeling was seen as most likely to succeed.

It took Commissioner Hayes to give this broad program life. The issue had been chosen as a "personal theme" for the new commissioner. Hayes was on record as supporting "cooperative" rather than coercive relations with industry, a position in tune with that of the Reagan administration. Along with Secretary Schweiker, Hayes held a meeting with 200 industry representatives to seek their cooperation. A year-long series of meetings and correspondence between FDA officials and industry representatives ensued. Hayes took every opportunity to push his sodium initiatives, making speeches, talking with the press, even appearing on television.[69]

Many observers saw Hayes as using the pending labeling legislation in a carrot and stick game. Such an intention is suggested by Hayes's public statements, in which he reserved the right to request mandatory labeling legislation if industry failed to reduce or label sufficiently.[70] Similarly, in a meeting with representatives of the Grocery Manufacturers of America, Dr. Sanford Miller, director of the Bureau of Foods, "cautioned that there was a lot of pressure for mandatory rules, and that this increases the importance of early success in a voluntary program."[71]

The FDA finally issued its proposed regulations for sodium labeling on 18 June 1982, after consultations with the USDA, and a lengthy review process within the Department of Health and Human Services and the Office of Management and Budget.[72] The proposed regulations declared that nutrition labeling would trigger sodium labeling, and set definitions for the use of sodium descriptors. By early 1983, approximately 55 percent of FDA-regulated processed foods bore nutrition labeling. In recognition of industry concern with many elements of the proposal, flexibilities in data accuracy were highlighted, as were possibilities for special exemptions and compliance extensions. Under the proposal, sodium labeling would be mandatory for those foods for which nutrition labeling is required, such as bread and diet soft drinks.

Along with the labeling proposal, the FDA's GRAS response was announced. Revision in the status of salt was deferred, pending an evaluation of the results of the voluntary program and the proposed labeling regulations. More drastic options, for example standards for salt content in all processed foods, were rejected as untenable. One senior Bureau of Foods official observed that "banning salt would be impossible; we aren't stupid."[73] The furor created by FDA attempts to ban saccharin surely played a role in heightening agency sensitivity to regulations likely to incite public irritation and ridicule. Still, the proposal explicitly notes that inadequate industry response could lead to more stringent labeling and other requirements under the provisions of the GRAS review.

The key element of the FDA's crusade was publicity. Agency activities generated abundant media coverage. The FDA sent sodium articles to newspapers and produced radio and television commercials, often featuring celebrities, advising Americans that "taking care of yourself is important. That may mean cutting down on salt."[74] The agency, along with the USDA and National Heart, Lung, and Blood Institute, also produced numerous pamphlets on sodium.

The FDA worked with other government agencies through interagency task forces. Besides its own advertising, the USDA also encouraged sodium labeling, and initiated technical efforts regarding sodium restriction in foods. And the FDA collaborated with the National High Blood Pressure Education Program, whose information efforts began to stress the role of sodium restriction in hypertension treatment.[75] In addition, the FDA attempted to involve health professionals and their organizations in its efforts. For example, a letter sent by Hayes to every U.S. physician sought to raise awareness of the sodium content in food and the role of sodium restriction in the treatment of hypertension.[76]

In sum, several agencies, but Commissioner Hayes and the FDA in particular, significantly raised public awareness of sodium as a possible health hazard. Hayes, by concentrating the authority and prestige of his post on sodium, amplified what might have been a rather low-key effort. The visibility of this effort may also have served to project an activist stance for an agency under pressure to minimize its regulatory efforts, and subject at the same time to criticism that it was abandoning protection of the public's health and safety.[77] Yet such a personalized approach was not without its risks. Hayes's emphasis on the need for general population concern with sodium, and his high public profile, led at least one senior official in the Department of Health and Human Services to state that Hayes was overstepping the bounds of scientific as well as political propriety.

Salt Sellers and Pickle Packers

Salt is more than a scientific or a political issue; it is a consumer product. Several industries have played central roles in the development of public concern about sodium. Sodium in processed foods, largely in the form of sodium chloride, comprises 50 percent of our daily sodium intake.[78] Thus, food companies have been the targets of organized efforts to reduce the sodium consumption of hypertensive or potentially hypertensive people. Although some food companies felt threatened by these efforts, others used new or existing product formulations to gain marketing advantages from the concern with sodium. Several firms, including salt companies, have sold products as explicit substitutes for salt. The salt industry sells its products to consumers as well as to food processors, and though it is not a likely target of regulation the industry is mindful of the impact of decreased salt consumption on profits.

The U.S. processed-food industry encompasses thousands of firms, including large conglomerate companies such as Procter & Gamble, General Mills, and Dart-Kraft, and more specialized producers of fresh and processed meats, dairy products, soft drinks, packaged goods, and canned foods. Each sector of the industry has its unique features, and for each, salt and sodium compounds are important, though to varying degrees. Firms are represented by a variety of trade associations, with the peak group being the Grocery Manufacturers of America. Often a food company belongs to several trade associations, which compete with each other for company support.

Nutrition issues have historically been important for the food industry, and in recent years attention has magnified as consumers have brooded about sugar, additives, fat intake, and of course, salt.[79] Such worries have led to a number of new products. This heightened sensitivity to nutrition issues has been reflected in the various publications reaching industry officials. Sodium, as part of the rising issue of diet and disease, was a constant, if often secondary presence.

Far smaller than the food industry, the U.S. salt industry includes some forty-seven companies, but only ten sell more than 1 million tons annually, accounting together for 80 percent of total U.S. production.[80] Of these forty-seven companies, only twenty-five produce dry salt, with the remainder producing brine for the chemical industry and other uses. The twelve U.S. members of the Salt Institute comprise over 75 percent of the U.S. dry salt market. The industry is not heavily reliant upon food salt sales, which are concentrated in a few firms.[81] For the year ending June 1982, when the sodium issue was on the rise, food-grade salt sales for Salt Institute members, which include salt sold to both consumers and food processors, were 911.4 thousand tons, or 4 percent of total tonnage.[82] This tonnage accounted for $125.5 million dollars, or 19.7 percent of industry sales. Data on profits are not available, but the ratio of tonnage to sales is far lower than that of any other salt use category, suggesting that food salt is highly profitable, a proposition readily supported within the industry. The major uses for salt can be seen in table 4.1, along with sales and tonnage figures.

The salt market, unlike that for processed foods, is mature. Annual growth in U.S. demand for salt is projected at 2 percent by the Bureau of Mines. Figure 4.1 describes the decade-long decline in per capita sales of the familiar round can of table salt. As measured by the Salt Institute, food-grade salt tonnage, which includes table salt as well as salt sold to the food industry, has also declined. By 1985 food grade sales had dropped to 886 thousand tons and 120.3 million dollars. Although it is impossible to

TABLE 4.1

Total Salt Sales by Major End Use

Use	Dollars (thousands)	Percentage	Tons (thousands)	Percentage
Water conditioning	108,999.5	15.7	1,930.0	8.4
Highway	103,623.8	16.3	9,787.3	42.7
Agriculture	101,838.4	16.0	1,868.5	8.1
Food grade	125,547.2	19.7	911.4	4.0
Chemical	52,872.9	8.3	3,825.3	16.7
Miscellaneous	142,994.2	22.5	4,597.5	20.1
Totals	635,876	100	22,920	100

NOTE: 1 July 1981–30 June 1982; Salt Institute members only.
SOURCE: Salt Institute.

attribute with certainty these changes to increased consumer concern with salt as a health hazard, such an interpretation is accepted by some within the industry. Others, however, assign much of the decline in table salt sales to a greater consumer reliance upon processed foods and restaurants.

According to salt industry sources, Morton Salt Company is the leader in table salt sales, with approximately 60 percent of the market.[83] Morton Salt is a division of Morton-Thiokol, Inc., formed by a 1982 merger of

FIGURE 4.1

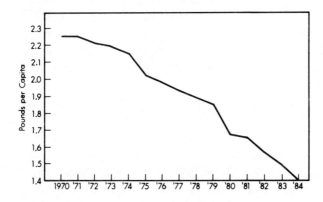

Per Capita Sales of Table Salt

SOURCE: A. C. Nielsen, Shelf Movement Data on Round Cans of Table Salt.

Morton-Norwich Products, Inc. and Thiokol, Inc., a chemical firm. Before this merger, Morton-Norwich had already expanded into pharmaceuticals, household products, and chemicals. In 1981, as antisalt pressures mounted, salt contributed 45 percent of Morton-Norwich's operating profits on 34 percent of sales. As illustrated by Morton's experience, diversification is an important strategy for salt companies facing declining markets, as are research efforts to find new uses and markets for salt.[84] Other companies undergoing such changes include Diamond Crystal Salt, a major producer of salt for the food-processing industry, and International Salt, a major producer of salt for de-icing and chemical production, which shifted away from table salt over the past decade.[85]

Unlike processed foods, salt is a basic commodity for which product differentiation and brand recognition are relatively unimportant. Morton does, however, market its table salt as a premium product. Private label sales are a major line of business, even for firms with their own brands. Because it is difficult to increase consumer demand for table salt, the product is not heavily advertised, and marketing emphasizes arrangements that produce shelf space, such as deals and discounts. Morton is the only national marketer of table salt. Other major producers of food-grade salt include regional producers such as the aforementioned International Salt and Diamond Salt companies, as well as Cargill, Inc., and Hardy Salt Co. These market characteristics suggest that there are significant limits to what any one salt firm will do to protect its products from public concerns with the health effects of salt intake.

Morton Salt has also dominated the salt substitute market. Over the past several years, sales of salt substitutes have been rising.[86] Morton sells two salt substitutes, Morton Salt Substitute, and Morton Lite Salt. The first is predominantly potassium chloride, which is bitter. It was introduced in the 1960s, and marketed to people on sodium-restricted diets. In the early 1970s Lite Salt was introduced. It is 50 percent sodium chloride and 50 percent potassium chloride, more palatable than the original substitute, and aimed at "normal healthy people who want to reduce their sodium intake."[87]

Until recently, Morton did not aggressively push its salt substitutes, perhaps because the market was seen as limited, and there was no desire to cast aspersions on salt. An additional reason for caution was a 1975 FTC consent decree, applying to Lite Salt, strictly limiting implied advertising links between sodium intake and hypertension, and requiring a warning on the use of the product by those on a salt-free diet. In 1983 Morton was granted a revision of this decree, which allows the firm to present medical opinions on the links between sodium and hypertension in its advertising.[88]

An earlier threat to the salt industry was criticism of excessive road salt use.[89] These attacks began in the early 1970s, and a number of communities and states passed ordinances regulating road salt use. In response, the industry began a public relations and technical effort, the "Sensible Salting Program." By 1981, public and government attitudes toward salt and hypertension became more worrisome for the salt industry, increasing significantly with the appointment of Commissioner Hayes. "Sensational" accounts in the popular press and the media, such as the 1977 polemic *Killer Salt* and the 1982 *Time* magazine cover story titled "Salt: The New Villain?" are decried by industry executives and seen as contributing to heightened public concern.[90]

The smaller salt companies did not put a lot of effort into defending salt. Morton Salt, with a very large stake in consumer salt sales, was somewhat more active. In general, all of the companies relied heavily upon the Salt Institute, at least as a "front." Because Salt Institute funding comes from its member firms, which have widely varying investments in food salt, major expenditures on salt and hypertension issues are likely to stimulate pressures for special program funding by the most affected firms.

GOVERNMENT PRESSURE, VOLUNTARY COMPLIANCE, AND THE MARKET

Food safety regulation (especially of suspected carcinogens), labeling rules, and official diet recommendations have all loomed large for the food industry since the mid-1970s.[91] Generalized industry opposition to government attempts to reduce sodium consumption arose when sodium became the sole focus of attack. Two elements were at work here. One is the reflex reaction by most food companies, and especially food industry trade associations, against any sort of regulation. Perhaps more important, mandatory sodium labeling was seen as linked to a larger regulatory agenda including saturated fats, sugars, and food safety.

The need to respond to government initiatives commanded the attention of a number of trade associations. Meetings of a "Food Industry Group" commenced in 1978, at the behest of the Salt Institute.[92] This coalition later worked to defeat H.R. 4031, the Gore-Waxman sodium labeling bill. They presented their views to the FDA on its sodium program, submitting comments, and meeting with officials. The Grocery Manufacturers of America, which must achieve near consensus in arriving at a position, was affected by the strong concerns of some members, particularly the soft drink, dairy, and meat industries. This group, and other trade associations and firms, went as far as the Office of Management and Budget in attempts to halt the FDA's sodium labeling rule.

With a focus much narrower than the food industry's as a whole, the salt industry promoted "sensible" use of salt by both consumers and food processors. Since 1978, the industry has publicly favored sodium labeling. It also supported regulations requiring sodium labeling if nutrition labeling is used. The Salt Institute even favored mandatory sodium labeling until the "concerns" of its food processing customers led it to drop this position. The institute's approach seems to be based on the realization that sodium content labeling is likely to have only minor impact on salt consumption, and that industry cooperation might forestall adverse regulatory efforts and attendant publicity.[93]

At the same time, the salt industry was quite sensitive to calls for sodium reductions for the general population. One industry statement asserted, "It is important that the general public not be left with the impression that it should restrict sodium intake on its own."[94] The Salt Institute opposed descriptors, "low sodium" for example, that can be used as marketing tools, noting: "We believe that the proper solution to the dietary sodium problem for individuals with hypertension . . . lies in sodium labeling and low-sodium products, not in reducing sodium in all foods and trying to scare everyone into cutting back on sodium and salt."[95] When Nabisco Brands ran an advertisement for unsalted Fleischmann's margarine, aggressively proclaiming the need for Americans to cut down on salt, a salt company official reports that words were exchanged between salt industry executives and Nabisco's legal department, and the advertisement was discontinued. Nabisco was seen as "breaking ranks."

Some firms, General Mills for example, were labeling for sodium content as early as 1978.[96] General Foods decided in 1980 to begin sodium labeling, and was able to announce its new policy at the Gore Hearings in April 1981.[97] Since the FDA stepped up its campaign for voluntary sodium labeling, many more firms joined this trend. The FDA estimates that by June of 1983, 39.6 percent (by dollar volume) of the packaged processed foods that it regulates were labeled, up from 13.4 percent in 1979.[98]

The cost of labeling is a matter of some debate, varying from industry to industry. Although not trivial, involving measurement, printing, and monitoring costs, the cost is not seen by industry officials as unduly high in most cases. Yet even those firms choosing to label sodium did not make it a selling point. Firms with low-sodium products emphasized that sodium content was low, not that it was reported on the package. Labeling may be a relatively cheap sop to those consumers who look at nutrition labels and worry about sodium, but it is more likely that most sodium labeling is a response to government pressure, or its anticipation.

Still, the food industry's increasing adoption of sodium labeling is an important element in what many perceive as an upsurge in sodium-related activity. In addition, by making firms more aware of the sodium content of their products, labeling probably increases the number of marketing approaches based on sodium content. It should also be remembered that under the food-packaging laws, claims about the sodium content of a product must be accompanied by labeling.[99] Industry executives generally credit Commissioner Hayes with the burst of industry interest in sodium. According to a food company executive, his efforts were seen as having "moved the issue out in the open," creating the possibility for more than a limited diet food market.

MADISON AVENUE MEETS KILLER SALT

Advertising, packaging, and product differentiation are salient concerns of the food-processing industry.[100] Competition for shelf space is keen, so companies produce endless variations on familiar themes; constant product change is characteristic of the processed-food industry. Recipes are not randomly arrived at. In the search for new products, companies often follow a long process of review, with taste panels, test markets, and the like. Salt, which enhances taste, texture, and product life, and performs these functions relatively cheaply, is often a key ingredient.

Some companies reported ongoing efforts to review the sodium content of their products. Results varied. At one firm, a corporate policy memo led to a reduction in sodium content in one product of 5 percent per year, with no announcement of the changes. The feeling was that incremental changes would allow for a gradual adjustment of consumer taste, without arousing any negative attention.

Standard Brands (now Nabisco Brands) established a nutrition policy, following its experience with the health-oriented marketing of Fleischmann's margarine. This policy called for salt reduction wherever possible, especially in new products. Products such as no-salt margarine and unsalted peanuts were introduced. Industry activity seems to have increased in 1981. Salt companies began to work with food processors on sodium reduction, including the use of salt substitutes in the baking industry. Still, interest in sodium reduction was mixed.

By 1983 new products specifically marketed as reduced- or low-sodium were proliferating.[101] Kellogg test marketed a line of low-sodium cereals. Del Monte presented, with great hoopla, a "no salt added" line of canned vegetables. S. S. Pierce, in a similar move, converted virtually its entire Libby line of canned vegetables to "no salt added." Even Vlasic Pickles presented a reduced-sodium pickle. Several supermarket chains introduced "private label" low-sodium brands.

Once salt content became a marketing problem the decibel level of the antisodium campaign took a quantum jump. There were two key elements to this change. First, the sheer volume of products and associated advertising increased. Second, there was a new perception that "low-sodium" products were no longer confined to the special diet market. For example, Campbell's market research identified 20 percent of consumers as "hard core," "concerned about salt as a health issue and willing to make a behavioral change to reduce salt in their diets."[102] But another 40 percent had become "conditioned to eat less salt," because salt was now a "good health issue."

Campbell marketed its low-sodium soups to the "hard core" population. Thus glossy advertisements appeared in the *New England Journal of Medicine* rather than *Newsweek.* Perhaps the recognition that its low-sodium soups are in a limited market, and that its regular soups are still fairly high in sodium, along with a concern that the 40 percent who worry about salt might simply avoid soups, has led the company to take its rather cautious approach.

At the other extreme were the broader-based efforts of Del Monte and Libby. Given a canning industry perception that "within three to four years, low-sodium will be 60 to 80 percent of the total canned vegetable category"—a declining market—it is no surprise that Del Monte mounted an expensive television campaign, and Libby's switched its entire line to no-salt.[103]

Products already low in sodium were "repositioned" to take advantage of the heightened interest in sodium. Carnation highlighted the fact that its Contadina tomato paste had no salt added, spurring a competitive response from Hunt-Wesson.[104] Riopan, an antacid identified as low in sodium at the AMA's 1978 Salt II conference, asked those choosing an antacid to "Consider the sodium factor," mentioning the Surgeon General's statements on sodium in its advertisements.[105] Fleischmann's "unsalted" margarine published an advertisement headlined "FDA Head Urges Less Salt in Food." Even Frito-Lay, having identified salt in its snack products as an area of consumer concern, introduced "back panels" noting that one serving of potato chips had less salt than two slices of bread.[106] Perrier, with less sodium than some other bottled waters, sponsored its own "symposium," and distributed a low-sodium diet booklet featuring, of course, Perrier.[107] Spice manufacturers praised the joys of cooking with seasonings other than salt. Sunkist suggested lemon juice as a flavoring for food, telling us to "Pass That Salt."[108]

A number of salt substitutes took advantage of the travails of the salt industry. Mr. Pepper, a black pepper product with a large mark-up, aggressively advertised that reducing sodium intake is a health goal for the entire population, citing Commissioner Hayes on this point on its salt "hotline."[109] In 1982, a division of Revlon introduced a new potassium chloride product, called NoSalt. NoSalt was marketed aggressively, particularly on television, posing the question, "Are you a saltaholic?" NoSalt quickly captured 58 percent of the salt substitute market.[110]

Salt industry executives were confident that NoSalt would fail, because its "unpalatable taste" and relatively high price would discourage repeat purchases by the general public to which the product was aimed. Marketing data did indicate the narrow peaked sales curve of a product that cannot generate repeat purchases.[111] Still, NoSalt's debut appears to have stimulated a more vigorous marketing campaign for Morton Lite Salt, which is said to be more palatable than a pure potassium chloride mixture. In an illustration of the fierce battles that accompany health-related product wars, the American Meat Institute filed complaints against Revlon with the Better Business Bureau and the FTC, charging that a NoSalt television ad misleadingly portrayed the amount of salt in hot dogs.[112]

Label descriptors are an important element of product formulation and marketing strategies.[113] For example, in its proposed regulation the FDA stated that products must have 75 percent of their sodium removed to qualify as "reduced sodium." This requirement was seen as unduly restrictive by many within the industry. One way for firms to evade such restrictions is to modify recommended serving size, so that the product has even less sodium per serving. For example, Ralston Purina reduced the serving size to one third of a can when it introduced a tuna with 50 percent less sodium.[114]

Another constraint on the marketing of low-sodium foods is that companies are restricted in the health claims they can make about their products.[115] Many got around this problem by saying something like "The Surgeon General says Americans eat too much salt." The FDA also considered allowing references to be made to the relationship between sodium reduction and blood pressure. Some firms used advertisements that implied sodium is somehow bad for you, as comedian Rodney Dangerfield did when pushing Lo-Sal, another low-sodium antacid, on television.

Trumpeting the absence of salt or sodium, without telling people why this is good, broadens the market for these products. If salt is seen as unhealthy, even by those unconcerned with hypertension, a generalized aversion may develop. The data from Campbell Soup and a 1982 FDA report suggest the existence of such feelings.[116] By engaging in rudimentary educational efforts, companies expand their own markets. Competitive practices supplement the government propaganda campaign. A large reservoir of such anxieties, even if shallow, will provide a basis for countless new products.

LIES, DAMN LIES, AND STATISTICS

Various trade associations, including the American Meat Institute, the National Food Processors Association, and the American Bakers Association, as well as some individual firms, sponsored studies on the functional and taste characteristics of sodium, and the possibilities for reduction. Most of this research is of recent origin.

A more interesting trend involves the sponsorship of medical research and the dissemination of its findings. Several firms, including Frito-Lay, General Foods, and Campbell, held internal seminars featuring scientists doing new research on hypertension issues. As one executive put it, "When we see an issue on the horizon, we seek the best available science on the problem." One important consequence of such efforts is that regulatory comments, position papers, and testimony are at hand before any problem crops up. Another is the development of contacts with academic researchers.

Scientists studying alternative hypertension hypotheses received grants from food companies and trade associations. Citing credibility problems, as well as cost, major salt companies apparently did not directly fund hypertension research. They were asked for money, but one senior salt company manager characterized such expenditures as "throwing money down the drain." Still, the industry closely follows the scientific debate over the role of sodium and hypertension. In an attempt to propound its view of the issue, the Salt Institute sponsored a scientific monograph titled Sodium in Medicine and Health. [117] This book, begun in the mid-1970s, and motivated in part by the issue of road salt contamination of drinking water, deals largely with sodium and hypertension. Its conclusion, presented by Dr. Fredrick Stare of Harvard University, an avowed enemy of "food fads," is that "moderation seems to be the best path to follow."

In 1982, at least two scientific meetings on the causes of hypertension were sponsored by food firms and trade associations. The first, presented by Campbell, was held in March 1982. The proceedings were published as a supplement to the Journal *Hypertension*. The second, organized by an industry-sponsored research organization, the International Life Sciences Institute (ILSI), was cosponsored by the National Kidney Foundation and the U.S. Department of Health and Human Services. It was published, at ILSI expense, as a supplement to *Annals of Internal Medicine.* The thrust of both conferences was to widen the scope of hypertension hypotheses, implicitly and explicitly minimizing the role of sodium.[118]

Originally formed to deal with industry needs for caffeine research, ILSI tried to sponsor the kind of credible scientific research needed by food companies in an era when food safety questions involve complex estimations of risk.[119] The ILSI's industry ties might suggest that its research is influenced by factors other than the normal constraints governing science. However, such bias, if it exists, is in no way requisite for the group's success. Support by ILSI of research, meetings, and publications that would otherwise lack funding exerts a powerful influence upon public and scientific agendas. The most active firms on the ILSI hypertension subcommittee were Frito-Lay, Kraft, Campbell, the Salt Institute, and Coca-Cola—the organizations most active in fighting governmental initiatives on sodium.

Industry executives repeatedly stressed the "uncertain evidence" linking sodium to hypertension. This stance often reflects a general approach to diet and health issues, leading to a call for, as General Foods has phrased it, "variety, balance, and moderation." Many in industry asserted that sodium reduction by the general population is not warranted by what are characterized as the medical needs of a small percentage of the population.

One executive explained that "alternative views of hypertension causation should be emphasized as part of [the firm's] strategy." Hypotheses involving potassium, calcium, and body weight are "pursued by bright young researchers"; another executive referred to the data on sodium as "old hat." It is obvious that this approach was central to the conference cosponsored by ILSI, "Nutrition and Blood Pressure Control: Current Status of Dietary Factors and Hypertension" (note my added emphasis on multiple *factors*). For example, a physician involved in planning both conferences has done recent work linking calcium deficiency to hypertension.

Industry is now trying to communicate with the public. The Potato Chip Information Bureau publishes articles noting that "salty snacks" are not particularly sodium laden.[120] General Foods puts on its corporate information program "Sane Talk About Food and Your Health." Trade associations and companies publish booklets discussing sodium and health, and listing the sodium content of foods. For example, *Straight Talk About Salt,* a pamphlet by the Salt Institute, was endorsed by the FDA and the National

High Blood Pressure Education Program.[121] After industry and FDA criticisms were resolved, 80,000 copies were printed.

Industry efforts to raise questions regarding the relationship of sodium and hypertension generated several magazine and newspaper articles doing just that. The principal aim of this campaign was probably not any exoneration of salty foods, but rather the undermining of the FDA's focus on sodium. Nevertheless, salt industry executives are relatively fatalistic about the effect of health concerns on their industry. Given their limited dependence on food salt, they appear to be engaging in a damage-limitation strategy.

SHAKING THE HABIT?

Viewed on the whole, industry responses to the rise of the sodium issue tend to have opposite effects, typifying the contradictory tendencies inherent in a scientifically based product controversy. Marketing efforts heighten consumer attention to sodium. Traditional government relations activities diminish the effect that these concerns have on the likelihood of regulation, but have little impact on the concerns themselves. In contrast, attempts by ILSI and its related firms to challenge the sodium hypothesis may actually erode worry about sodium intake. These efforts may be directed at regulators and even scientists, rather than the public, but the effect is the same. Within a particular firm, each of these activities may be undertaken, although a significant sodium-based marketing effort by a company probably means it will not try to minimize the issue. Likewise, firms that seek to reduce concern are usually those without much marketing investment in low-sodium products. Of course, firms threatened by heightened awareness about salt may engage in defensive sodium-based advertising, which also contributes to public awareness of the issue.

Issue erosion lags behind the expansionary effects of marketing. The press, happy to identify salt as a killer, is equally pleased to discover that salt was never a problem in the first place. Reporters look for "news," and the link between sodium and hypertension is no longer new. Yet the visibility of the sodium issue creates a context for critical stories and "spin-offs."

The title of an April 1982 article in *Science* says it all: "Value of Low-Sodium Diets Questioned."[122] The author attacks Commissioner Hayes's statement that "sodium reduction must remain a general health goal for our nation." The views of prominent skeptics of the sodium hypothesis set the article's tone. Although not stated in the piece, the 1982 seminar sponsored by Campbell was the article's principal source. The ILSI-sponsored conference had a similar result, generating a *New York Times* article headlined "Experts Challenge Low-Sodium Diet," and a *Newsweek* report asking, "Is Salt Really That Bad?"[123] The seeds of an eventual reversal were planted.

The sense within the hypertension community that sodium was only one of many potential dietary factors in essential hypertension accelerated through 1985. For example, in her description of a 12–14 March 1984 "Workshop on Nutrition and Hypertension," sponsored by the National Institutes of Health (NIH), Dr. Artemis P. Simopoulos, Chairman of the NIH Nutrition Coordinating Committee, noted that the 1982 conference cosponsored by ILSI, HHS, and the NKF "was the first conference on this subject and truly revolutionized the field by taking, so to speak, the scepter away from the dietary sodium and letting other nutrients claim a portion of it."[124] Simopoulos portrayed the 1984 NIH conference as a direct outgrowth of the initial 1982 efforts. In the literature, the hypertension link with calcium was especially prominent. In 1985, the journal *Hypertension* printed a "Debate" between Dr. David A. McCarron and Dr. Graham A. MacGregor on the relative importance of calcium and sodium in essential hypertension.[125]

In the short run at least, more Americans are likely to consider themselves hypertensives, attempting to restrict their sodium intake, often at their doctor's request. As people with a diagnosed "disease," they are the targets of dietary advice from health professionals and organizations, and are not apt to be greatly influenced by the changing media tone. In addition, a marketing-driven focus on sodium will be with us for some time.

The more generalized concerns of the nonhypertensive population, who worry that salt might cause them to develop hypertension or other problems, will probably recede. This waning concern will be hastened by the media's rising skepticism about sodium's threat. Sodium will be relegated to the ever-expanding list of health fads, retarding its legitimacy as a general health concern, if indeed such distinctions matter for a public with a remarkably short attention span. Although a substantial array of low-sodium products will remain, stabilized markets will be accompanied by a decline in the aggressive advertising that has been responsible for fueling much of the public's awareness of salt's threat.

Aside from regulatory concerns unrelated to consumer perceptions of a product's saltiness, whether a firm desired issue expansion or contraction depended on its major product characteristics. There was no single industry position. Most processed foods contain salt, but some contain more than others—and many of these rely on salt for their key characteristics.

More important, some foods are perceived by consumers, physicians, and the press as particularly high in salt: canned soups, pickles, chips, canned vegetables, snack crackers, hot dogs, and cold cuts.[126] Companies that depend on these items, and for which salt reduction consistent with reasonable cost and taste is not feasible, tended to favor issue contraction. The degree to which minimizing concern was actively sought appears to increase with the size and rank of a firm, and to diminish with a firm's degree of diversification. Diversification spreads the threat to a particular product line over many products. Examples of industry leaders that are heavily reliant upon "salty" foods include Frito-Lay and Campbell, two companies that engaged in issue-dampening activities. Although they produced low-salt versions of their products, they fretted that consumers who worried about salt might simply cut back on soup or chips rather than accept diminished palatability.

For many other firms, however, the furor over sodium represented market opportunities. These companies introduced their own low-sodium products and view diminishing public concern with sodium as undesirable. The widespread low-sodium marketing response suggests that if regulatory efforts decline, the number of companies interested in actively fighting antisodium efforts will likewise decline. Sodium will be less and less a regulatory issue, and more and more defined by normal competitive factors.

Conclusion

Issues rise and issues fall. What we have seen in the sodium case is that the seeds of an issue's demise may be present in those factors most responsible for its growth. This dialectic is particularly relevant for the health scares that have become a familiar part of the American consumer landscape. Scientific advances provided new evidence of the role of sodium in hypertension, and revealed the importance of treating people with lower ranges of high blood pressure. But science moves on, and new hypotheses are constantly raised, revised, and discarded.

Similarly, the rising concern with diet–health links led to an outpouring of reports and recommendations. Sodium was swept along in the process, creating what many saw as a new consensus, and stimulating the interest of government agencies and private health organizations. These groups had varied institutional approaches to nutrition issues, however, and ultimately produced divergent recommendations on sodium policy. Thus, on specific scientific and policy issues, the apparent consensus began to unravel.

Eventually, sodium gained significant attention in its own right. A process of agenda building had made the issue ripe for the accelerating actions of key public actors. In particular, the issue enabled the Reagan administration, which was under attack for doing too little to protect the health of citizens, to take an activist health stance. The food industry responded to government pressure and competitive forces, acting as a vehicle for the communication of sodium concerns to the public.

Ironically, the issue's heightened visibility made it a symbol. For scientists and government officials it represented an application of knowledge that some saw as improper, and others as long overdue. Those favoring an activist stance toward sodium drew the wrath of a business community, in particular the food industry, that had thought "regulation" was finally in retreat. Salt reduction became a target for scientists and industry. Their attacks were news, with the potential to modify opinion about sodium's relationship to hypertension, and the proper responses to this link. Thus sodium's connection with a dread disease set the stage for widespread interest in rather esoteric scientific and regulatory challenges.

Chapter 5

The Political Reality
of Artificial Sweeteners

LINDA C. CUMMINGS

In April 1977 the Food and Drug Administration (FDA) declared saccharin to be a carcinogen and initiated proceedings to eliminate the use of the artificial sweetener in foods, beverages, cosmetics, and most drugs. The FDA's decision generated such vigorous protest from consumers and the diet food industry that Congress passed legislation to prevent the FDA from restricting the use of saccharin until further research could be conducted. President Carter signed the Saccharin Study and Labeling Act in November 1977. Often called the "saccharin moratorium," the law has been extended several times. The moratorium stands as testimony to the FDA's failure to understand the politics of product risks.

The public outcry was prompted by the FDA's attempt to curtail the availability of the only artificial sweetener still on the American market. In 1950 the federal government removed the artificial sweetener dulcin from the market; hardly anyone noticed. In 1969, when the agency decided to ban the sugar substitute cyclamate, it encountered some opposition and even a lawsuit from one diet food manufacturer. Serious doubts were raised about the validity of the scientific studies that were cited in support of the ban. The objections to the cyclamate decision were neither as well-organized nor as widespread as what followed the proposal to limit saccharin usage.

Before cyclamate became available, the use of artificial sweeteners was associated with illness. Since the early 1900s, saccharin had been used almost exclusively by diabetics, primarily as a sugar substitute in liquids. In its most common tabletop version, saccharin resembled aspirin or other tablet drugs. Moreover, many people experience an unpleasant aftertaste with saccharin, which did nothing to dispel the notion that it was a medicine.

Between 1955 and 1965, however, a substantial diet food industry developed, based chiefly on cyclamate, which had been discovered in the 1930s. At the time of the cyclamate ban in 1969 almost all diet products were formulated with a cyclamate and saccharin combination, making it extremely difficult to identify the separate health effects of either ingredient. When the FDA removed cyclamate from the market, saccharin was the ready, if less tasty, alternative for those seeking slimness. Subsequently, the evidence against saccharin has mounted while that against cyclamate has declined. With cyclamate banned, however, it has been impossible to act against saccharin. It is only recently that another sweetener, aspartame, has become available, but it too has been challenged as a health risk. Thus, the consequence of the FDA's action against cyclamate is the continued marketing of substitutes, which are not necessarily less dangerous.

Sweeteners and Light

Cyclamate and saccharin are nonnutritive sweeteners, providing no calories. Aspartame is classified by the FDA as a nutritive sweetener because it is metabolized by the body as a protein and has a slight caloric value. The three differ in the intensity and flavor of their sweetness, in the variety of foods in which they can be used, and in their cost. But they have a similar purpose—to provide a low- or zero-calorie alternative to sugar. They also share the experience of ongoing controversy about their effect on the health of consumers.

The producers of artificially sweetened products were surprised to learn in the 1950s that most of their sales were to people interested in losing weight. The companies, beginning with Abbott Laboratories, the leading cyclamate manufacturer, quickly modified advertising campaigns to stress the usefulness of artificial sweeteners as a dieting aid. This shift in marketing strategy shortly eradicated the popular notion that the use of artificial sweeteners was linked with illness, an image that still predominates in other countries. In the United States, 70 million men and women now consume artificial sweeteners on a regular basis, most of them hoping to become or remain slim.[1]

The market for artificial sweeteners continues to expand rapidly as sugar substitutes are introduced to flavor an ever-growing range of products, including toothpaste and drugs.[2] The bulk of the consumption, though, is in the form of soft drinks, a submarket once the exclusive domain of saccharin but now being usurped by aspartame.

A variety of products containing NutraSweet, the brand name for aspartame, became available in the early 1980s. These include cereals and powdered drink and dessert mixes. In the summer of 1983 the FDA granted permission for the use of aspartame in beverages. The major soft drink companies have since introduced aspartame-sweetened versions of their diet brands to the U.S. market. Under the label Equal, aspartame is also sold in one-ounce envelopes and in tablet form for tabletop use.

The regular consumers of artificial sweeteners include most of America's 10 million diabetics. The sweeteners are considered by diabetics to be an important aid to controlling their weight (obesity is often associated with adult diabetes and is a serious health concern) and in bringing variety to their restricted diets. Sixty to ninety percent of those who classify themselves as diabetics in this country are thought to use saccharin extensively.[3] The plight of the diabetics was a significant influence in the enactment of the saccharin moratorium.

The American obsession with slimness generated most of the public protest, however. In 1959 the American Medical Association called weight reducing "a national neurosis."[4] The dieting craze has continued unabated, if not intensified, over the years. The use of artificial sweeteners has expanded largely on the unexamined assumption that they help in weight reduction. The press and the public, guided by the diet industry, appear to have accepted a straightforward relationship between replacing sugar with an artificial sweetener and losing weight.

A greater number of dieters consume artificial sweeteners than do non-dieters, and the greatest users are females between twenty and thirty-nine years of age. (In the past, women of all ages consumed much more of the sweeteners than did men, but the margin of difference has narrowed considerably.) Congress and the FDA received many letters during the debate over possible restrictions on saccharin from young women who were convinced that artificial sweeteners were essential for weight control.

A saccharin ban would have a devastating effect on the American diet food industry, at least until aspartame is fully accepted as an alternative. Over 20 percent of the soft drink market is in artificially sweetened sodas, worth more than $4 billion annually. The major soft drink producers, Coca-Cola, PepsiCo, Seven-Up, Dr Pepper, and Royal Crown, as well as some smaller companies, manufacture diet drinks. Coca-Cola has over a third of the total U.S. soft drink market; Pepsi has about a quarter.[5]

The FDA holds responsibility for ensuring the safety of the American food supply, including food additives. The agency regulated cyclamate, saccharin, and aspartame in different ways (see table 5.1). At its behest hundreds of scientific studies have been conducted with the three sweeteners, some demonstrating potentially serious health effects and others exonerating the products. The extent of the actual risk to human beings for each of the additives, however, remains uncertain. Contradictory scientific evidence about the dangers of artificial sweeteners has permitted the divergence in regulatory approaches. With an indeterminate scientific base for regulation, the role of nonscientific factors has assumed decisive importance in policymaking.

Scientific Uncertainty

In 1902, Dr. Harvey Wiley, an official in the federal Bureau of Chemistry, the FDA's predecessor agency, formed what was dubbed "Wiley's Poison Squad," teams of young men to test the toxicity of preservatives and coloring agents. For five years these volunteers (Wiley thought young men were the most resistant to possible adverse effects) sampled a variety of foods while Wiley monitored their physiological reactions.[6]

Dr. Wiley conceded that the results of his poison squad tests were difficult to interpret given the lack of controls and standards. Experimental methods have greatly advanced, of course, since the turn of the century, but the increased sophistication in scientific techniques has not always made data interpretation less problematic. Definitive answers are virtually impossible in evaluating the safety of a food additive. Some degree of risk is associated with any substance depending on the extent to which science is able to identify harmful effects, on the quantities in which it is used, or on the susceptibility of the population using it.[7]

The testing of toxic substances is today done with animals; in the case of artificial sweeteners, most often with mice or rats. Of the 35 extrinsic substances known to cause cancer in people, 34 of these are also known to be carcinogenic in mice and rats.[8] Yet cancer that develops at one organ

TABLE 5.1

Artificial Sweeteners

	Discovery	Sweetening Equivalent[a]	Cost/lb.	Uses	Health Concerns[b]	U.S. Regulatory Status
Saccharin	1879	300×	$ 4.00	Baking Beverages Food mixes Tabletop	Bladder cancer	FDA restrictions on use delayed by Congress; available for all uses
Cyclamate	1937	30×	$ 1.93	Baking Beverages Food mixes Tabletop	Bladder cancer Embryotoxic effects Testicular atrophy	Banned in 1969; up for reconsideration
Aspartame	1965	200×	$ 90.00	Beverages Food mixes Tabletop	Brain lesions Prohibited for phenylketonurics Alterations in brain chemicals	Approved for dry foods in 1981; carbonated beverages 1983

[a]Compared to sugar.
[b]Health concerns raised in animal studies

SOURCES: *Beverage Industry Annual Manual 1982*; Gene Bylinsky, "The Battle for America's Sweet Tooth," *Fortune* (26 July 1982): 30; Chris W. Lecos, "Sweetness Minus Calories = Controversy," *FDA Consumer* (February 1985): p 23; telephone interview, National Soft Drink Association official, December 1985.

site in animals may occur at a different site in humans. Once a human carcinogen is identified, it is possible to find animal cancers developing in the same organ, but the reverse is not always true.[9] Extrapolating the results of animal testing to determine the effect of a substance in humans, therefore, is a controversial activity.

It is standard practice to administer large doses of a substance to test animals in order to compensate for their short life span relative to humans, for the increased rate at which animals metabolize and excrete chemicals, and for the small numbers of animals used in a study.[10] Nevertheless, critics of the animal studies that were conducted with cyclamate and saccharin often charge that a person would have to consume hundreds of cans of diet soft drinks a day to approximate the test dosages. They argue that the high animal dosages make the test results of questionable use in determining any harmful effects on humans.

Epidemiological studies are also an important source of information in evaluating the safety of an additive. A British journal noted recently that with the exception of tobacco, saccharin may be the substance most tested by epidemiological studies.[11] Epidemiology has its limitations, however, and these are often pointed to by critics on both sides of the artificial sweeteners controversy. Those in favor of keeping cyclamate or saccharin on the market argue that the lack of adverse epidemiological data is evidence that the sweeteners are safe for human consumption. Those opposed describe epidemiology as a relatively insensitive measure of low-level risks.

Conducting a useful epidemiological study is an arduous task; a great deal of data is required from large numbers of people, sometimes over extended periods of time.[12] Any number of variables may affect the results, and it is unlikely that all the confounding variables can be identified. Even with the most careful design, cause and effect for one individual can almost never be determined, although it is possible to arrive at an estimate of risk for an entire population.

The National Bladder Cancer Study, the largest epidemiological evaluation of artificial sweeteners ever conducted, was initiated in 1978 in response to a congressional mandate. Because cyclamate–saccharin mixtures were in general use until 1970, it was impossible to distinguish between them to determine specific exposure. Conducted by the National Cancer Institute, the study involved 3,010 persons with recently diagnosed cancer of the urinary bladder. The investigators found no association in the total population between the incidence of bladder cancer and any past consumption of artificial sweeteners. A slightly greater risk appeared as consumption increased among two subgroups, nonsmoking white females and white males who were heavy smokers.[13]

Despite the scale of the study, interpretation of the data has been disputed on the grounds that chance, not any causal factor, explains the positive finding of increased risk for the two subgroups. Critics contend that it is beyond the current capacity of epidemiology to demonstrate conclusively when risk increases in evaluation of low-level hazards such as saccharin.[14]

Efforts to arrive at more precise estimates of the hazards of a chemical have contributed to specialization among scientific disciplines and, on occasion, confusion over test results. The improved capacity to detect minute quantities of a substance has not always been matched by the ability to interpret their significance. When disagreement occurs among disciplines, it becomes difficult to accept the policy implications of even the most carefully designed study.

Formulating regulatory policy for a controversial chemical is further complicated by the problem of establishing a cause and effect relationship between consumption of a substance and the development of cancer. Chemically induced cancers generally have a latency period of ten to forty years from initial exposure to when symptoms of the disease appear.[15] If an individual were to develop bladder cancer, it would be impossible to attribute the disease to the two packages of saccharin he added to his daily coffee and not to where he lived, what else he ate or drank, the number of cigarettes he smoked, his occupation, or any number of other factors.

It would also be highly unlikely that one particular substance could be singled out as the cause of a disease from all the additives that currently are allowed in the American food supply, a number of which are under suspicion. The FDA has jurisdiction over 3,000 direct additives, used as ingredients in foods, and as many as 10,000 indirect additives, those that may migrate during processing, packaging or storage. In 1981 it was estimated that each American consumed 139 pounds of food additives annually, sugar accounting for 80 percent and salt for 10 percent of the total.[16]

Those additives in widest use are intended to enhance the appeal of the food to the consumer. Critics of the food industry charge that the use of chemicals is excessive and can be traced to the convenience of the retailer or the manufacturer in their search for products that are pleasing to look at and that have extended shelf life. The FDA requires a manufacturer to establish that a substance is "safe" under the proposed conditions of use, but the agency is not required to consider the potential benefits of an additive. The manufacturer must demonstrate that a proposed chemical

entity is functional, that it will accomplish the intended physical or technical effect in the food: the FDA "must be satisfied that an emulsifier emul-
sifies and that a stabilizer stabilizes. But the agency is not authorized to
determine whether society needs another emulsifier or stabilizer."[17]

If a manufacturer can establish reasonable certainty of no harm, a new
substance stands a very good chance of being approved. Charges of industry fraud in safety studies are rare. A company's concern for its reputation
with the public and with the FDA, where past credibility figures significantly in the approval process, serves as assurance that safety testing will
be thorough. But safety is only one element in the product development
process that also includes attention to aesthetics, shelf life, and profits.
Product liability laws have little relevance in the food additive area because
of the difficulty of establishing a cause and effect relationship. The scientific evidence submitted in support of a food additive petition may serve
to reduce uncertainty about the health risks of a substance, but cannot be
relied upon as a guarantee of its safety.

Interest groups on both sides of risk issues have utilized the equivocal
aspects of the science. The diet industry has been the principal sponsor of
studies concluding that artificial sweeteners cannot be shown definitively
to have any ill effects on humans. By contrast, public interest groups have
argued that the very ambiguity of the data is a compelling reason to curtail
the use of artificial sweeteners until conclusive evidence is available. Even
the regulators who must choose among the studies find advantage, for they
gain in the uncertainty a policymaking flexibility that would be otherwise
denied them.

Cyclamate: Serendipity and Slimness

Cyclamate was discovered in 1937 by Michael Sveda, a doctoral student
in chemistry at the University of Illinois. Sveda's discovery was accidental;
he was conducting experiments on sulfamic acid and its salts and noticed
a sweet taste on a cigarette that had touched his laboratory bench. From
the twenty compounds with which he was working at the time, Sveda
identified the sweetener as sodium cyclohexyl-sulfamate or cyclamate.

Sveda took out a patent on cyclamate that he later assigned to DuPont
where he went to work in 1942. Dr. Ernest Volwiler, president of Abbott
Laboratories, a major pharmaceutical firm, heard of Sveda's discovery on

one of his periodic visits to DuPont. Because DuPont lacked experience in the manufacturing of over-the-counter drugs (which is what cyclamate was then considered to be), the company licensed Abbott to develop cyclamate for commercial use.

In 1950 Abbott asked the FDA for permission to market sodium Sucaryl, a tabletop sweetener containing cyclamate. The approval was delayed because the FDA had reservations about the quality of the safety tests submitted by the company in support of the application. The FDA conducted two years of additional animal feeding studies on its own, and approved Sucaryl as a nonnutritive sweetener. It was required to carry the warning label that it was intended for use "only by persons who must restrict their intake of sweets."[18] Abbott produced cyclamate in three forms: cyclamic acid, sodium cyclamate (the most commonly used product), and calcium cyclamate, which was recommended for those needing low-sodium diets.

Although cyclamate is less sweet and more expensive than saccharin, it was considered by the food industry and by many consumers to be an almost ideal sugar substitute. (Cyclamate is 30 times as sweet as sugar while saccharin is 300 times as sweet as sugar.) Its primary advantage is that it is free from the bitter aftertaste that many people experience with saccharin. Cyclamate is also more versatile; it can be used in both dry and liquid food applications, and it maintains its sweetness when heated or frozen. Most food and beverage preparations added cyclamate and saccharin in a 10:1 combination, a synergistic mixture in which the two together were sweeter than the sum of their individual ratings. In a 10:1 ratio, cyclamate and saccharin each contributed about half of the final sweetening power.

In 1955 DuPont's patent and exclusive licensing of cyclamate to Abbott expired. Other companies began to produce cyclamate for the bulk market and for home use in tablet or liquid form. In response, Abbott undertook a campaign to expand the use of Sucaryl from a product limited to diabetics to one used by all sugar-avoiding people.[19] To do so, the company began to place advertisements in women's magazines describing Sucaryl as a diet aid and as a way for children to avoid the dental caries associated with sugar.

The interest in dieting that developed in the 1950s gave Abbott the incentive to promote cyclamate as a weight reduction aid rather than as a product for diabetics. The FDA, however, was instrumental in making the new use a success. In 1958, as required by the amendments to the Food, Drug, and Cosmetic Act, the FDA compiled a list of food additives "generally recognized as safe" (the GRAS list). Scientists in a national survey were asked to indicate any reservations about the substances on the list including cyclamate and saccharin. Of the 900 asked about cyclamate, the 355 who responded said they knew of no ill effects from it. As a result, cyclamate was exempted from the testing that was to be required of new food additives. Saccharin was also listed as GRAS.[20]

Under Abbott's initial petition in 1950, cyclamate's use was restricted to special dietary foods carrying a warning label. By placing cyclamate on the GRAS list, the FDA made it possible for manufacturers to add cyclamate to any food, in unrestricted amounts, and often without any warning label. Cyclamate's GRAS status and the American preoccupation with dieting encouraged the food and soft drink companies to develop diet products.[21]

Until 1958 artificial sweeteners were available only in liquid and tablet form. That year the Cumberland Packing Corporation introduced one-serving packages of the cyclamate-saccharin mixture in powdered form under the brand name Sweet 'n Low. Expecting that the convenience of their product would appeal mainly to diabetics, Cumberland Packing was surprised to receive letters from nondiabetic consumers who praised Sweet 'n Low's taste and declared their belief that it helped in dieting. When the advertisements were modified to appeal to dieters, sales of Sweet 'n Low climbed dramatically.

No other product has had as much consequence for the diet industry and for the development of the controversy over artificial sweeteners than have soft drinks. Americans today drink more soft drinks than any other beverage. Although sales are now slowing, per capita annual consumption of soft drinks more than doubled from 18 gallons in 1963 to almost 40 in 1982. Diet drinks have been the fastest growing component of the soft drink market.[22]

The first soft drink manufacturers to use cyclamate also did not anticipate the popularity of the low-calorie drinks with dieters. Soft drinks sweetened with saccharin were produced initially in 1947. Their sales were insubstantial until the late 1950s when Kirsch Beverage, a minor producer, introduced its No-Cal soft drink sweetened with Sucaryl and began a marketing appeal directed toward the dieter. Almost immediately, the No-Cal drink was outselling all other Kirsch brands and attracting the attention of the industry majors.[23] The first of the nationally marketed low-calorie brands was Royal Crown's Diet Rite Cola, introduced in 1962. Coca-Cola and Pepsi followed the next year with their own low-calorie products, Tab and Patio Diet Cola. Soon all of the national soft drink companies were producing a diet beverage.

By the late 1960s, cyclamate was an ingredient in over 250 products, many of which were developed specifically for the weight-conscious. Consumption in 1969 had reached 18.5 million pounds per year with a retail value of $1 billion. Someone in almost three quarters of American families was using cyclamate.[24] Cyclamate's popularity, however, drew attention from the scientific community and with it the concern of federal regulators.

The Cyclamate Ban

At several points during the 1960s the Food and Nutrition Board (FNB) of the National Academy of Sciences, which had an advisory contract with the FDA, cautioned the agency about the potential dangers of increased use of artificial sweeteners in diet drinks. The FNB feared that a large portion of the population was being placed at risk and wished further study of the potential hazards. By 1968 the FNB decided that the evidence of significant risk was at hand and recommended to the FDA that cyclamate be removed from the GRAS list. Japanese studies had found that although cyclamate was not absorbed by the body it was metabolized into cyclohexylamine, a toxin. Two FDA-sponsored studies provided additional causes for concern. One reported that cyclohexylamine produced chromosome breakage in test animals. The other study noted deformities in chicken embryos after injections of cyclamate.[25] The FDA chose not to act.

Scientists were not alone in worrying about the effects of increased artificial sweetener consumption. The sugar industry also sought FDA action on cyclamate. Soft drink producers had long been the largest purchasers of refined sugar. By the 1960s the cost of a cyclamate-saccharin mixture formulated for soft drinks was about half per pound as that for sugar.[26] The practice of soft drink producers was to price diet drinks exactly the same as their sugared brands, making their diet lines quite profitable. The sugar industry though was apprehensive that cyclamate-laced drinks either would eventually become competitively priced or would grow in popularity to the point that the market for sugared drinks would erode.

The industry's counter to artificial sweeteners was orchestrated during the 1960s by Sugar Information, Inc., an organization that represented cane sugar refiners, beet sugar processors, and raw sugar producers. Bold to the task, Sugar Information sponsored advertisements in popular periodicals and trade food journals that contrasted "synthetically" sweetened soft drinks with "real" sugar, alleging that diet soft drinks robbed children of the energy that sugar provided.[27] Another series contended that sugar could actually help the dieter lose weight by curbing the primary cause of overweight—overeating. "Do you use artificial sweeteners and still gain weight?" it asked. Sugar was portrayed as benefiting weight reduction because it provided a means of satisfying hunger with "no aftertaste."

Royal Crown responded with full-page advertisements in newspapers across the country that stated: "Guilty of upsetting the sugar cart! We plead guilty. . . . If it's wrong to do millions of people a favor by taking the sugar out of cola . . . Diet-Rite pleads guilty." Abbott also sponsored a campaign that concentrated on television viewers. Commercials for Sucaryl proclaimed that the consumer could save 180 calories daily using it instead of sugar. Other manufacturers increased promotion of tabletop sweeteners, emphasizing their convenience when used in beverages.

Ironically, a study sponsored by Abbott Laboratories, cyclamate's prime producer, forced the FDA's hand. Abbott was hoping to demonstrate the safety of long-term cyclamate use. In the fateful study, test animals were divided into four groups, one for control and three fed varying diets of cyclamate-saccharin combinations for two years. The high-dose group, fed the equivalent of 3,000 Sucaryl tablets per day, were found to have developed testicular atrophy. Worse still, many of them had bladder tumors, half of which were diagnosed as cancerous.

On 13 October 1969, Abbott, as it had to, notified the government of the tumor findings and other test results. On 18 October 1969, cyclamate was removed from the GRAS list in a ruling that cited the Abbott study and a second one done by the FDA that also found bladder tumors in a small number of animals fed a calcium cyclamate and saccharin combination, the sodium-avoider's artificial sweetener.[28] Immediately, cyclamate was banned in soft drinks, general purpose foods, and nonprescription drugs. Within a year it was ordered removed from prescription drugs as well.

Post-ban Questions

The cyclamate ban has received more criticism on scientific grounds than either of the FDA's subsequent decisions on saccharin or aspartame. Although the tumor results cited in the ban raised serious concerns, the FDA failed to note that the study sponsored by Abbott was not designed to evaluate cyclamate alone. Abbott argued, plausibly, that cyclamate, saccharin, or cyclohexylamine might have been the culprit for the tumor findings. The agency also failed to verify the results of the two studies through additional tests. In fact, subsequent animal studies with cyclamate failed to produce statistically significant evidence of bladder tumors.[29]

At the time the two cyclamate-saccharin tests were conducted, it was generally assumed that cyclamate was responsible for the harmful results. Although critics of saccharin had been warning of ill effects of one sort or another since its discovery, there was no solid evidence to warrant serious concern. The fact that cyclamate was used in greater proportion in the standard mixture also contributed to the belief that cyclamate was at fault. Moreover, the National Academy of Sciences reports had repeatedly cautioned only against excessive cyclamate consumption.

After the ban, it became known that the bladder tumors were more likely the result of the saccharin rather than the cyclamate. Since 1970, many long-term animal studies of cyclamate's carcinogenicity and cocarcinogenicity have been conducted, and all have been negative.[30] The studies of cyclohexylamine to date are inconclusive. Dr. Bernard Oser, who led the Abbott-sponsored chronic toxicity study, later expressed doubts about the way the results had been employed as the basis for a ban.[31]

A report by the National Cancer Institute summarized the findings that cyclamate, when tested with appropriate protocols, was not carcinogenic.[32] The president of the National Academy of Sciences opened a forum on sweeteners with the remark that the FDA cyclamate decision derived from a set of experiments that "were badly designed, were inconclusive with respect to the actual findings, and did not warrant any action at the time."[33]

After the ban, Abbott, as the principal cyclamate manufacturer, tried to enlist allies among others in the diet industry, but without success. The availability of saccharin as a substitute served to mute both consumer and industry protest. Some consumers wrote angry letters to the FDA and to Congress, but others said that they felt "grateful" that the government was protecting them from a potential carcinogen. The scale of public opposition to the ban was much less intense and widespread than the protest that followed saccharin's attempted ban seven years later.[34]

The ban affected the companies using cyclamate with varying degrees of severity. Most firms were able to switch quickly to saccharin without much market disruption. For example, Cumberland Packing, whose Sweet 'n Low tabletop sweetener was originally formulated with a cyclamate-saccharin combination, had a new saccharin-only product on store shelves by the Monday following the Friday announcement of the ban. In fact, for this relatively small company (its total sales, 90 percent of which are from Sweet 'n Low, were about $60 million in 1984), the cyclamate ban turned out to be an unexpected asset. The company's timely reaction to the ban enabled it to edge out the competition, and its product became a household word that dominated the tabletop sweetener market until the introduction of aspartame.

The soft drink manufacturers were able to reformulate their products using saccharin and to have new inventories available within a few weeks. Seeking to turn adversity into advantage, the firms acted as if they had sought the ban. "Cyclamates? Diet Pepsi Can Do Without Them," one ad proclaimed. The phrase "Cyclamate Free" was prominently displayed in print advertisements and on packaging. Consumers adjusted to the new taste of saccharin-sweetened diet drinks. The sales of these products quickly reached new highs.

Only one other segment of the diet industry was affected as severely by the ban as Abbott. The California Canners and Growers, an 1,100-member cooperative group, initially claimed to have lost over one fifth of its expected 1969 sales of $110 million. The Diet Delite line of low-calorie fruits and vegetables produced by the association was prepared with cyclamate, and the year's harvest had just been canned when the ban was announced. The canners and the soft drink industry backed a bill cosponsored by thirty-four legislators that provided the companies with millions of dollars in reimbursement for their cyclamate losses. Despite support from President Nixon, the bill was defeated. Nevertheless, the canners' eventual loss was greatly reduced through foreign sales and tax write-offs.[35]

From the beginning it has been Abbott's policy to seek a reinstatement of all cyclamate use, including that in soft drinks. Some lawyers have argued that if Abbott had been more accommodating it could have won back part of the market for the sweetener. An attempt at a partial reprieve as a tabletop sweetener might meet less resistance. Others only wanted its use in soft drinks to be banned.

In 1973 Abbott submitted a petition to the FDA that included 300 toxicological reports which it claimed exonerated cyclamate. The FDA offered Abbott the opportunity to submit its case to an independent board of inquiry. When that concession was refused, the FDA slowly sifted the evidence itself, rejecting the petition in 1979. Abbott petitioned the FDA again in 1982, asking the agency to review 59 studies attesting to cyclamate's safety. On the basis of those studies and other data, the FDA concluded that the available evidence does not establish cyclamate as a carcinogen, although the agency asked the National Academy of Sciences (NAS) to review the data. The NAS concurred that cyclamate by itself does not cause cancer, but it raised other issues for more investigation. The NAS recommended further evaluation of cyclamate's possible role as a tumor promoter or cocarcinogen and of the concerns that cyclamate causes testicular atrophy and genetic damage.[36]

When the FDA banned cyclamate use it did not consider the impact of its decision on any potential review of saccharin. Yet it should have been obvious that if cyclamate was unavailable consumption of saccharin would increase and that there would be a need to consider again saccharin's safety. Other artificial sweeteners were years away from the market; until one or more of them were ready, saccharin would be the only approved sugar substitute. Nevertheless, the FDA did not pause to make a comparative risk assessment of cyclamate and saccharin. By removing cyclamate so quickly from the market, the agency unwittingly helped to precipitate the saccharin crisis that came seven years later. As it turned out, saccharin appeared to be the more hazardous of the two sweeteners.

Saccharin: Tried but Untrue?

The oldest nonnutritive sweetener, saccharin is a coal-tar derivative first synthesized by Ira Fahlberg and Charles Remsen at Johns Hopkins University in 1879. The infant organic chemical industry in America displayed little interest in saccharin, and its earliest manufacturers were German. In 1901, however, the Monsanto Chemical Company in St. Louis, Missouri, began producing saccharin for sale to food-processing companies.

Six German firms, known as the "Dye Trust," attempted to halt Monsanto's production by driving down the price of saccharin. Their efforts were unsuccessful, and Monsanto continued in the saccharin business until 1970 when sluggish performance caused the company to phase out a number of its operations including saccharin. Today the Sherwin-Williams Company of Cleveland, Ohio, is the sole domestic producer of saccharin with 60 percent of the market. Imports from Japan and Korea account for the remainder.[37]

Saccharin was initially used as an antiseptic and food preservative, but its sweet taste quickly led to its use as a cheap substitute for sugar.[38]

Virtually from the beginning of its history as a sweetener, saccharin was the source of controversy. Early concerns focused on appetite and gastrointestinal problems that were reported in an 1886 study conducted in France.[39] In the early years of saccharin's use, much of the criticism was generated by the sugar industry.

In 1912 saccharin was banned from foods in the United States, not because it was considered unsafe, but because, given the availability of sugar, the Department of Agriculture considered it "unnecessary." Saccharin was reinstated during the sugar shortages of World War I. In fact, both world wars boosted saccharin consumption. During World War II especially, the use of the artificial sweetener grew substantially, particularly in Europe.

Outside of wartime, saccharin's availability was restricted until the mid-1950s by numerous state regulations. Most states required that synthetic sweeteners be identified as products for special dietary purposes, and any foods containing saccharin were labeled "dietetic." Only three states allowed artificial sweeteners to be marketed without inhibiting regulation. Seventeen states placed limitations on their use; ten states specifically banned saccharin, and the remainder required dietary labeling. In Massachusetts and Florida, consumers had to have a doctor's prescription to buy a synthetic sweetener.[40] Many of these laws were enacted under pressure from soft drink bottlers and food processors who feared competition for their higher-priced sugared products. When cyclamate became popular as a diet aid, these laws were relaxed or repealed, often at the urging of the same manufacturers who had been against saccharin.

From 1961 to 1977, saccharin use increased at the rate of nearly 25 percent per year, largely because of the growth in diet soft drink consumption. The National Academy of Sciences first reviewed saccharin in 1955, but was asked to evaluate its safety again in 1967 because of the growing market for diet soft drinks. In 1968 the NAS reported that consumption of saccharin at the level of 1 gram or less per day by an adult presented no apparent hazard, but also recommended the conduct of further, more sophisticated studies.[41]

There has been little scientific interest in assessing the effectiveness of artificial sweeteners as a weight reduction aid, probably because it is virtually impossible to consider all the variables or to measure their benefits quantitatively.[42] What evidence does exist is inconclusive. The 1968 NAS report found saccharin's usefulness as a diet aid to be unsubstantiated, but suggested that it may satisfy the psychological desire for sweets among diabetics and others who must control their sugar intake. Through advertising, the diet food industry has been primarily responsible for promoting the association of artificial sweetener consumption with weight control. The few studies that have been conducted on dieting with artificial sweeteners demonstrated that the substitution of sugar with saccharin or cyclamate produced no weight loss. In many cases the calories a person avoided by using artificial sweeteners were simply consumed in other forms.[43]

Unlike the work that was the basis for the 1969 cyclamate ban, the studies reviewed by the FDA in its 1977 saccharin decision constituted a series of carefully refined experiments that demonstrated that saccharin was an animal carcinogen, and that it alone, not impurities created during the manufacturing process, was responsible for the findings of bladder tumors.[44] In the early 1970s a number of animal experiments were conducted with saccharin. A 1972 study by the Wisconsin Alumni Research Foundation, partially sponsored by the Sugar Association, found that saccharin increased the incidence of bladder tumors in male rats, especially in the second generation. The following year an FDA experiment produced similar results.[45]

In response, the agency removed saccharin from the GRAS list and published regulations intended to discourage general use by consumers. The FDA requested the NAS to conduct yet another review of the toxicological data. The NAS report released in 1974 came to no conclusions about saccharin's carcinogenicity and emphasized the uncertainty about the effect of orthotoluenesulfonamide (OTS), an impurity in commercial saccharin. Finally, in 1977 a long-awaited study by the Canadian government corroborated the Wisconsin and FDA second-generation experiments. The Health Protection Branch, the Canadian equivalent of the FDA, evaluated the relative toxicity of saccharin and OTS in a two-generation rat study. The results indicated that a saccharin level of 5 percent of the diet increased the incidence of bladder tumors in the male rats (especially in the second generation) and that saccharin, not OTS, was responsible for the findings.[46] On 9 March 1977, saccharin was banned in Canada.

The next month, the FDA proposed a ban on the use of saccharin in foods, beverages, and cosmetics. The FDA action did not actually constitute a total ban because the agency indicated that it would consider applications for marketing saccharin as a single-ingredient drug, without prescription, but carrying a label warning of a cancer risk. Nevertheless, saccharin's availability for most people was to be drastically reduced because it would no longer be allowed in prepackaged foods such as canned goods, soft drinks, and tabletop sweeteners.

There is little scientific disagreement that saccharin is an animal carcinogen, albeit a weak one. A great deal of contention remains, however, on extrapolating the data from animals to humans. Unlike most other carcinogens, saccharin does not undergo chemical changes in the body, does not appear to attach directly to genetic material, and is excreted rapidly and almost entirely unchanged. Saccharin apparently acts as a promoter, enhancing the carcinogenic potential of other substances.[47]

There has been no increase in bladder cancer rates among the general population or among diabetics that can be attributed to the growth in saccharin use since World War II. Epidemiological studies have also failed to establish a link between saccharin consumption and bladder cancer. A review of the major epidemiological studies from 1974–83 concluded that "there appears to be a consensus that saccharin is not a potent or even moderate human bladder carcinogen."[48]

Yet these findings are inconclusive for several reasons. It is unlikely that a small effect of the degree likely to be caused by saccharin would be detected, and other potential causes of bladder cancer (smoking, occupational hazards) have also grown in the postwar years. Because the latency period for bladder cancer is twenty to forty years, it is still too soon to detect a rise in rates, especially among the children of women who consumed a great deal of saccharin in the years of its heaviest use, 1965 to the present. Finally, diabetics generally smoke less than the rest of the population and have elevated mortality risks from causes other than bladder cancer.[49]

The Saccharin Study and Labeling Act of 1977 (the saccharin moratorium), required that all foods containing saccharin bear a label warning that it had been shown to cause cancer in laboratory animals. Congress asked the NAS to review saccharin still one more time. Reflecting on new evidence, the NAS concluded that saccharin was indeed an animal carcinogen and a possible carcinogenic risk to humans as well, but one of low potency. Epidemiological studies did not provide "clear evidence to support or refute an association between past saccharin use and bladder cancer in males." However, the NAS noted that "even low risks to a large number of exposed persons may lead to public health concerns."[50]

The Food, Drug, and Cosmetic Act was last updated with the 1958 amendments that produced the GRAS list. Section 401, often referred to as the Delaney clause after its congressional sponsor, was cited by the FDA in its saccharin decision. The operative line in the clause states that "no additive shall be deemed to be safe if it is found to induce cancer when ingested by man or animal."[51]

Part of the public controversy over saccharin has centered on the apparent willingness of the FDA to use the Delaney clause. Only twice before had the FDA invoked the Delaney clause, in both instances to ban minor food-packaging components.[52] With saccharin it was proposing to use the clause to eliminate a major food additive. Industry groups feared the precedent, believing that the Delaney standard failed to recognize the widespread, but essentially harmless presence of carcinogenic substances in commonly used products, and thus was unnecessarily strict. Almost immediately they sought revision of the clause. Others, especially public interest advocates, rallied to its defense, arguing that the Delaney clause would provide vital public health protection if applied routinely.[53]

Congress equivocated. The saccharin moratorium legislation demonstrated both congressional responsiveness to the crisis of the moment and distaste for dealing with tough long-term issues. Any unpopular application of a zero-risk cancer standard would be continually stymied, but there would be no revision of Delaney's zero-risk cancer standard. With the saccharin moratorium, Congress is saying that Americans can have their cake and eat it too, even if it is slightly carcinogenic.

Reaction to the Proposed Saccharin Ban

Both the American Diabetes Association and the Juvenile Diabetes Foundation, voluntary health organizations committed to the welfare of diabetics, reacted strongly to the FDA attempt to restrict major uses of saccharin. They sought to make government officials and the public aware of the great dependence by diabetics on artificially sweetened products. The message of the Juvenile Diabetes Foundation was particularly poignant. Without easy access to saccharin-sweetened soft drinks and foods, the nation's 300,000 children afflicted with diabetes would be further denied a normal childhood.[54]

Through their local affiliates, the diabetes associations organized an intense letter-writing campaign seeking congressional intervention to block the ban. The intent of the associations was to assure that existing saccharin-based products would continue to be available. Diabetics should be advised to moderate their consumption of saccharin and additional research should be done to identify saccharin's true hazard, but, with cyclamate already banned, the associations had to defend the right of diabetics to have unrestricted access to saccharin, the only noncaloric, nonnutritive sweetener still on the market.

Because saccharin was thought to be a carcinogen, it might be expected that the American Cancer Society would take the opposite position in the debate over the ban. Instead, the society chose to abstain. Not until three years after the FDA proposed the ban did the society issue its first statement on saccharin, one cautioning moderate use of all artificial sweeteners particularly by children and pregnant women. The statement also noted that if any of the current cases of bladder cancer could be attributed to saccharin consumption, the number would likely be very small.[55] The American Cancer Society has not sought a termination of the congressionally imposed moratorium.

The participation of the diabetes associations complicated the FDA decision-making process. The agency was under pressure by these organizations to temper the effect any regulatory action would have on diabetics. Their impact on the actual regulatory outcome, however, was less important than the public affairs strategies adopted by the manufacturers of artificial sweeteners and artificially sweetened products.

When the FDA announced its proposal to restrict saccharin, Sherwin-Williams, unlike Abbott Laboratories with cyclamate, found strong commercial allies in its opposition to the FDA decision. The soft drink companies and Cumberland Packing saw the market for their diet-oriented products collapsing without saccharin. Although a number of alternative sweeteners were under development at the time, approval of an acceptable substitute was thought to be years away.

The diet industry watched the saccharin issue develop, following closely the studies conducted by the National Academy of Sciences and others over the years. Because no substitute for saccharin existed, it was possible to mobilize the industry when the ban was proposed. Cyclamate had provided a valuable lesson. This time there would be a concerted effort to contain the issue through the molding of public opinion.[56] The Calorie Control Council would take the lead for the industry; the soft drink firms preferred to remain off center stage in order to protect their marketing images as the purveyors of wholesome goods.

The first need was to discredit the scientific case against saccharin. Given the fear that a cancer link evokes, this could be expected to be difficult. Inadvertently, the FDA provided the vehicle. In announcing the agency's decision, FDA Commissioner Donald Kennedy had sought to prevent public panic by mentioning that the dosage given to the tumored test animals was the human equivalent of drinking 800 cans of diet soda a day.[57] Soon the Calorie Control Council was heralding the 800-cans-a-day figure in newspaper advertisements to ridicule the FDA's action. The advertisements urged consumers, dieters, and diabetics alike, to protest this absurd concern about saccharin's safety by writing their congressmen. The deluge of mail reached record levels.[58]

Because sales of saccharin-based Sweet 'n Low represented nearly all of its revenues, Cumberland Packing was the company that would have suffered the most under a saccharin ban. The 500 jobs the company provides in an economically depressed section of New York City would surely have been eliminated. With the subtle direction of the soft drink firms, media attention often focused on the plight of this small company and served to personalize the economic effects of the FDA's decision.

The diet industry averted the saccharin ban because it was able to mobilize public support. Instead of the issue being perceived as "cancerous cola," it became one involving deprived dieters, competing scientists, and the individual against big government. The FDA helped create this situation by its removal of cyclamate with insufficient consideration of the implications for a saccharin decision. Without a substitute, millions of people, persuaded by over two decades of advertising that artificial sweeteners were effective in dieting, were unwilling to give up saccharin in order to protect themselves against what they were convinced was a trivial risk.

Aspartame: Equal to the Task?

Aspartame was synthesized initially by a British company, Imperial Chemical Industries, but it was a chemist at the G. D. Searle Pharmaceutical Company in Skokie, Illinois, who in 1965 discovered its sweetening powers.[59] James D. Schlatter was working with amino acids, apparently licked his fingers, and was surprised by a sweet taste. Aspartame is composed of three substances, aspartic acid and phenylalanine, two amino acids that are present in food proteins such as hamburger or milk, and methanol, which also occurs naturally in some foods. Imperial Chemical Industries holds the patent on aspartame though it has granted Searle the exclusive right to aspartame's use as a sweetener.

Almost 200 times sweeter than sugar, aspartame can be used in such small quantities that the calories produced are negligible. It is less versatile than either saccharin or cyclamate, losing its sweetness when heated and therefore making it unsuitable for baking. Aspartame is not completely stable in a soft drink solution for longer than four to six months, which partly accounted for a delayed FDA approval for its use in beverages.

In 1973 Searle petitioned the FDA for permission to market aspartame as an ingredient in dry foods and powdered beverages under the brand name NutraSweet and as a tabletop sweetener under the brand name Equal. Approval was granted a year later with the stipulation that products containing aspartame carry a warning label for people suffering from phenylketonuria (PKU), a protein-metabolizing deficiency that affects approximately 1 in 15,000 people and is usually detected at birth.[60]

Before aspartame could be marketed, however, formal objections were filed by a professor of psychiatry at Washington University, Dr. John Olney, and by James Turner, a lawyer who had been involved earlier in the cyclamate dispute. Olney and Turner alleged that aspartame was linked to findings of brain tumors and could cause mental retardation. They also expressed concern about the vulnerability of children or pregnant women to any toxic effects from aspartame and the possibility that some people unknowingly carry a recessive PKU trait and might be adversely affected. In 1975 the FDA stayed the regulation authorizing the marketing of aspartame and, with the Searle company's consent, reviewed fifteen additional safety studies.

In 1979 with the concurrence of Olney, Turner, and Searle, the FDA selected a public board of inquiry composed of three academic scientists to review the aspartame data. The board ruled in 1980 that aspartame should not be allowed on the market until further animal tests were conducted to resolve the brain tumor question. Searle submitted still more data and two of the three scientists reversed their earlier negative decision. In July of 1981 aspartame was approved for dry use, carrying the PKU and baking warning labels. In addition, Searle was required to monitor consumption levels and report the information to the FDA.

The 1981 ruling on aspartame did not include its use in beverages because of concerns that, in storage for long periods of time, the sweetener broke down into a substance called diketopiperazine (DKP). One possible effect of DKP is the formation of carcinogenic nitrosamines. In the spring of 1983 the FDA was prepared to approve aspartame for soft drink use, convinced that Searle would be able to overcome its stability problems, when evidence surfaced of additional health effects.

Richard Wurtman, a specialist in neuroendocrine regulation at the Massachusetts Institute of Technology, wrote to the FDA expressing his concern over the unrestricted consumption of aspartame in soft drinks. Wurtman, who in 1980 had testified on behalf of aspartame at the board of enquiry, noted that aspartame in soft drinks in conjunction with eating carbohydrates, could cause changes in brain chemicals. These chemicals affect behavior and body functions and could be especially detrimental in people with latent brain diseases. The Center for Science in the Public Interest also wrote to the FDA urging it to "proceed cautiously" in view of Wurtman's apprehension. The FDA decided to approve aspartame despite these concerns, after evaluating Wurtman's data and stating that the agency's review did not support his findings. In July 1983 the FDA granted Searle permission to market aspartame as a sweetener in soft drinks and in certain wet foods such as peanut butter, jelly, canned fruit, and ice cream.[61]

In February 1984 the FDA provided the Centers for Disease Control (CDC) with the results of 517 interviews of consumers who complained about aspartame's ill effects. The CDC reported that although some people are unusually sensitive to aspartame, the data did not "provide evidence for the existence of serious, widespread, adverse health consequences attendant to the use of aspartame."[62]

The sugar industry has not been active in the controversy over aspartame's health effects as it was in the cyclamate and saccharin controversies. Competition from corn sweeteners has replaced artificial sweeteners as the sugar firms' major concern. Food and soft drink companies have increasingly substituted corn sweeteners for sugar in their products because these sweeteners are cheaper and less price-volatile than sugar. A major setback for the sugar industry occurred when Coca-Cola and Pepsi began using formulations of 50 to 100 percent high-fructose corn syrup. As a result, corn sweeteners are now expected to gain at least half the total sweetener market in the United States. Plunging demand has caused a collapse in world sugar prices and the enactment of a federal support program for domestically grown sugar, which is quickly accumulating large surpluses.[63]

But not only corn sweeteners are making inroads against sugar. Searle's advertising portrays aspartame as a replacement for both sugar and artificial sweeteners. Aspartame's flavor is far closer to sugar than is saccharin's; in a number of tests, consumers have found aspartame to be indistinguishable from sugar. Just as cyclamate expanded the diet market in the 1950s and 1960s, aspartame is likely to increase the number of consumers for low-calorie products. Surveys indicate that many of the new users of Equal and other aspartame products are switching from sugar rather than from saccharin.[64]

Aspartame sales have been growing at a nearly 40 percent annual rate and now approach the billion dollar mark. Although patent protection is expiring, aspartame's margins are expected to remain high thanks to Searle's clever marketing of the sweetener as a branded product.[65] In fact, its prospects are so good that Monsanto, once the leading producer of saccharin, has reentered the artificial sweetener market by acquiring Searle.[66]

Of course, aspartame's market is not guaranteed. It still costs a great deal more than does saccharin and is not suitable for use in baking. Moreover, there is lingering uncertainty about its health effects. It is not surprising that new sweeteners are under development, including a calorie-free form of sugar.[67]

Conclusions

The regulation of artificial sweeteners produced strange outcomes. Cyclamate, the sweetener that now appears relatively safe, is banned. Saccharin, its replacement, survived an attempted ban even though there are persistent doubts about its safety, in large part because it was the only available sweetener. Aspartame, not fully free from questions, came to market with little regulatory challenge, it would seem, because there is a need for an alternative to saccharin.

The science of sweetener risk is inherently ambiguous. Doubts about artificial sweeteners remain despite hundreds of studies. The only certainty is that judgments made about one sweetener will affect the judgments about others.

The FDA's rush to ban cyclamate prevented a ban of saccharin and assures that there will be a search for other, safer sweeteners. Pressured by the public's fear of cancer and the sugar industry's fear of artificial sweeteners, the FDA acted quickly to remove cyclamate from use on rather weak grounds. Criticized for its haste, the FDA then marshaled carefully the case against saccharin. When the Canadian government, which had been agnostic on cyclamate, banned saccharin, the FDA thought it safe to act. The wrath of diabetics and dieters, abetted by the politically savvy soft drink firms, quickly fell upon the agency. A congressionally mandated moratorium on the saccharin ban serves to remind the FDA of the importance of having substitutes for widely used substances available when it judges product risks.[68]

Others learned more quickly. After losing cyclamate, the diet industry began to monitor developments affecting artificial sweeteners. When saccharin use was threatened with restrictions, the industry was able to organize the coalition required to suspend the ban. The political skills the industry demonstrated in the saccharin case seem to have intimidated the critics of artificial sweeteners. Sugar producers now worry more about government price supports for the natural product than they do about discovering a fatal flaw in the artificial one. Public interest groups advocate caution about the introduction of new artificial sweeteners or the return of an old one, but do little about the continued use of the artificial sweetener for which there is most scientific concern.[69]

The diet industry clamors not at all for the return of cyclamate, tainted in the public mind as it is by the ban. Only Abbott, the maker of cyclamate, attempts to correct the record. It seeks vindication and the return of a lost market. Until other artificial sweeteners become available as alternatives to aspartame, the industry is unlikely to surrender the use of saccharin. In the diet business there is no substitute for having substitute sweeteners.

Chapter 6

Tampons and Toxic Shock Syndrome: Consumer Protection or Public Confusion?

SANFORD L. WEINER

The *New York Times* reported in 1985 that in the four and a half years since toxic shock syndrome first became a household word, reaction to the disease has caused significant changes in the tampon-buying habits of women. "I think about toxic shock every time I reach for a box of tampons," said one woman.[1]

This study describes the growth of concern about toxic shock syndrome, and its impact on perceptions about and sales of tampons. In contrast to many other product risks, toxic shock syndrome (TSS) is in the category of newly recognized public health threats, and one that led to almost immediate public action. In only four months, TSS went from a virtually unknown disease to the cause of a multimillion dollar recall.

The case of TSS is an extreme but revealing example of the pressures that shape perceptions of the safety of consumer products. From the physicians who made the initial discoveries, to the public agencies and corporations that evaluated the science, the constraints of time and public scrutiny were intense. A dramatic and possibly deadly new disease aroused great media attention. But public understanding hardly kept pace with public information. The collective impact of all the actors involved was first to distort the magnitude of the danger and then to dramatize a solution of limited value.

The case begins with the scientific understanding of TSS itself and then traces the responses by public health officials, the tampon industry, and the national media.

The Scientific Detective Story

THE PEDIATRICS PROFESSOR FINDS A SYNDROME

So much of the toxic shock drama was played out in full view of the press that the total obscurity of its first phase is remarkable. The contrast demonstrates how selective media attention is, even as the overall amount of medical and scientific news continues to grow.

In 1978 Dr. James Todd published a short paper describing seven cases of a new syndrome in "older children" that had appeared in Denver.[2] Three boys and four girls had experienced high fever, vomiting, diarrhea, and an intense sunburn-like rash. They soon developed very low blood pressure and went into "severe prolonged shock." Five of the children recovered after about a week in the hospital (though a layer of skin peeled from their palms and feet), but one died and another developed gangrene of the toes. Dr. Todd had isolated staphylococcus (staph) bacteria from some of the cases, but found that a toxin produced by the bacteria was the probable direct cause of illness throughout the body. Todd called the disease toxic shock syndrome.

A few isolated case reports, stretching back to 1927, had described vaguely similar illnesses, but there had never been a cluster with such distinct and striking symptoms. On the other hand, a number of very rare children's infectious diseases, including several attributed to new staphylococcal strains, had recently been described, and one more created no stir whatsoever. There was negligible medical response and no press attention.

Dr. Todd is a conservative, clinically oriented pediatrics professor. By January of 1980 he had collected ten male and twenty-five female cases to bolster his contention that TSS was indeed a new disease, but he had published none of the additional data. Although he noted that the boys averaged about twelve years old, in contrast to nearly twenty years for the women, he did not pursue any epidemiological studies. The next physicians to detect the problem had a very different professional style, with dramatically different results.

THE EPIDEMIOLOGICAL CYCLE

In December 1979 Dr. Joan Chesney encountered three young women in Madison, Wisconsin, hospitals with symptoms identical to those described by Todd. Three cases in one week for a very rare new syndrome seemed so unusual that she called in the state health department epidemiologist to investigate. Dr. Jeffrey Davis found that all the women had been previously healthy, and had nothing in common save that their illness had struck while they were menstruating. A review of hospital records turned up two more cases from the previous summer, and another two were hospitalized in January 1980. A check with the neighboring Minnesota Health Department revealed that they had found five TSS cases as well. All twelve cases had occurred in young women, and eleven of the women had been menstruating.

Both states had youthful, aggressive health departments, and a dozen cases of a rare disease of unknown causation, no longer limited to children, challenged them to act. Following established routine, they notified the Centers for Disease Control in Atlanta, which established a national case register. Each state health department then began a vigorous epidemiological case-finding project.[3] In Wisconsin, Dr. Davis sent a memo to 3,500 local physicians, describing the syndrome and requesting notification of other cases, and opened a formal case-control study to ascertain what possible causal factors the victims might share. His Minnesota counterpart, Dr. Michael Osterholm, put the information in the department's public health newsletter, and began meeting an average of once a week with physician groups around the state to describe the latest findings. Osterholm also circulated a monthly TSS questionnaire to the state's infectious disease specialists.

Within a week these professionally oriented information efforts had also spilled over into the local newspapers, which ran prominent stories about the latest medical mystery. The combined effect was that a substantial number of new cases were found—which produced a feedback cycle in earnest. From this point on in the toxic shock investigation each new cluster of cases would create greater concern among public health officials, stimulating them to publicize TSS more widely. The publicity would then bring in yet more case reports from physicians and victims, and create still greater concern, starting the cycle all over again.

The steadily rising curve of case reports that resulted would bedevil state and federal physicians all spring and summer, for it is one of the most difficult epidemiological events to interpret. A rising disease curve reflects the intermixture of two separate phenomena, the behavior of the disease itself and the performance of the reporting system. A sharp increase in case reports may simply be a classic epidemic spreading across the country. At the other extreme, the increase could reflect a new disease that has stabilized, but where a steadily larger share of the actual cases are being recognized and reported. In practice, new infectious disease curves often simultaneously reflect new spread and better reporting. No firm conclusions about the real slope of the curve and, thus, the long-term danger, can be drawn until the reporting approaches 100 percent. To do that on a national scale, with a disease that was not so rare after all, was to prove exceedingly difficult.

CDC JOINS THE CYCLE

By May 1980 the Centers for Disease Control (CDC) had accumulated fifty-five cases, enough to put toxic shock on the national agenda. The CDC is the most activist part of the federal health bureaucracy and has historic organizational interest in charting new infectious diseases. Its notable successes, such as finding the source of Legionnaire's disease, and its greatest failure, the swine flu vaccination program, both stem from the same organizational preoccupations.

The CDC perception of toxic shock victims was now transformed from that in Todd's original paper. Of the fifty-five cases, seven had died. Of those that became ill, 95 percent were women, average age twenty-five, and 95 percent of the women were menstruating at the time. One third had experienced renewed symptoms during a later menstrual period. Most of the cases were from Wisconsin and Minnesota, and from Utah where the health department had also been active; but there were scattered reports from ten other states as well. The CDC distributed its warning of "a serious disease of unknown etiology" through its *Morbidity and Mortality Weekly Report,* the major national communications channel of the public health community.[4] The *Report* is also carefully monitored by the national news organizations, and toxic shock made a front-page debut in both the *Washington Post* and the *Los Angeles Times.* As had happened on the state level, the effect was electric. About ten TSS cases a month had been reported. Now the CDC was receiving three to four calls per day about possible cases and the number of confirmed reports would more than double in June 1980 alone.

Moreover, toxic shock syndrome was about to acquire much greater salience for a wide segment of the population. The epidemiologists had been pondering a long list of menstrual-related practices that might encourage staph bacteria, which are often present on the body in any case, to overgrow enough to produce disease. Now Dr. Davis reported that the Wisconsin case-control study was almost finished, and only one major difference had shown up: in 97 percent of the TSS cases the women were using tampons compared to only 76 percent of the controls. The numbers were small, but the conclusion was striking. The CDC decided to undertake its own study, to be drawn from the fresh cases now streaming in. But the pressures—the media attention, the increasing number of cases, the Davis study—were mounting, and the study was a hurried affair. A hundred cases and controls were questioned and tabulated in six days, and the results were published a week later. The results were very similar to Wisconsin's. This time 100 percent of the cases used tampons, compared with only 86 percent of the controls.[5]

A possible association with a product regularly used by 35 million women immediately confirmed toxic shock syndrome as a serious national health issue even if it remained a rare disease. The *New York Times,* the Associated Press, and United Press International all carried major stories on the tampon and TSS link.

It was obvious that tampons per se could not be the only causal factor; too many million women used them without incident. It seemed likely to the state and federal biologists now working on the project that a new strain of staphylococcus, which often mutates every few years, was involved, a strain that somehow circumvented the immune response in a small number of women. Yet tampons had also changed significantly over the preceding two years. New superabsorbent materials had been introduced and captured over half the market. The timing was close enough to raise further suspicions.

Neither of the case-control studies had shown any notable differences by tampon brand. The CDC staff members, however, felt that methodological problems might have obscured such differences. Although all their cases were newly reported, some had actually taken place months or years earlier. Only with the recent publicity had women realized that their illnesses in April or September 1979 matched the symptoms described in the press. With an emotional issue and year-old experiences there can be significant recall distortions. A new study was designed that would employ only cases of recent onset. But though the overall number of cases had doubled again, to 272 by 5 September 1980, far too few were appropriate for research. Some were months old and many were already being used in the ongoing state studies. Yet the death count had now reached twenty-five and, with the pressures still mounting, the CDC went ahead with the study anyway, this time completing the interviews in four days. To make up for the mere 50 cases, 150 controls were matched to try to increase the statistical power. The new findings, however, focused entirely on the cases. This time the overwhelming majority of toxic shock victims had used Procter & Gamble's Rely, the brand with the most innovative superabsorbent fibers.[6]

The use of Rely tampons by the women in TSS cases in this new study was twice that found in the CDC's first study in June 1980, and a half-dozen methodological reviews have never satisfactorily resolved the difference. The CDC staff stressed that they had used all the available *reported* cases, thus minimizing sampling bias. But this argument assumes that the reports received by CDC were a significant part of all occurring TSS cases, or at least an unbiased subsample.[7] With the total case-reporting curve still climbing sharply, this was an impossible criterion to fulfill, for no one could say what the ultimate total would be.

Just a slight bias in case reporting by brand could greatly shift the results.[8] The study was based on only forty-two single-brand tampon users, of whom thirty used Rely. If press speculation about superabsorbent tampons had inspired a slightly disproportionate number of Rely cases to be reported, these few extra cases (out of forty-two) could sway the percentages. In California newspapers, for example, Rely had been specifically singled out in TSS stories. When the California cases were removed from the CDC figures, the reported cases tied to Rely dropped from 71 percent to 61 percent (table 6.1).[9] It is impossible to know how much media-influenced case reporting biased the overall study, but such small numbers left little room for error.

Enter the Food and Drug Administration

The CDC had created a double-edged sword. It had a study whose raw figures were fragile, but whose percentages created a powerful indictment. If two thirds or even half of a still growing health problem could be tied to one brand of tampons then the public health bureaucracy could hardly be idle. In fact, the federal officials concerned moved with extraordinary

TABLE 6.1

Tampon Use by TSS Cases and Controls
(CDC Study, July–August 1980)

Brand	Cases (42)	Controls (114)
Rely	71%	26%
Playtex	19	25
Tampax	5	25
Kotex	2	12
O.B.	2	11

NOTE: Centers for Disease Control, "Follow-up on Toxic-Shock Syndrome," *Morbidity and Mortality Weekly Report* 29 (19 September 1980): 443.

swiftness. Within a week, in September 1980, the CDC staff had analyzed the data and shared their findings with their colleagues at the Food and Drug Administration (FDA)—and a decision had been made to seek the complete withdrawal of Rely from the market.

Tampons had become the FDA's concern under the 1976 Medical Devices Act. Inspired by problems with faulty pacemakers and artificial heart valves, Congress had passed legislation covering 1,800 different types of medical devices, from tongue depressors to dialysis machines. Even the FDA found the law's provisions "so complex that they boggled the minds of laymen and lawyers alike," and had spent four years just sorting out the few devices that needed full drug-style controls.[10] Tampons had not been placed in this category, and had been, on the whole, ignored.

A major product recall, though, went beyond the concern of the Medical Devices Bureau, to the FDA commissioner's staff offices, including the general counsel and public affairs. In the Carter administration the FDA's senior leadership had been aggressively pursuing the implications of new studies, and welcoming the resulting controversies. In 1978 under Donald Kennedy, the agency had attacked nitrates as likely carcinogens, and his successor, Jere Goyan, had voiced strong concern about caffeine and birth defects.[11]

In decisions about health risks the key point is where scientific expertise is integrated into broader policy concerns. For the FDA, this merger of expertise and policy took place in the interactions between the Medical Devices Bureau and the senior staff. But the process of the TSS review was extremely flawed. The combination of a weak bureau and an aggressive senior staff resulted in strong policy without the needed expertise to guide it.

Goyan was a relatively weak commissioner and power had devolved onto his senior assistants, particularly those nonscientists responsible for regulatory and legal affairs. They tended to take the lead when problems arose.

The Medical Devices Bureau had been extremely troubled throughout its three-year history, and was accurately described in a congressional report as "the FDA's neglected child."[12] It had begun under a cloud, for its congressional mandate—to write product standards for 1,000 different devices—was impossible to complete in this century. The agency had assigned it low priority in personnel and location. It was staffed by transfers from other FDA bureaus (remembered by their former colleagues as "castoffs"), and given office space 10 miles from the main FDA complex ("sitting above a hair transplant shop . . . we saw them [the bureau staff] only at retirements and funerals").[13] The bureau was dominated by engineers who evaluated the medical hardware, with few clinicians and no epidemiologists.

The outcome of this sorry history was that the bureau had limited scientific expertise to evaluate the CDC's work, and even less credibility with its own superiors. The senior FDA staff simply did not trust the bureau's scientific judgment and this was crucial in the FDA decision process. More powerful FDA bureaus, such as the Bureau of Drugs, have often differed with the CDC over the importance of particular studies in their area, thus creating several policy alternatives. On toxic shock, though, the CDC's activity took center stage unchallenged. One of the senior staff members recalled the feeling of "extraordinary luxury . . . having first-class scientists on our side."[14]

The CDC had completed the study interviews on 8 September 1980. They presented their conclusions to an FDA group in Atlanta on 12 September. The group immediately returned to Washington for the first of almost daily crisis meetings. The CDC had pushed their conclusions about Rely tampons persistently, and the senior FDA staff soon saw Rely in the same light as did the CDC. As one participant remarked, "We were very concerned about the data and [thought] that unless the company had a justification for keeping the product on the market, we would ask that the product be withdrawn immediately."[15] An FDA staff member not directly involved described the conclusion as "a half scientific and half guts call."[16]

By September 16 the FDA had arranged a joint meeting with the CDC and Procter & Gamble (P&G) to discuss the recall. The company's offer of warning labels instead was rejected. The P&G staff then began criticizing the study. The FDA staff replied that the company had a week to present compelling counterevidence or Rely would have to go.

The FDA also decided to spread the message through the media. The day after the meeting, the CDC study was released not just in its *Weekly Report,* but with a full FDA press conference, whose theme was regulating actions to come. Wayne Pines, the FDA's press officer, continued the media orchestration:

> Throughout the series of events, we made sure the press was notified so as to keep the story alive. We wanted to saturate the market with information on Rely. We deliberately delayed issuing press releases for a day to maximize the media impact. There was quite a concerted and deliberate effort to keep a steady flow of information before the public.[17]

The media campaign added to the growing pressures on P&G, a company noted for its particular sensitivity to its public image.

But as Nancy Buc, the FDA general counsel, noted, "Procter & Gamble isn't somebody you're going to roll over lightly."[18] The FDA legal staff started preparations to obtain an immediate federal injunction that would force a recall if needed. One lawyer stated, "I was prepared to go to District Court in Cincinnati (where Procter & Gamble is headquartered) and say 'People are dying.' "[19]

With its public relations staff collecting negative headlines from across the country (as extreme as "Rely Causes 25 Deaths"), P&G first halted production, and then voluntarily recalled the product on 22 September 1980.[20] Many of the press accounts noted the small irony that Procter & Gamble's advertising slogan had been "Rely. It even absorbs the worry." The stories missed the larger irony that the FDA's press campaign was successfully using Rely to absorb the worry about toxic shock.

Procter & Gamble and the Tampon Industry

The recall of an entire brand is comparatively rare, and for a thorough and determined company like Procter & Gamble it was unprecedented. To understand the cross-pressures that motivated the senior P&G management to reluctantly accept the FDA's demands, rather than to fight or delay, we first need to consider their corporate strategy for the tampon market.

The menstrual products field was historically divided between two dominant corporations. Kimberly-Clark, the large paper products firm, made Kotex sanitary napkins; and Tampax made tampons. Though still a single-product firm thirty years after it had introduced tampons, Tampax was an extraordinarily profitable one. With 90 percent of the market in the late 1960s and low advertising costs, its return on investment approached 40 percent.[21]

Neither company's commanding position, however, survived the 1970s. From 1972 on, napkin and tampon ads were allowed on television, opening the doors for new products to be aggressively marketed. Johnson & Johnson introduced beltless pads, and by 1980 it had taken over 55 percent of the market, reducing Kotex from 60 percent to 35 percent.[22] Playtex became the main competition on the tampon side. Its advertising edge was a scented "deodorant" tampon which helped it gain a 35 percent market share in 1978. Johnson & Johnson and Kimberly-Clark also diversified into tampons. For a time Tampax was shielded from the costs of its eroding market share, because the overall tampon market continued to expand as women's preferences shifted from napkins. But its refusal to compete on television until 1978 finally took a heavy toll. Its near monopoly had fallen to 55 percent by 1978 and only 43 percent in 1980.[23]

Procter & Gamble was also eager to compete in both the menstrual pad and tampon markets. A company dedicated to internal growth through new products had found its primary detergent and food brands approaching market saturation in the early 1970s. The paper products division had become the new success area; P&G's marketing approach had always stressed products with a slight technological edge that could be employed to win a dominant market share. The first synthetic detergent (Tide) and fluoride toothpaste (Crest) had shown the way. The company's paper division had developed the first disposable diapers (Pampers) into the company's best-selling brand. After a decade of further development the same superabsorbent fibers in Pampers were now to be used for tampons and pads.[24]

In its first test markets P&G's Rely did have a competitive edge ("twice as absorbent as the leading tampon" said the ads), and it quickly gained a 25–30 percent share to equal Playtex and Tampax.[25] But P&G's four years of painstaking test marketing gave each of its rivals time to develop their own "Super" and "Super Plus" versions. In the spring of 1980, when it finally went into national distribution, Rely was still P&G's most promising new product, backed by a $15 million advertising campaign. Another $10 million was devoted to sending free samples to 80 percent of the households across the country, and its market acceptance rose month by month to 17 percent in June 1980. A Rely pad was set to follow, and P&G anticipated that at least 25 percent of the overall billion-dollar menstrual products field would soon be its reward.[26]

Procter & Gamble's chief executive, Edward Harness, was personally familiar with Rely's progress. He had been the paper division's chief, and the division's success had assisted his climb up the corporate ladder. Harness had multiple reasons, then, to react to the CDC findings by being "determined to fight for a brand, to keep an important brand from being hurt by insufficient data in the hands of a bureaucracy."[27]

But product momentum and executive frustration would not be sufficient to overcome a weak tactical position. Companies seeking to defend products under attack rarely succeed unless they find a way to split some part of the opposition, whether the scientists, the government agencies, or the concerned consumers. Procter & Gamble, however, would not be able to inspire a dedicated group of users who would insist that their product had a unique and compelling value (unlike the case of saccharin discussed in chapter 5). The CDC and the FDA appeared united in their opposition, and there was no other likely agency to assert competing jurisdiction. The company's only hope lay with challenging the scientific premise behind the recall. (This task was made even harder when yet another small study, this one involving twenty-five Utah TSS victims, also pointed at Rely.)[28] Procter & Gamble assembled its own panel of outside scientific consultants. They agreed that the available evidence was weak, but there was no immediate way to refute it. "That was the turning point," Harness recalls, "We didn't know enough about toxic shock to act, and yet we knew too much not to act."[29]

Harness's approach to regulatory issues is to "keep the ball in your own court, if you can. Do it right before somebody else does it wrong for you."[30] Procter & Gamble announced a voluntary recall on 22 September 1980. The FDA, however, refused to be preempted. It still had the threat of a mandatory federal recall, which would imply that safety standards had been violated. To avoid this implication, which would have been damaging in the liability suits that were sure to follow, P&G accepted the FDA's proposal that it conduct the largest recall publicity campaign ever mounted.[31] The two groups jointly composed a vivid newspaper ad. Procter & Gamble put its entire marketing organization in full reverse. For a month, "stop using Rely" ads ran on 600 television stations, 350 radio stations, and in 1,200 newspapers.[32] The paper products division salesmen were sent to retrieve the product from all their clients. And salesmen from other P&G divisions were detailed to buy up Rely cartons whenever they still appeared on supermarket shelves.

The key to Procter & Gamble's response in this case is that the FDA forced the company to examine its basic priorities. The initial publicity had already wounded Rely and any recall was going to permanently tarnish the brand name. P&G's future in the tampon business lay in a return to basic research until the TSS problem was understood, and in the reformulation of a new brand. More fundamental was P&G's concern over its overall corporate image. It has spent decades cultivating the belief that it is a dependable supplier of safe, high-quality products, and the potential success of Rely was marginal by comparison. (Rely sales of $250 million would still be only 2 percent of an $11 billion company.) Even the resulting $75 million write-off was an acceptable price to pay for preserving the Ivory Snow company. As Chairman Harness put it, "We couldn't have moved any slower or else we would have gotten into a blood bath of wholly negative publicity."[33]

Media Routines

Each phase of the toxic shock story, and especially the Rely withdrawal, produced an escalation of media coverage. James Todd, the cautious physician who published the first TSS paper, has bitterly denounced the press attention as "toxic shlock syndrome."[34] Yet most of the press activity was quite predictable, given the professional norms and operational routines of media organizations. Newspapers define their work as conveying stories of salience and immediacy to their readers. A mysterious, possibly deadly disease, striking healthy young women, and linked to a widely used, rarely questioned product, was bound to be intensively reported.

To help determine which events count as news, reporters and editors frequently rely on routine story categories and toxic shock matched several of these perfectly. The initial reports combined the "scientific detective" story with the "possible disaster" story. Even when the lead paragraph was strictly factual, as in this *Washington Post* page-one report, the story was captivating: "A new disease that most frequently strikes young women and can produce death within a few days is being called to the attention of doctors across the United States."[35] Once alerted to an ongoing science mystery, the press carefully monitored professional journals and meetings for signs of progress. The conjectures and speculations that are a normal part of medical research on a puzzling disease were printed in the *Lancet* or the *New England Journal of Medicine* as usual. The difference was that, with the press watching over their shoulders, the doctors found their ideas carried the same day by the *New York Times* or the *Boston Globe,* no matter how conjectural they may have been.

Another routine story category is the interview with disaster or disease victims, and TSS was no exception. Even the *New York Times,* the "newspaper of record," ran a story that began:

> Linda Imboden's hands curve like claws, most of her waist-length hair has fallen out and gangrene has cut off the sensation in her fingertips and two toes. The cause is toxic shock syndrome, a newly discovered disease associated with menstruation and tampon use.[36]

Because the logistics of news gathering put a premium on accessible sources, and reporters compulsively read each other's work, the same incidents appear again and again.[37] Mrs. Imboden's serious injuries (which resulted in a $5 million lawsuit against Rely) were described in the *San Francisco Chronicle, Time, Newsweek, People,* the *American Journal of Nursing,* and even the London *Observer.* Reports from the Associated Press, United Press International, and the *New York Times* News Service were carried by papers across the nation.

Local television news stories tend to concentrate almost exclusively on the human interest side of the issue, obscuring its context completely. A classic example was a report on KCRA, Sacramento:

> A fifteen-year-old girl is dead tonight, the apparent victim of complications resulting from the use of a tampon. . . . Diane's mother had heard of Toxic Shock Syndrome brought on by the tampons and had warned her girls. But Laura and Diane used them one more time—in Diane's case, one last time.[38]

Finally, the apparent denouement of the mystery story in which Rely was revealed as the villain, quite naturally attracted the most attention of all.

Getting the Message

All of this media attention had serious consequences for the public's understanding of the syndrome and its relevance to their own personal behavior. Marketing studies report that 95 percent of all women aged fifteen to fifty heard about the tampon–TSS link. The reaction in the marketplace was immediate and sharp. Tampon sales dropped 20 percent in favor of napkins. The percentage of women who used tampons at all dropped from about 70 percent to 55 percent–5 to 10 million women who were worried enough to forgo their normal preferences. Among those who continued to use tampons there was also a marked shift among brands in favor of Tampax. As *Fortune* described it:

> In the wake of TSS, Tampax got a second lease on life. To the dismay of its competitors it has successfully capitalized on its image as the old, familiar, and (by implication) safer product.... Recognizing what one Wall Street analyst called "the opportunity of a lifetime," Tampax continued to spend heavily on promotion.[39]

All the other companies reduced or ended their advertising while waiting for the situation to stabilize. Tampax sought to differentiate itself in every way possible. The FDA had requested that all tampon companies include TSS warning labels and package inserts with their products, while the agency formulated a regulation to make them mandatory. Tampax refused to put a label on the box, so that an apparent distinction was created on drugstore shelves.[40] (The company's lawyers told the FDA that "a frightening death warning" was unjustified and "could have a drastic effect" on a one-product company.) In addition, the TSS information inside the Tampax box, though technically accurate, was much milder than the FDA's proposed text. The set piece of the Tampax campaign was the return of its least-absorbent model—driven off the market three years before—as the new, "natural" 100 percent cotton "Original Regular" style, with ad copy that stressed "no super-absorbent synthetic materials."[41] No mention was made of the superabsorbents that remained in all the rest of the company's styles.

Simple Perceptions and Complex Realities

For a time it seemed that the bold public health moves, reinforced by the various advertising campaigns, were paying off. After peaking in August and September 1980, new toxic shock cases reported to the CDC fell off sharply (figure 6.1). This could be attributed to the absence of Rely, the drop in overall tampon usage, or the new system for case reporting that referred callers to their state health departments, who then reported to CDC. The CDC staff stressed the first and discounted the last.

Yet only a few weeks later, new evidence began to accumulate to remind those involved how complex TSS really was. Wisconsin and Minnesota,

FIGURE 6.1

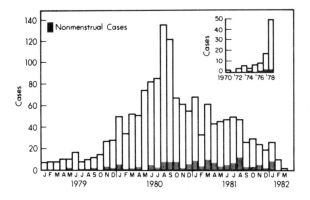

Confirmed Cases of Toxic Shock Syndrome, January 1970–March 1982

NOTE: Centers for Disease Control, "Toxic-Shock Syndrome, United States, 1970–1982," *Morbidity and Mortality Weekly Report* 31 (30 April 1982): 201.

which had started the cycle a year before, had now gathered enough cases (along with Iowa) to break down the user pattern by absorbency styles within brands. Their data presented a very different picture from the earlier studies.[42] They found that greater TSS risk correlated directly with greater absorbency, whatever the brand. Rely was only slightly "riskier" than other tampons of similar absorbency. During that period Rely had about half the market for "Super" tampons, and about half the TSS victims. The direct implication was that Rely had been singled out as much for its marketing success as for its distinctive risk.

By the summer of 1981 it was clear that TSS was not fading away. The CDC was still receiving a steady 40–50 case reports a month (figure 6.1). The eventual 1981 total would be 492 cases and 15 deaths, compared with 867 and 44 the year before. More disturbing yet were additional data strengthening the Minnesota case. They had continued the active search for cases and, in stark contrast to the national data, had found no TSS drop-off whatsoever (table 6.2).[43] The correlation with absorbency continued, so that the only difference after September 1980 was that the victims now tended to use Tampax Super or Playtex Super, in place of Rely.

The controversies engendered by these studies remain unsettled, and more research is slowly being done. The fact that the earlier studies have

TABLE 6.2

TSS in Minnesota Before and After Rely Recall

Brand Used	Jan.–Sept. 1980 (n = 55)	Oct. 1980–June 1981 (n = 59)
Rely	45.5% *	1.6% *
Tampax	12.7	45.7
Playtex	20.0	30.5
O.B.	3.6	1.6
Kotex	5.4	13.5
Pursettes	1.8	1.6
Multiple Use/Unknown	10.9	5.0

NOTE: Michael T. Osterholm et al., "Toxic-Shock Syndrome in Minnesota: Results of an Active-Passive Surveillance System," *Journal of Infectious Diseases* 145 (April 1982): 462.
*Due to rounding, columns do not add up to 100 percent.

been questioned by ones at least as persuasive, however, has received little public attention. Within the FDA the "shell-shocked" Medical Devices Bureau was reorganized (into the National Center for Devices and Radiological Health) and given new leaders, who found that it was "hard for the folks here to explain what had happened." Comparing the CDC Rely study to the regulatory standards used in his prior work, one new official concluded that "I would have had a hard time calling for a recall." Another newcomer felt the same: "If Rely had stayed on the market, by the summer of '81 we would have handled it no differently than any other super [tampon]."[44] But these doubts have been voiced in public only very cautiously. There is a natural bureaucratic reluctance to challenge their colleagues at CDC or the former FDA leadership.

The disposition not to rock the boat is so strong that in 1985 a major research study, which cast strong doubt on the original perceptions, brought policy changes with virtually no public awareness. A Harvard research team finally developed a plausible laboratory model for the interaction between tampons and staph bacteria. They found that toxin production by the bacteria was greatly influenced by subtle changes in the magnesium level of the surrounding environment. And superabsorbent fibers are particularly good at absorbing magnesium, leaving a magnesium-deficient environment that greatly increases the amount of toxin. The polyester foam used in Rely stood out as a magnesium collector. But the polyacrylate rayon that was the basis for all the other super tampons also showed the same propensity, so any super tampon could deplete the magnesium and support toxin growth. When these results were reported in the spring of 1985, the remaining super tampons were reformulated "to make them safer."[45] Few drew the contrast with the earlier public advice.

Conclusion: Public Understanding or Public Confusion?

Toxic shock syndrome stands as a powerful example of the distinction between dramatic deaths and statistical ones. There is no question that, as the latest FDA warning puts it, "TSS is a rare but serious disease that may cause death." But the massive volume of TSS information destroyed any comparative public health perspective on "just how rare is rare." The differing ways of viewing the disease are strikingly illustrated by Nan Robertson's *New York Times Magazine* cover story on her own experience with toxic shock. In poignant and moving detail, the story begins with Robertson near death after a Thanksgiving family dinner, and describes the months of painful recuperation needed to regain the use of her fingers after partial amputations. But it ends triumphantly: "I have typed the thousands of words of this article, slowly and with difficulty, once again able to practice my craft as a reporter. I have written it—at last—with my own hands."[46] The piece won several journalism awards, including the Pulitzer Prize. Though the body of the article accurately portrays all the scientific evidence about TSS, the very power of the writing conveys one simple message: toxic shock can strike anyone, anytime—even a fifty-five-year-old woman who had not used tampons for a decade—and with devastating impact.

Doctors and epidemiologists working on TSS find Robertson's message so misleading that some even miss its strength as journalism. One scientist commented, "I was utterly dumbfounded when it got a Pulitzer."[47] For the overall statistical picture is quite different. Although TSS victims require immediate and intensive hospital care, most go home a week later with no lasting impact on their health. Two thirds of the victims are women twenty-five or younger. Other age groups are attacked much less frequently. At the time Robertson was stricken, less than 10 of the 1,400 cases then counted by the CDC had occurred in women over fifty. It is generally agreed that the 500 cases a year reported to the CDC underestimates the true TSS incidence. Minnesota appears to have collected far more complete data, but even extrapolating that state's results gives a national estimate of only 5,000 cases per year, or 9 out of 100,000 menstruating women. As

TABLE 6.3

Rates of Diseases and Other Events in the United States
(Number per 100,000 Population per Year)

Syphilis, deaths	0.1
Legionnaire's disease, incidence	0.2
Toxic Shock Syndrome, deaths (menstruating women only)	0.5
Tuberculosis, deaths	0.8
Accidental falls, deaths	5.0
TSS, incidence (menstruating women only)	9.0
Homicide rate	11.0
Syphilis, incidence	12.0
Suicide rate	13.0
Tuberculosis, incidence	13.0
Motor vehicle accidents, deaths	24.0
Gonorrhea, incidence	450.0

NOTE: American Council on Science and Health, *News and Views* 4 (March–April 1983): 15.

shown in table 6.3, that places toxic shock about equal to tuberculosis in the realm of serious infectious diseases. That makes it a notable public health threat, but a very rare one.

Conveying to the public that a new disease is very serious but very infrequent is a difficult task. In this case that balanced explanation was never achieved. After allowing the syndrome to be oversold, public health officials then exaggerated the withdrawal of Rely as an equally compelling "solution." The gap between expertise and policymaking within the FDA left the agency blind to how fragile its answer really was. For its part, the media effectively dramatized the problem and its apparent resolution. Much was made of the need for public information. Far too little was done to put that information in perspective.

Chapter 7

Banning Formaldehyde Insulation: Risk Assessment and Symbolic Politics

SANFORD L. WEINER

Formaldehyde is a ubiquitous chemical. Its properties as a preservative and germicide make it useful for biologists, embalmers, and mushroom growers. It is also an inexpensive chemical adhesive that forms the basis for particle board and permanent press fabrics. It is not surprising that a chemical that appears in so many guises might come to the attention of several regulatory agencies.

During the last decade, in fact, four separate federal agencies have considered the issues posed by formaldehyde-emitting products. What makes formaldehyde an interesting case of risk assessment is that from almost the same evidence each agency has drawn strikingly different conclusions. The Consumer Products Safety Commission (CPSC) banned outright the use of urea-formaldehyde foam insulation in housing. The Department of Housing and Urban Development (HUD) though, settled for a mild standard for mobile homes, where formaldehyde levels from particle board are much higher. Meanwhile the Occupational Safety and Health Administration (OSHA) has changed its mind twice about the risks of urea-formaldehyde resins used in garment factories. And the Environmental Protection Agency (EPA), whose jurisdiction overlaps everybody else's, has also reversed itself twice on whether to get involved at all. A federal appeals court, reviewing this situation, found

these contrary pronouncements . . . disconcerting. Regulatory agencies such as these were created to protect the public from latent risks. For them to be effective, the public must be confident in their ability to determine which products are unsafe, which drugs are dangerous, and which substances are carcinogenic. Interagency disagreement undermines such confidence.[1]

In understanding the bureaucratic processes that produce these differences three themes stand out. First is the extremely limited scientific base on which all the regulators were forced to rely. Second, in the absence of scientific findings to constrain the debates, the controversies were unusually ideological in nature. Advocates on both sides invoked broad concerns toward cancer or regulation. Third, many of the battles have been essentially symbolic, intended to set precedents for other formaldehyde uses, or other chemical carcinogens altogether. The CPSC's deliberations about banning foam insulation, for example, took place as the industry was already dying.

The Rise and Fall of Foam Insulation

It was the use of formaldehyde resins for home insulation that first brought the chemical to the attention of regulators. In contrast to other "dangerous product" cases, health concerns were generated not by new scientific discoveries, but by angry consumers using the political system, whose complaints were amplified by the media. Formaldehyde itself has been widely used in industry for decades without attracting particular notice. But foam insulation, when improperly installed, could give off unpleasant fumes throughout a house, and there were many complaints to local health departments. In this respect the formaldehyde case shares some characteristics of environmental issues.

Urea-formaldehyde can be sprayed as a liquid foam into the exterior walls of old houses, where, under appropriate conditions, it will harden into an effective, fireproof insulation. It had considerable use in Europe over the past twenty years, but came to America only in the wake of the first oil price increases in 1973–74. With heating fuel prices soaring and conventional insulation (Fiberglas) factories pressed to capacity, a number of small chemical firms worked to adapt European urea-formaldehyde foam techniques to create new insulating material for the American market. They were extremely successful. From about 25,000 homes insulated in 1975, sales jumped to over 150,000 homes in the peak year of 1977.[2]

There was a three-tier distribution system. The raw materials were produced by the major chemical companies. (Celanese, Borden, and Du-Pont control about half the formaldehyde market.) About thirty small specialty chemical firms made the foam combination and the necessary applicators, though Rapco Foam had over half this market before it went bankrupt in 1981. Finally, thousands of local independent contractors did the on-site installing and spraying.

Steadily escalating adverse publicity about the troubles when the installation went wrong soon reversed the sales trend (figure 7.1). The major problem stemmed from the variability in the local contractors. Industry representatives now readily admit that the booming market had a negative impact on their ability to control distribution: "Getting into the foam business was easy and cheap. We got some fly-by-night guys who didn't go by the manufacturer's standards. They'd do a bad job and then leave town."[3]

Even the established contractors had problems. Many installers had previously worked on storm window and siding renovations. But foam insulation is mixed at the home, and is a technically demanding process. The age of the resin, the exact foam mixture, and the outdoor temperature and humidity must all be just right, and the foaming equipment must also perform precisely. Should any of the variables be incorrect, the foam will not cure properly and will eventually crumble inside the wall, with little residual insulating effect. More important, the uncured foam may release formaldehyde gas into the home. Some homeowners found their newly insulated houses had a distinct odor and other families developed eye and throat irritations and other respiratory problems.[4]

These installation failures soon resulted in complaints to local consumer protection agencies and health departments, and local media coverage across the country. A typical story began:

A few hours after their house in upstate New York was insulated with urea-formaldehyde foam the young couple developed headaches and a burning sensation in their eyes. The baby cried all night. Within days the pet rabbit died. After a week with the heavy strong smelling fumes, the family moved out.[5]

FIGURE 7.1

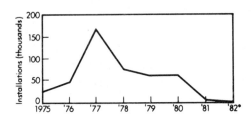

Urea-Formaldehyde Insulation Use, 1975–1982

*Estimated.
SOURCES: Consumer Product Safety Commission; industry estimates. Reprinted with permission from
Chemical and Engineering News (29 March 1982): 35. Copyright 1982, American Chemical Society.

As complaints were the only way to gauge the extent of the problem,
media coverage played a key amplifying role. Each story made additional
homeowners wonder if their less-dramatic illnesses had the same source,
and they asked local officials for help as well. A *Redbook* feature, "Our
House Was Endangering Our Health," exactly captures the rebounding
fears produced by a local newspaper:

> We had already experienced the sinus problems and irritations the article listed.
> . . . We'd always blamed them on Michigan's fickle weather. . . . The thought of
> our newborn daughter's spending 24 hours a day in an environment that could
> jeopardize her health made our tight, energy-efficient home seem like a prison.
> [After the health department checked the house] . . . The figures were infinitesimal,
> measured in parts per million. We had no idea what they meant. But they shouldn't
> have been there at all.[6]

This family was hardly alone in its confusion. From local investigators
to federal regulators, it was to prove very difficult to distinguish normal
respiratory complaints from formaldehyde sensitivities, and regular background formaldehyde readings (given off by furnishings and other sources)
from those caused by foam insulation.

There were enough clear-cut horror stories, however, to inspire consumer protection offices in several states, including Wisconsin and
Colorado, to issue strong calls for tougher state and federal standards. (The
consumer offices had been concerned from the beginning about the in-
flated, sometimes fraudulent claims that all types of installation firms had
resorted to.) The Massachusetts Department of Health began gathering
cases to ascertain whether foam insulation should be banned as a hazard-

ous substance. Similar complaints also surfaced from those living in mobile homes, which are tightly sealed and filled with formaldehyde-based particle board.

At this point numerous state officials sought scientific backing for their complaint-derived hypotheses. They were to find the science of formaldehyde exposure unready for policy application.

The Elusive Effects of Formaldehyde

A National Academy of Sciences study on indoor pollutants concluded that "the existing data base is, for the most part, derived from pilot studies or anecdotal reports."[7] Regulators trying to employ this data base to gauge the health impacts of formaldehyde exposure were continually frustrated. The federal appeals court that eventually reviewed the CPSC decision on foam insulation, for example, complained that the thousands of pages offered in evidence failed to answer the most basic questions: how many consumers were exposed to how much formaldehyde with what consequences?[8]

There were two reasons for the primitive state of the science.[9] The field was relatively new, and the policy questions far surpassed the research funding. But the more fundamental reason is that these studies are unusually difficult to design and carry out.[10]

It is a technically demanding process just to measure formaldehyde at levels of one part in 10 million. The original equipment had been designed for factory use and did not adapt well to mobile field studies. As one review noted, these "systems are unwieldy, difficult to operate, expensive, and unreliable."[11] Newer techniques were also plagued with problems. In 1980, the National Institute of Occupational Safety and Health (NIOSH), which helps set technical standards in this area, described an entirely new system. Two years later they published a paper retracting their advice, since they had found variations of 50–75 percent in test readings during actual studies.[12]

The protocols for conducting measurements in the home are no better established. There are obvious confounding variables such as the indoor temperature and humidity, how long the windows have been closed, and the presence of cigarette smoke (which contains significant amounts of formaldehyde). Controlled laboratory studies have also revealed more subtle biases.[13] Formaldehyde concentrations can also be influenced by the temperature *outdoors*, for the indoor/outdoor contrast determines how much the house will "breathe." Seasonal conditions, or even a different time of day, can escalate the reading. Table 7.1 demonstrates that different conditions in the same house might change formaldehyde levels tenfold.

Reliably pinning down the source of the measured concentration can also be challenging. Most emissions from foam insulation decline steadily over the first 12–18 months, and then level off or end completely. This month's measurement may not match last month's effects. The overlapping impact of the seasonal and aging trends is very hard to disentangle. Foam emissions are also influenced by their microenvironment. The wallboard may itself absorb the formaldehyde from the foam, and only slowly emit it into the room. Room concentrations, in turn, depend on the interaction of all potential emitters, and these can include carpeting, curtains, and wall paneling. If the insulation is releasing formaldehyde, this will partially suppress other sources—they will not be additive. (Technically, any emission depends on the existing concentration.) But the effect works both ways: should the insulation be removed or sealed off, the other sources will increase and keep the room levels from dropping all the way back. Thus a meaningful answer to the question of how much formaldehyde is given off by foam insulation requires a large-scale survey with reliable equipment, consistent testing protocols, and controls for temperature, humidity, age of foam, and other major formaldehyde sources.

After measurement, the formaldehyde readings have to be related to the possible health effects. Most of the early formaldehyde studies were based on complaints investigated by industrial hygienists, whose normal procedure is to match the illness to an obvious noxious chemical. But where the

TABLE 7.1

Potential Effects of Temperature and Relative Humidity on Formaldehyde Air Concentrations (ppm)

Temperature	Relative Humidity				
	30%	40%	50%	60%	70%
59°F (15°C)	0.08	0.11	0.14	0.17	0.19
68°F (20°C)	0.15	0.19	0.24	0.29	0.33
77°F (25°C)	0.24	0.32	0.40	0.48	0.56
86°F (30°C)	0.40	0.53	0.66	0.79	0.92

SOURCE: Environmental Protection Agency, Office of Toxic Substances, "Preliminary Assessment of Health Risks to Garment Workers and Certain Home Residents from Exposure to Formaldehyde," unpublished draft, May 1985, p. G-15.

measured concentrations are highly variable and the typical illnesses re semble colds and allergies, full-scale epidemiological studies are needed. Because of the seasonal effects, these need to be done over an entire year, with control groups to establish background formaldehyde rates (in nonfoam-insulated homes), and average respiratory disease rates.

The final element that makes large-scale studies mandatory is that individual susceptibility to the same formaldehyde concentration varies greatly. Measured levels in houses often range from 0.5 ppm to 0.05 ppm. Most of the population (80 percent) will not notice any effect below 0.25 ppm. But some people, often those with asthma or allergies, are irritated by levels as low as 0.1 ppm. The key question, then, is what levels cause illness in what proportion of the population, and how often those thresholds are reached. In the mid 1980s, five to seven years after these questions first came to attention, the necessary studies have begun. If the curve described foam-insulated homes, the federal court would have found the sensitivity curve in figure 7.2 to be highly relevant, for example. But this study (published in September 1984) is still a small-scale, nonrandom, pilot study of mobile homes, which can only provide a rough estimate of how often formaldehyde burns the eyes.[14] Mobile homes are used in these studies because they are more standardized than on-site foam installations, but the results do not apply directly to conventional homes. Virtually all the other available studies can be severely challenged on one or more of the confounding variables just described. That makes it hard for regulators to know where to set limits, and harder still to defend those limits.

Then CPSC Finds a Role

Through 1977–78 the complaints and publicity at the state level increased. Yet the issue had hardly surfaced in Washington. The Department of Energy, EPA, and CPSC were gingerly avoiding claims of jurisdiction. The complaints were diffuse, usually undocumented, and the overall scientific evidence was so weak that foam insulation was not on anybody's priority list. As the *New York Times* described it: "No agency is planning to investigate the effects of long-term exposure to relatively low levels of formaldehyde in the air. And, in sort of a Catch 22, no agency is willing to take steps against products containing formaldehyde without knowing more of what its effects are."[15]

FIGURE 7.2

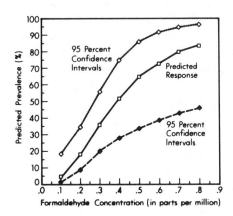

Prevalence of Eye Irritation at Various Levels of Formaldehyde Concentration

NOTE: L. P. Hanrahan et al., "Formaldehyde Vapor in Mobile Homes," *American Journal of Public Health* 74 (September 1984): 1026.

Then the CPSC got a new chairman and a new mission. Since its establishment in 1972, the commission had defined product safety primarily in terms of accidents. Armed with hospital emergency room surveys of product-related injuries, the CPSC had overseen the redesign of chain saws, cribs, bicycles, and Christmas tree lights. Susan King, a consumer activist appointed by President Carter in 1978 as chairman of the CPSC, wanted the agency to get involved in the long-run chronic hazards, such as birth defects or cancer. These issues had a much higher scientific content and usually much greater visibility than, say, court battles with the lawn mower industry. She made clear that this was "the most important initiative undertaken by the agency in the last few years" and beefed up the scientific staff with new expertise.[16]

A small agency with limited budget and staff has to pick its issues carefully, however, and preferably ones that other agencies have not already staked out. The new group began by investigating asbestos in consumer products, which led to a widely publicized hair dryer recall. They also began collecting data in the spring of 1979 on formaldehyde and foam insulation, as a possible future issue. For some staff members it soon became clear that "there was no justification for a product that bad being sold to consumers . . . this wasn't a defective toaster, it made your house defective."[17] Moreover, the foam manufacturers seemed much less willing to modify their product than other trade groups CPSC had dealt with. As one staff member recalled, "Not only were they unresponsive, they were technically ignorant."[18] (The commission's new executive director was also well versed in the issue. He had just come from the attorney general's office in Massachusetts where a state-level ban of the foam was also under consideration.)

Then in October 1979, a completely unexpected report made the CPSC look prescient. The major chemical manufacturers had sponsored animal studies designed to refute the concerns over formaldehyde sensitivity. They were particularly interested in forestalling tighter exposure standards in chemical and textile plants. As is customary in these studies, rats had been subjected to quite high doses, so as to maximize the treatment effect for a given number of animals. After breathing in formaldehyde over 12–24 months, though, 50 percent of the rats exposed developed nasal cancers, which are usually extremely rare.[19] (Over 10,000 rats used as controls in similar studies had never developed *any* nasal cancers.) Formaldehyde could, therefore, act as an animal carcinogen.

This finding immediately changed the face of the issue for several agencies. At CPSC a senior official recalled that the finding created a fair amount of additional interest. As he saw it, regulating a new possible carcinogen would put the agency "at the cutting edge of scientific knowledge." With cancer as the spur, CPSC mapped out a two-pronged attack on foam insulation. Both the respiratory complaints and the cancer findings would be pursued, and then the combined findings would be used for regulatory action.

The CPSC moved first on the respiratory illness front. Hearings on urea-formaldehyde foam were held in four different cities, producing a fresh burst of publicity (though the insulation's image, according to a staff comment in the *Washington Post,* was already that of "shrink and stink").[20] In March 1980, the commission released to the press a consumer alert on the various respiratory hazards attributed to formaldehyde in the home.

Meanwhile the CPSC staff moved to assemble what scientific studies were available. The staff had a good deal of skepticism about reported formaldehyde levels. After combining various state and CPSC records, the staff totaled 1,100 complaints, which had led to 384 investigations and 114 in-home formaldehyde readings. Yet only about 40 of these readings could be rated high quality. Some outside studies showed more respiratory complaints soon after foam had been installed, but had no actual readings. Another had higher formaldehyde levels in insulated homes, but the complaints did not match the levels very well, perhaps because of differences in individual sensitivities. The CPSC staff tried to find a pattern, drawn from the better studies, of measured levels where complaints became significant. They concluded that the evidence, as disorganized and conflicting as it was, supported the clinical impressions that foam insulation in place could cause serious illness. But it remained a qualitative argument, not a statistical one.

The CPSC's alternative at this point was to sponsor a full-scale epidemiological field study that could provide firmer data. But for insiders this was never a realistic option. Staff members were not willing to accept the two to three years of additional harm to consumers while waiting for science to catch up. Moreover, the commission was not in the major research business. As one staff member put it, "This agency is never going to have the money."[21] A million dollars for a study would have been greater than the entire formaldehyde project budget, and unprecedented in an agency whose total budget was only $39 million.

The commission staff did arrange for a special series of laboratory tests, in which urea-formaldehyde foam was installed in sample wall panels under controlled conditions. From this small study they concluded that even state-of-the-art installation techniques still permitted significant formaldehyde emissions. Though industry disputed the testing procedures, the CPSC staff became convinced that the only solution was to ban the product altogether—no standards could reform an unstable product.

Cancer by Consensus

While this activity was taking place within the CPSC, its staff also participated in a governmentwide scientific panel, the Federal Panel on Formaldehyde, which had been formed to evaluate the case of formaldehyde as a carcinogen. The 1979 animal study had come at an opportune time. Historically, government regulation of carcinogens had been done on an ad hoc, lengthy, case-by-case basis, with each new chemical and regulation serving as precedent for the next. The science-oriented agencies in the Carter administration had been trying to produce general principles for carcinogen regulation that could be used by all. Now formaldehyde, a chemical that spanned the jurisdictions of EPA and OSHA as well as CPSC, would be a fine working example.

The group's underlying assumptions were simple.[22] For prudent public policy, substances that caused cancer in animals, no matter what the dosage, would be assumed to have the same potential for humans. On the other side of the coin, because no convincing threshold model of carcinogenesis had been established, the lowest possible human exposure to the chemical should be sought. Epidemiological studies of actual human disease were valuable. But because many occupational carcinogens took decades to reveal their potential in humans, regulation should not wait for the cancers to manifest themselves. The conscious philosophy of these assumptions is "when in doubt, err on the side of safety." Prudence, then, required that no animal dose could be high enough to be disregarded, and no human exposure could be low enough to escape concern.

From this perspective, the validity of the animal tests became a key question. The governmentwide review panel reported in the fall of 1980 that the tests had been properly conducted and thus "formaldehyde should be presumed to pose a carcinogenic risk to humans."[23] Further evidence arrived in August 1981, when Arthur Upton (a former National Cancer Institute director) reported that his laboratory had replicated the first 1979 study, and could provide "decisive confirmation" of formaldehyde's carcinogenic activity.[24]

Bans and Precedents

Given the statistical problems concerning respiratory illness, the CPSC staff sought to tie formaldehyde to cancer as specifically as possible. The staff argument went far beyond the generalities of the government's formaldehyde panel. Though no one could be sure that the chemical even caused human cancers, the staff utilized a computerized, mathematical model that transformed dose-response effects in rats into estimates for humans. For the 2 million people residing in the 500,000 homes that had urea-formaldehyde foam insulation, the model predicted up to 89 extra cancer deaths. This was a highly speculative exercise. Looking back, staff members concede that their portrayal of the cancer numbers made them appear "more realistic than was intended."[25] Roy Albert, a scientist who had helped apply this computer model at EPA where it was developed, explained the point at a congressional hearing:

> The way in which EPA has put the quantitative risk assessments was always to emphasize that they are crude ballpark estimates. They provide what might be regarded as a plausible upper limit estimate. Things could be as bad as these

TABLE 7.2

Leading Producers of Formaldehyde

Company	Output capacity (millions of pounds)	Percent of U.S. output
Celanese	1,734	20.1
Borden	1,575	18.2
DuPont	1,470	17.0
Georgia-Pacific	1,045	12.1
Reichhold Chemicals	820	9.5
Monsanto	690	8.0
Getty Oil	280	3.2
Tenneco	265	3.1
Others	750	8.7
Total	8,629	

SOURCES: SRI International; *New York Times* estimates. Reprinted by permission of The New York Times Company, copyright © 1981.

TABLE 7.3

Leading Uses of Formaldehyde

	Percent of total consumption
Industrial Chemicals*	33.0
Particleboard	20.3
Plywood	9.2
Polyacetal Resins	7.5
Insulation	6.7
Hard Plastics	5.3
Fiberboard	3.7
Paints and Lacquers	2.1
Paper and Paperboard	2.0
Textiles	1.8
Specialty Uses†	4.5
Other	3.9

*Includes pentaerythritol, butanediol, nitroparaffin derivatives and others.
†Includes embalming fluids, drilling muds, disinfectants, dyes, cosmetics, and others.
SOURCE: The Formaldehyde Institute. Reprinted by permission of The New York Times Company, copyright © 1981.

estimates point out, but they could also be less. So that when you are talking about sacrificing people, I think that is putting it a little strongly. We are not so sure that we are dealing with dead bodies lying on the ground. We are dealing with estimates that have a certain amount of plausibility, a certain amount of uncertainty, and I think the issue is the extent of prudence which is to be exercised in dealing with these matters.[26]

Without such careful qualification, the CPSC evaluation was easily undermined. In a widely quoted open letter to the commission, John Higginson, the former director of the International Agency for Research on Cancer, dismissed the whole idea:

Today few experienced experimental oncologists would make any attempt to extrapolate mathematically the degree of human risk from animals. . . . Exact estimates as to the number of cases of a cancer that might be expected to occur in man based on a single experiment are silly and simply ignore biological realities. The fact that no better methods exist does not make these statements any better or more valuable.[27]

Even if predictions were possible, the computer model's 89 deaths hardly stand out among the 200,000–400,000 deaths from cancer ordinarily expected among 2 million people.

The commission staff pressed on, nonetheless. By October 1980 the staff had combined the respiratory case and the cancer case into a public recommendation that formaldehyde foam be banned.

The various industry groups were quite differently situated to oppose the staff report. By 1980 the actual foam installers in the field were fading away as the adverse publicity about their product mounted. There were only several hundred left. They were represented by essentially one Washington lobbyist who generated press releases, but did not have the resources to compete in what was an increasingly technical debate. (When the battle was finally lost, he could only issue a bitter statement that the CPSC staff had lied to the commission—a charge that even one of the commissioners who voted against the ban labeled "hogwash.")[28]

The small foam manufacturers were only slightly more organized than the installers. By contrast, the large chemical producers, who make formaldehyde itself, including DuPont and Celanese (see table 7.2), had established the Formaldehyde Institute in 1978, with a multimillion dollar budget for research and lobbying in defense of the product. (The 1979 rat study had been intended as their first defensive effort.) Although foam insulation absorbed only about 2 percent of the 6–8 billion pounds of formaldehyde sold annually, the precedent was vitally important. As *Fortune* was quick to observe,

In labeling the formaldehyde in foam insulation as a potential cause of human cancer, the CPSC immediately raised questions not only about one small industry, but about the formaldehyde used as adhesive or preservative in hundreds of other products with billion dollar markets—plastics, plywood, textiles, cosmetics, drugs and food.[29]

The Formaldehyde Institute attacked on all fronts, from press releases to scientific critiques. As the CPSC was legally bound to evaluate and respond to all comments on proposed regulations, the agency staff began to suspect they were being deliberately weighted down with 500-page tomes. The industry's institute questioned each of the staff findings. No clear-cut foam-caused illness had been demonstrated. Properly installed insulation gave off minimal emissions. Complaints had not been properly documented. Banning foam would be a valuable product loss to consumers, and an economic loss to small business concerns. The industry then focused squarely on the carcinogen findings. There were methodological problems with the rat studies. In any case, extreme doses, beyond normal human tolerance, were unrepresentative of human biology. As James Ramey of Celanese put it: "Epidemiology, not animal studies, is the most accurate and definitive way to assess human health risk. Neither historical experience nor recently reported epidemiology results link formaldehyde to cancer in humans."[30]

In the last days of the Carter administration, the commission tentatively voted three Democrats to two Republicans in favor of the ban. It was widely assumed that the new Reagan-appointed chairman would reverse the vote. But over the ensuing year a complex interplay of personality and organizational politics took place. Nancy Steorts did not prove to be the ideological Chairwoman her sponsors may have intended.[31] And the CPSC, with four hold-over members, had far more continuity than similar executive branch agencies. Although the former executive director departed, all of the key scientific staff who had made the formaldehyde case stayed on, and slowly won the confidence of their new leader.

As they gathered still more exposure data to counter the industry critiques, they also convinced Steorts that her preference for voluntary standards could not be applied to a product manufactured on site, where no quality control was possible. As there was no middle ground, she agreed that such a dangerous product would have to be banned.

By the time of the final vote, it was mostly symbolic—the industry had evaporated. Both sides were hoping to use the vote for a precedent before other agencies. Even the CPSC admitted that particle board had uses and risks too varied to be simply banned, but producers were put on notice that manufacturing standards might be applied there too.

Carcinogen Politics: Round One

Formaldehyde outlook: The main concern of formaldehyde producers is that health questions, which have all but wiped out the urea-formaldehyde foam insulation business, do not spread to formaldehyde's biggest market, resins for particle board. All depends on the decisions of government regulatory agencies.[32]

The carcinogen policy advocates had the greatest hopes, and the most disappointments. They thought the CPSC's official recognition of formaldehyde as a carcinogen would help pressure EPA and OSHA to strictly limit occupational exposures. In the fall and winter of 1980, an interagency task force prepared a background paper that mapped out consistent and coordinated regulatory actions for both agencies. The EPA concluded that the animal carcinogen findings, along with estimates that several million people were regularly exposed to formaldehyde, triggered a section of the Toxic Substances Control Act. This provision gives the agency six months to propose an action plan when evidence is found that a chemical may pose "a serious risk of widespread harm for cancer."[33] OSHA, under its own legislation, had similar priority categories.

In May 1981, at the end of the six-month period, staff recommendations at both agencies for an intensive regulatory effort were met head-on by the Reagan appointees newly arrived in the senior posts. They, too, saw formaldehyde as a precedent that could open the gates to the expanded regulations that they were in office to prevent. Explicit instructions were sent down the bureaucratic chain to rewrite the draft papers to fit the opposite conclusions.

The Reagan officials differed from their predecessors on each of the key assumptions about cancer policy. In their view, thresholds might well be important in human cancer, so that animal studies by themselves were inconclusive. Some epidemiological evidence of demonstrated risk to humans was also necessary.[34] At EPA this general philosophy was adapted to formaldehyde through extensive meetings with industry-sponsored scientists, who presented detailed information on the uncertainties needing resolution before regulation would be appropriate.

That an important test case had been decided was clear to both sides. A reporter for *Science* commented, "Many scientists believe that EPA could not have a clearer candidate than formaldehyde. An EPA official who declined to be quoted by name said, 'I find it hard to imagine that we could find a substance to qualify if formaldehyde doesn't.' "[35]

Defeated in the regulatory agencies, the anticarcinogen advocates have been forced to rely on the courts or on more clear-cut epidemiology, but neither recourse has been much help, compared to holding office and setting policy.[36]

THE TRIALS OF EPIDEMIOLOGY

During 1980–83, twelve new studies of workers potentially exposed to formaldehyde were reported, all of them inconclusive.[37] One review of the evidence concluded that "The epidemiological findings on formaldehyde and cancer are scant. Certainly if there were no positive laboratory findings of mutagenicity and carcinogenicity in cells and animals the human findings alone would be little cause for concern."[38] A number of factors make the epidemiology of occupational cancer a frustrating enterprise:

1. Long latency periods. It can take twenty to thirty years after the initial exposure for the cancers to show up. Two or three decades of retrospective employment data are often incomplete.
2. The need for lifetime exposure levels. Only crude estimates are available for how much formaldehyde was present thirty years ago, and which workers were actually exposed. (As most of these are mortality studies, worker interviews are not possible.)
3. Competing risks. Chemical plants typically expose workers to many substances that could be the real causal factor.
4. The "healthy worker" effect. For simplicity, cancer rates are usually compared with those of the general population, but long-term employees are generally healthier than those outside the workforce, often by 20–40 percent. This can mask elevated disease rates within the workforce.
5. Small numbers. It is hard to obtain data for a population large enough to show statistically significant variations. The largest formaldehyde study to date, for example, combined six British chemical factories with nearly 8,000 workers.[39] But only 605 of them had over five years of high exposure plus twenty years of follow-up observation. (Several other major studies are still in progress.)

The formaldehyde studies have carried two additional burdens. Because of the finding of nasal cancer in rats, the human studies have looked for respiratory tract cancers as the most likely index cases. Yet human nasal cancer is exceedingly rare (only eight cases per million per year) and *none* of the workers in the study populations have died from it.[40] On the other hand, lung cancer is all too common, and confounded by smoking histories, which are rarely available. Thus significant increases might not surface at all.

One major group of studies looked at professionals who might have been exposed to formaldehyde—anatomists, pathologists, morticians. Their overall cancer mortality, including lung cancer, is far below average, probably because of reduced smoking. (An Ontario study, though, found high levels of cirrhosis of the liver among undertakers, which was attributed to their drinking habits.)[41] In these professions, there was a very small but consistent increase in brain cancer and leukemia, however. This fragmentary evidence has aroused considerable interest and concern.

Studies of chemical plant workers have gone in the opposite direction. No excesses of brain cancer or leukemia have been detected. But the large British study mentioned earlier did find an excess of lung cancer in the highest exposure group. The authors of the study downplayed this finding, noting that the rate was above national levels, but close to the regional level for the plant's location (in the Midlands). Considerable controversy has arisen over what the appropriate comparison should be, and how far crude exposure estimates can be pressed.[42]

In late 1983, a Consensus Workshop involving industry, government, and academic scientists was sponsored by EPA in an effort to establish a common framework for formaldehyde debates. Their careful review of these studies found that conclusions in either direction were still premature:

> The data are sparse and conflicting and do not yet provide persuasive evidence of a causal relation between exposure to formaldehyde and cancer in man.
> In view of the . . . various methodological limitations of the studies, it is not possible from the available epidemiological data to exclude the possibility that formaldehyde is a human carcinogen.[43]

One additional study has only added to the controversy.[44] A Danish group started with cases of nasal cancer and worked back to their estimated occupational exposure. They found some elevated risk for those probably exposed to wood dust plus formaldehyde, but when the wood dust is controlled for, the formaldehyde risk drops below statistical significance. An unpublished Dutch study found similar results.[45]

Thus, each study and new technique carries its own built-in limitations. Though the suspicions and perplexities rise with each report, the conclusions get no firmer. Only the established partisans on each side find useful ammunition.

In many other health and safety issues, the courts have been successfully used by public interest lawyers to force regulatory action, but formaldehyde has been a disappointment here, too. The major case concerning CPSC's foam insulation ban may have been decided by some competitive jurisdiction shopping. The industry had made it clear that it would file suit to overturn the ban on the first possible day. They chose the Fifth Circuit Court of Appeals in New Orleans, which had a track record of severely questioning federal regulations. Though it supported the CPSC ban, the Public Interest Litigation Group, the legal arm of the Nader groups, had found a technical issue that would allow it to also appeal the CPSC ruling. This was intended to produce a more favorable jurisdiction for the appeal. They chose the District of Columbia Appeals Court, then much more liberal on these issues, and their suit was filed at ten seconds past noon on the same day. However, the clock in New Orleans lacked a second hand, so the court clerk there accepted the industry appeal at exactly noon, thereby sending the entire trial to the Fifth Circuit Court.[46]

This maneuvering proved important because in March 1983, the court in New Orleans did indeed overrule the CPSC. In an unusual opinion the court chose to make its own evaluation of the scientific evidence, and it found the commission's reasoning unsupported in several areas. (The court made a number of scientific errors of its own, however.) In the hands of a hostile court, the commission's attempt at statistical precision became its own undoing. The court observed that no elaborate computer model for predicting cancer deaths could be of any use if the actual data on home formaldehyde exposure were of such poor quality: "To make precise estimates, precise data are required."[47] As the whole cancer argument had been tied to the model, the court found it easy to dismiss the rest as well. Though its findings about the cancer risk were sufficient to overturn the ban, the court went on to attack the other elements of the CPSC case, advising that each deserved reversal on its own.

The CPSC protested that the judges had misunderstood the science of the matter and moved for a Supreme Court review. But even though the commission is an independent agency, it is represented in court by the Justice Department as if it were part of the executive branch. The Solicitor General sets his own priorities for appealing cases to the Supreme Court, including the case's importance as a precedent, the likelihood of success, and overall administration policy. Despite CPSC protests, he refused to appeal their case, leaving the ban permanently overruled. (By state action urea-formaldehyde remains banned in Massachusetts and Connecticut, but it is no longer on the market in any state.)

Carcinogen Politics: Round Two

OSHA DELAYS

The legal sparring over whether OSHA should strictly regulate occupational exposure to formaldehyde began in 1981 and shows no signs of resolution. Indeed, the legal maneuvering has grown ever more complex as OSHA's tactics in defense of its position have grown more subtle.

In 1981, the Reagan appointees were eager to wave the banner of deregulation on all occasions. Having decided not to regulate formaldehyde, they removed OSHA's sponsorship of a newly issued joint NIOSH /OSHA statement warning of its carcinogenic potential. They then attempted to fire Peter Infante, an OSHA scientist who had remained outspoken about formaldehyde's possible dangers. The move was prompted by an angry letter from the lawyer for the Formaldehyde Institute who demanded to know "How do you control members of the bureaucracy who seem to be operating freely within and without government?"[48] (After a congressional hearing and much press coverage, Infante remained in place.)

In January 1982, OSHA formally rejected a petition from the United Auto Workers and thirteen other unions urging emergency action on formaldehyde limits. With assistance from Nader's Public Citizen Litigation Group, the unions filed suit to force the agency to act.

From that point the pace markedly slowed. Two years passed before a federal district judge ordered that OSHA should take a new look at the evidence. By this point the new epidemiology had been reported, with data for all sides. With more experienced leadership, OSHA discovered that infinitely slow-motion regulation was as effective as deregulation, and much easier to defend in court. Again and again OSHA asked for more time to gather data and weigh the complexities of the issue. Eventually a federal appeals court warned that since "petitioners have shown the Agency's actions to be unduly delayed and its explanations for delay to be questionable . . . [We] will look with extreme displeasure on any variance from the schedule."[49] Eight months after that scolding, the court finally demanded an immediate response and threatened "necessary and appropriate action to compel compliance."[50]

But the draft regulation OSHA brought forth was completely in character.[51] It acknowledged that the existing formaldehyde standard (3 ppm) was out of date and should be replaced. But it said the agency needed still more information before deciding whether it should be regulated as a carcinogen, or merely as a respiratory irritant.

Even if it did adopt the more serious carcinogen standard, OSHA did not propose to demand much change. The agency had its own quantitative model for estimating human risks, with a different set of assumptions than used at CPSC or EPA. By its calculations workers exposed to up to 1 ppm had only a slight additional lifetime risk of cancer (between 1 and 20 per 100,000), with the risk declining sharply below that. OSHA also estimates, however, that 95 percent of the workers exposed to formaldehyde are *already* below the possible 1 ppm standard. By this reassuring analysis, if and when OSHA decides that there is a problem, the problem has already been solved.

The public interest lawyers fully realize that their only impact is to "prod an agency that is inert into *some* kind of action," rather than to see policies reversed.[52] But this suit is part of a much larger long-term effort to set the agenda for occupational health. The Nader group and the activist unions (auto and chemical workers) are old allies dating back to the establishment of OSHA. At the moment they are in court over benzene, radon, and ethylene oxide as well as formaldehyde.

HUD MAKES A RULE

It is slightly ironic that the only agency with a formaldehyde regulation now in force is HUD. Though foam insulation received the bulk of the media attention, formaldehyde levels detected in mobile homes averaged four times higher, as much as the average factory using formaldehyde.[53] Yet HUD, with no expertise in health sciences, was content to let other agencies take the lead for nearly four years. Announcements in 1979 and 1981 of future regulations led nowhere.[54]

By 1983, however, the close working relationship between the department and the mobile home industry became a force for regulation. In classic fashion, this industry has always sought federal standards to preempt state efforts. The overall regulation of mobile homes (under a 1976 law) has resulted in a national building code, explicitly overriding local initiatives. The federal code has also brought the industry laggards up to the level of the largest and most progressive producers. One of the federal standards provides for the homes to be airtight for energy efficiency. That standard combined with the urea-formaldehyde resins in the particle board used within the mobile homes led to the high emission levels.

When it became clear that Wisconsin and Minnesota intended to regulate those levels, with California possibly following, the industry reacted strongly. While the state regulations were challenged in court, a voluntary industry standard was created. (The loss of several formaldehyde liability suits also helped spur action.)[55] Then the mobile home industry urged HUD to finally issue a regulation. They testified that no level below the voluntary level was economically feasible—and HUD accepted that contention as its own rationale.

By law, HUD must get its health advice from CPSC and there were extensive consultations. But when the CPSC staff saw the regulation, they wanted the record to show that health effects had been outweighed by presumed economics.

As a result, by the time the regulation took effect, in January 1985, it was already becoming obsolete. Both the mobile home industry and their particle board suppliers (which include such major chemical firms as Georgia-Pacific) have been sensitized to the issue. They are pressing on with more stable resins that already emit much less than HUD demands. But, of course, they are doing it at their own pace.

A group of states have joined a suit in 1985 asking HUD to tighten the limits. The department has had the mixed blessing of seeing the mobile home industry and the Formaldehyde Institute join the case in defense of the current regulation.

Carcinogen Politics: Round Three

THE EPA

The EPA has also been in court. The Natural Resources Defense Council (NRDC), an environmental interest group, filed suit to force the EPA to treat formaldehyde under the Toxic Substances Control Act six-months provision.[56] The NRDC was also focused on the larger agenda, as that action-forcing section of the law had never before been invoked in court.

But it took a strong change in agency leadership to actually get the policy reviewed. The EPA Administrator Anne Burford and Interior Secretary James Watt represented the hard right of the conservative antiregulation movement. When Burford was forced to resign in 1983 amid charges of scandal and conflict of interest, twenty of her senior staff members also left, and William Ruckelshaus returned as head.[57] Ruckelshaus's mission was to restore the agency's credibility for environmental concern. In this context EPA took another look at formaldehyde and announced in June 1984 that it belonged on the high-priority list after all.

In the ensuing months a protracted tug of war has shaped the regulatory review. The "pursue the science as far as it goes" and "be credible to the public" factions keep running into the "do no more than the law demands" advocates. Thus, while accepting priority review status for formaldehyde, the EPA at the same time arranged a legal maneuver to sidestep the law's action-forcing timetable. There is no longer a deadline. (The NRDC stopped pressing its lawsuit, out of frustration. They have decided that toxic substances enforcement is to be found in congressional action to tighten the law.)

The EPA's technical staff has been writing and revising a lengthy risk assessment since the summer of 1984. As a matter of agency policy, EPA always uses quantitative models that project the highest potential risk, to err on the safe side. (Much of its clean air program would lose its rationale if anything but the highest plausible figures were used.) The EPA projections are at least 10–100 times higher than OSHA's from the same rat data. On this basis, EPA's analysis provides support for regulating garment factories at levels much lower than OSHA has proposed.

Yet, late in 1985 the legal faction won out, and the entire occupational exposure option will be left to OSHA's decision alone. That leaves EPA with the mobile home problem. HUD had explicitly deferred to EPA on the cancer problem, dealing only with respiratory effects. Here again the model could support a much tighter standard. At its current pace, EPA staff members have projected a final regulation in 1988, four years after they started work, and nine years after their predecessors first initiated a priority review.

Conclusion

This regulatory history cannot be considered an encouraging chapter in risk assessment. Without any scientific evidence as a bench mark, the agency actions reflected almost entirely their internal shifts in priorities and ideologies. For more than three years concerned consumers with foam insulation in their homes received no response to their complaints from Washington at all. Then a shift in priorities at CPSC—and the attraction of cancer control—set off a prolonged rule-making process for what was already a dying industry. At the same time, the highest levels of residential formaldehyde have consistently been found in mobile homes, but there has been no sustained interest in the problem at the Department of Housing and Urban Development, and whatever concern did arise came only at the mobile home industry's behest. The diminishing foam insulation problem remained the focus of attention because it was a convenient test case for much broader concerns, not because its danger seemed compelling.

The major long-range issue remains the control of formaldehyde exposure in factories where it is produced or used. Although EPA and OSHA have gone through a full cycle of ideological responses, the "best practice" in chemical plants such as those operated by DuPont is already to minimize exposure to levels significantly below the norms of ten years ago. Because formaldehyde is likely to remain a chemical under suspicion, the prudent elimination of unnecessary exposure will eventually become government policy as well. But how many more regulatory cycles it will take to reach that policy is difficult to predict.

Chapter 8

The Politics of Product Controversies

HARVEY M. SAPOLSKY

Personal experience is usually sufficient to allow consumers to cope with the hazards of the marketplace. Consumers learn quickly to count their change, to check package weights, and to discount the promises of sales-people. Consumers do not expect much from product warranties and are seldom disappointed. They are deluged by advertisements, but make their own choices. They either comparison shop or pay the price for convenience and full service.

But product health risks are a different sort of market hazard. Few consumers feel comfortable with the measure parts per million, let alone parts per billion. They cannot easily check what has been sprayed upon crops, dumped into the oceans, or fed to livestock. And how many know whether they should use margarine with monounsaturated or polyun-saturated fat? Personal experience affords no protection from products that may be slowly clogging arteries or producing cancerous lumps. Instead, consumers must rely upon the risk interpretations of intermediaries—scientists, government officials, reporters, policy advocates, and others—to guide their behavior.

The preceding case studies analyzed the experience of several products accused of endangering the health of consumers. Each of the controversies has unique features. The participants differ, as does the exact nature of the harm suspected. Some of the products remain for sale while others do not. And yet there is a common lesson in their separate stories.

The lesson is that intermediaries often provide consumers with misleading advice. The intermediaries' views on product risks are shaped by persistent professional and organizational interests that encourage the misrepresentation of dangers posed by products. The tendency is to exaggerate health risks, although producers of accused products certainly attempt to minimize them when they can. The net effect is to distort consumer perceptions of product hazards. Small risks become big and big risks bigger, and not proportionally: consumers are easily confused, thinking health risks are more alike than they actually are.

No one, of course, knows what are the true risks that consumers face. Lurking on pantry or bathroom shelves may be products that will someday be revealed as silent killers. But it is clear in the analysis of behavior and opinion surveys that the public has difficulty in distinguishing between the risks of cigarette smoking and failing to wear seat belts and those of consuming pesticide-laced muffins or living near a nuclear power plant.[1] The case studies explain why this is so. It is the prism of institutional interest that distorts risk perceptions.

The argument is not that consumers are intentionally misled. On the contrary, much of the distortion is the unavoidable consequence of professions and organizations competing with one another for scarce resources, in this instance the patronage of a population frightened by the recognition of its mortality. The responsiveness of institutions is to be admired. It is this responsiveness, after all, that distinguishes our society from others.[2] Every human need in America, including the compulsion to be informed of all possible threats to life, becomes a market to be served. Where one succeeds others soon follow. In the competitive din that results, it is not surprising that perspective is lost, that only the latest or the most unusual health threat is best remembered.

The Contribution of Science

Scientists, it would seem, prefer a different, more orderly world. Their most articulate representatives constantly convene at the nation's resorts and universities to discuss schemes that would substitute disinterested analyses of risks for the kaleidoscope of self-serving assessments to which consumers are currently subjected. For scientists, risk assessment is a solvable technical issue best dealt with by the scientifically sophisticated. And yet science, the dedication of its practitioners to rational analysis notwithstanding, contributes greatly to the public confusion over risk.

Each discipline works within a set of professional norms that define for its members the important research problems and the appropriate research methodologies. In the case of the health disciplines these norms also include definitions of acceptable risks. Epidemiologists, for example, describe themselves as being conservative in analyzing the public policy implications of their work. That is, they believe it is their obligation to warn society of avoidable dangers no matter how inconclusive the evidence.[3]

Science is an extremely competitive undertaking. Scientists compete within disciplines for recognition and research support. And disciplines compete within research institutions for status and budgets.

Reward in science comes with priority. The first to discover a new disease or a new cure is remembered. Those who follow are often forgotten though they provide the necessary confirmations and refinements. The first scientific study identifying a risk is likely to be considered important, the third or fourth reporting the same risk is not. The pressure for priority pushes scientists into ever more esoteric corners. If the biggest health risks have been identified, then the smaller ones become fair game. The hypotheses become bolder even if the evidence is weaker. Promotion and recognition in science depend upon laying unique claim to novel findings.

Advances in measurement technologies aid the scientist's quest by lowering the threshold of discovery. As the toxic shock syndrome case illustrates, reporting systems for vital statistics can now identify anomalies at the fifty deaths per year level. Similarly, new dangers in food and drink appear as the metric for substance identification has become parts per billion rather than parts per million. It is the small health risks and the hazards inherent in small doses that we now worry about with increasing frequency.

The public's heightened interest in health risks both compromises the scientific process and is in part the cause of the public's confusion over its risk exposure. The validity of a scientific finding is established through open debate among scientists in which hypothesis challenges hypothesis and research procedures are closely reexamined. It is a time-consuming process, but one that is intended to permit no permanent errors. In the service of an anxious public, however, the news media now broadcast the initial presentations of such professional publications as the *New England Journal of Medicine, Lancet,* and the *Journal of the American Medical Association.* Every scary finding is presented to the public, without their accompanying caveats, and well before they have been critically evaluated. The inevitably truncated interviews with the scientist authors merely increase the potential for premature hysteria. It also gives incentive to search for more disturbing findings.

Some scientists seek the publicity, convinced their work has health implications that require regulatory action. The resulting media and governmental attention confirms that they are doing important studies and that they are among the leading experts in their fields, deserving of tenure and extra rewards. A few even are willing to overstate the validity or significance of the evidence in order to increase the likelihood of action. Colleagues may point out the discrepancies, but not usually in settings where the public will notice. Instead, the exaggerations are repeated and extended in the media, gaining the status of conventional wisdom.[4] Consider the well-known "fact" that half of the motor vehicle deaths in the United States are alcohol-related. Careful analysis of the available data does not support such a conclusion. The few studies that have been done are so poorly constructed and so variable in result that they do not lend themselves to national extrapolation.[5] Yet every local reporter and state legislator now believes that alcohol causes half of the nation's motor vehicle deaths and that there is a need to control drunk driving.

The science disciplines also encourage their members to be expansive in their claims about hazards because group opportunities depend upon public perception of the relative importance of fields of enquiry. For example, environmental scientists and biomedical researchers argue over the proportion of cancer deaths due to particular causes. Environmental scientists claim that 40–80 percent is attributable to chemical hazards, whereas biomedical researchers see life-style factors as more important.[6] (Small variations in definition and assumptions can cause large variations in risk estimates.) Technical subtleties aside, this is a debate over budget shares. If a significant portion of cancer deaths is due to chemical hazards then the environmental sciences deserve to gain relative to the biomedical disciplines in the allocation of public and private research dollars. But if these hazards are of only minor importance, then it is the support for clinical investigations and prevention that should benefit. Further conflict develops between the clinicians and the preventionists over the relative merit of behavioral changes and early detection on the one hand and treatment on the other in saving lives.[7] The participants in these debates seek to buttress their claims for budgetary priorities by obtaining official endorsements of favorable estimates. The public, which may be unaware of the competition among disciplines but not unaware of their expansive claims, can easily be confused by the contradictory assertions, and may even believe that the risks are cumulative.[8]

Choosing an Interest

The objective of the Nader-type public interest groups in product risk controversies is almost invariably governmental action of some sort—the enactment of bans, the rendering of a punitive judgment, or the issuance of restrictive regulations. In contrast, the American Cancer Society, the American Heart Association, and other voluntary health associations, whenever they can be aroused by such issues, tend to favor private initiatives to control risks, usually limiting their own efforts to exhortations for individuals to abandon harmful practices. Born in the era of expansive government, the Nader groups recognize only government as the individual's savior.[9] The health associations instinctively know government to be their most formidable competitor in the collection and distribution of charity.[10]

Care in issue selection is vital to the organizational health of public interest groups because they mobilize support on the basis of issue attraction to particular audiences. In the case of most public interest groups, this means picking issues that appeal to middle- and upper-middle-class liberals and the students of elite universities.[11] Their leaders must calculate the potential for arousing public concern as well as the seriousness of the public wrong to be corrected. Some issues, attempts to limit smoking and drinking perhaps, involve decisions that are considered by potential supporters so clearly reserved for individuals to make that they cannot be expected to have much appeal. Only when they are couched in terms of the effect such behavior has on others, e.g., drunk driving or side-stream smoke, can mobilization occur, as the success of Mothers Against Drunk Driving (MADD) and Group Against Smokers' Pollution (GASP) illustrates.

Advocacy groups also search for issues that lack established champions and functions that are unique so as to avoid competition for support. While GASP concentrates on state legislation to curtail smoking, Action on Smoking and Health (ASH) works on federal regulation and judicial interventions to achieve the same end. Janet Levine and Mark Segal note in their cases (on diet and heart disease and salt and hypertension, respectively) the care with which the leadership of some public interest groups approach the decision to intervene in product controversies. The Center for Science in the Public Interest, active in both the cholesterol and the salt controversies, selected dietary-related issue categories for attention after a lengthy review by its senior staff of the available (that is, unclaimed) alternatives.

As policy advocates, public interest groups seek to sway public opinion. A prime technique is to guide media interpretations of scientific studies. Evidence supporting favored positions is gathered to be presented along with analyses stressing some, but not all, possible implications of the work. The usual setting is a news conference during which much anguish is expressed over the dangers consumers face because of a product and the irresponsibility of those who profit by continuing to sell it. Of course, industry groups use very similar tactics when attempting to defend the accused products. They bring attention to supporting scientific studies and cite the many thousands of consumers who use the product without ill effect.

What is interesting about the public interest groups' efforts is not that they are made, but rather how much credibility they are afforded. The financial and technical resources of industry are enormous in comparison to those of the public interest groups. And yet, when it comes to discussions of product risks or scientific evidence, the news media treat the groups as industry's equals, and sometimes better than that. Surely, in some corporate boardrooms it must appear that the poor have inherited the earth.

Some observers have argued that this situation is the result of the political biases of reporters and editors. There is no doubt that reporters and editors are more liberal than their employers, than employers as a class, and than the society that they seek to inform.[12] But it is also apparent that the public interest entrepreneurs, unlike most businessmen, are sensitive to the imperatives of the news media. Reports of serious risks in the use of commonly consumed products are captivating stories, certain to interest many readers. If the reports are denied, there is potential for major confrontation. Reporters are trained to provide media access to both sides of a public controversy. Their presumption in product disputes is that the affected businesses will always have media access because of their ability to advertise; thus, their job becomes one of balancing access by publishing the accusations of the public interest groups. More important, the public interest groups provide the more arresting news copy because they willingly discuss political motives and often assert their charges in personal terms. In contrast, business representatives always worried about the potential of liability suits and the impact of the controversy on product sales, tend to avoid nontechnical discussions and prefer to save their political insights for quiet lobbying efforts intended to prevent any adverse governmental actions. These are controversies in which one side usually strives to make news and the other does not.

The term "public interest group" should be used generically and not just reserved for advocacy groups. Voluntary health associations deserve inclusion under that heading because they seek to serve society's interest, in their case by fighting specific diseases and afflictions. Unlike the organizations mentioned previously, they are not mere extensions of the personalities of individual entrepreneurs. Rather, they are loose coalitions of interests concerned with the collection and distribution of charitable resources.

Until recently, most of the associations were dominated by medical researchers who used the organizations as a source of funds to expand their scientific investigations. Although each has important scientific units or affiliates, they are not entirely scientific organizations. Lay involvement is necessary in order to raise funds. Thus, much of the associations' activities have been directed toward motivating lay participation by conferring status with the distribution of associational titles. The use of status incentives is facilitated by the associations' decentralized structure, a network of state and local chapters that vastly increases the number of presidencies and board memberships to be awarded.

As I noted earlier, the voluntary health associations are chary about government because public charity can at some point be viewed as a substitute for private charity. Why give to the American Cancer Society when you already pay for the National Cancer Institute, the Veterans Administration's Department of Medicine and Surgery, and the Health Care Financing Administration which funds the Medicare and Medicaid programs? The growth of the federal government's support for health care research and services meant some accommodation was unavoidable. This was most easily accomplished in the distribution of medical research funds, as the scientists who are prominent within the associations are also among the government's leading advisors in the distribution of medical research grants. The voluntary health associations now champion government support for medical research. More difficult has been the accommodation of preventive health and medical care service interests, which have increased in importance due to governmental initiatives. Much of the internal politics of the associations is now focused on the balance between these health care service-related interests and the medical researchers Gradually, the medical researchers are losing their dominance within the associations.

Product controversies also impinge upon the associations. To the extent that discussions of product health risks increase public fears about specific diseases the associations are beneficiaries, because it is the fear of disease that moves many to donate funds. But the reverse is probably true as well. The extent to which the associations in their campaigns for contributions increase fears of disease helps exacerbate the public's fears about product risks. The product risk controversies themselves pose difficulties for the associations, moreover, as the associations are often pressured to endorse positions that could alienate important constituencies (for example, wealthy donors with connections to affected industries or segments of the medical community that are committed to a different perspective on risk). When the victims of disease disbelieve in the existence of the risk, as in the case of diabetics discounting the dangers of saccharin, the voluntary health associations' choice is clear; they must side with the victims. Similarly, when a strong consensus on risk exists (cigarettes are the best example) the associations will act if only to prevent being attacked publicly by advocacy groups for their temerity and, therefore, jeopardizing the flow of contributions.[13] Not infrequently though, the associations are caught between contending forces, scientific as well as industrial.

The Media: No Good News

In some senses our news media are extraordinarily free. There are few secrets in America; our society is too open and our media too inquisitive to permit many of them. Governmental processes are especially porous. Moreover, news is part of our entertainment and is frequently and colorfully presented.

In other senses, however, the media are quite constrained. The drive to attract and maintain large audiences, an economic necessity, limits attention to the most exciting incidents. The pressure of deadlines and inability of most audiences or reporters to comprehend technical information keeps the major stories simple, some would say superficial. The most boring television, the kind least able to hold an audience, is a so-called "talking heads" show, where experts discuss a complex topic.

The problem for the mass media is to fill vast amounts of space and time in ways that will attract the most attention. Genuine scoops are rare. Instead, the herd descends upon the same stories, marshalled by enterprising press agents or drawn by the scent of apparently threatening events. Even the media's health and science specialists have little opportunity to master the subject at hand before the words must flow.

Product risk stories are well covered; they are considered exciting, especially when they involve frightening possibilities and have an element of mystery. (Which hotel rooms harbor the Legionnaire's disease germs? Does your bottle of Tylenol contain the poison?) A finding of potential danger is quickly broadcast.[14] And then the routines of the media take hold, forced by editors and the tastes of the audience. Much attention will be paid to officials or other sources sensitive to the needs of the media for quotable, easily absorbed, and timely information. There will be interviews with handy or visible scientists, but with no attempt to distinguish among them because all experts are assumed to be unbiased (except, of course, industry-employed experts) and equally able. Film shots of the product lined up on shelves ready to strike the unknowing consumer will be shown. And invariably, there will be interviews with the victims or near victims to personalize events. "How do you feel about the tragedy?" they will be asked.

Unless new developments occur, though, the story will quickly fade. Old news is stale news; the familiar is uninteresting. Not surprisingly, advocates search for unusual twists. This year's Great American Smokeout will feature guerrilla theater; last year's had a mass burning of cigarette packs contributed by quitters. Another report that links cigarettes to lung cancer will not cause much interest, but one that reports that smoking may affect hearing or sexual performance, even if only slightly, will.

The conventions of the media make us forget some concerns and remember others. Unless a victim is especially prominent, lung cancer or another gruesome but commonplace end will not usually be reported as a cause of death. (Instead, it is a "long illness.")[15] But if our community contains a toxic shock victim, even one who does not die, we will all know it.

We judge the importance of things by coverage provided in the media. The square inches of newspaper columns devoted to a story are measured by business firms and media critics, as is the time allotted on television. And yet the media are always measuring us too, counting subscription renewals and last night's viewers, and this too becomes news. The lack of balance and depth that we see in the media is likely our own.

Government: Responsively Irresponsible

Social theorists have argued that the bureaucratization of government facilitated the development of capitalism.[16] Government by the whim of officials inhibited long-term investments. In contrast, the attributes of bureaucracy—written rules, depersonalized administration, record keeping —encourages capitalistic calculation, for it promises consistency in governmental behavior. American businessmen, working within the constraints of a regulated economy, probably think otherwise, however. In contemplating investments, they often worry most about the uncertain direction of public policy and blame the bureaucracy for their unease.

But it is our government's democratic structure, rather than its bureaucratic tendencies, that causes public policy to seem erratic. Each agency has a long-term policy agenda from which it would prefer not to deviate. Most are linked closely to a profession which has predictably rigid norms and predictably self-aggrandizing goals. That policies are contradictory within and between jurisdictions, and that they may change as does the calendar, is due to the fact that the agencies are subject to political masters who must respond to pressures in order to retain office. Berating the bureaucracy is only the politically acceptable means of expressing the frustrations we all experience when others as well as ourselves exercise cherished democratic rights.

Convinced that they must appear responsive to every public fear, officials make no effort to pursue a consistent, carefully designed policy toward health risks. Whatever the scare of the day, officials stand ready with hastily conceived congressional testimony, briefing papers, news releases, and research programs that demonstrate their commitment to protect the public. The scale of the response matches the fear, not the threat. A frightful new illness is identified—Acquired Immune Deficiency Syndrome (AIDS)—striking several thousand in a population of nearly 240,-000,000 and the secretary of the Department of Health and Human Services announces that its control is the federal government's number-one health priority.[17] Ignored in the secretary's statement is the fact that the same priority designation had been only recently used by the department to describe the unfinished efforts to control cigarette smoking, drunk driving, drug abuse, and teenage pregnancy.

If priorities are always changing, so too are the officials who proclaim them. Every change of leadership brings another shift in policy emphasis, a different personal interest requiring the attention of subordinates. One secretary of the Department of Health and Human Services is a reformed smoker wishing to spread the word; another is a long-time civil rights advocate determined to improve the health services available to minorities. One commissioner of the Food and Drug Administration seeks the mantle of consumer advocate; another wants to be known as a friend of industry. Conservatives recapture the Federal Trade Commission from liberals while an antiabortionist replaces a preventionist as Surgeon General. Only the publishers of Washington's hundreds of insider newsletters find pleasure in the never-ending parade of personal interests that is public policy.

The malleability of the policymaking process is not lost upon business interests or their opponents. No matter how much they may complain about the policy inconsistencies that result, they eagerly exert their own distorting influences upon the process. Policy conflict takes place on two dimensions. First, there is a struggle for a favorable jurisdiction, a level of government or a particular agency setting or court that will be most sympathetic at a given moment to a desired outcome. Second, there is a struggle over the extent of governmental intervention that is acceptable. Businesses usually prefer less intervention whereas their critics usually, but not always, prefer more.

In the case of product controversies, the jurisdictional struggle is especially important. For example, the proponents of beverage container deposit laws sought referenda in liberal states such as Massachusetts and Oregon, but also action in larger states such as California and New York where success, if achieved, seemed likely to force a national solution. Similarly, tobacco interests in the Congress have kept the Food and Drug Administration away from the cigarette issue because of the agency's reputation as a strict regulator. They mind not at all that the Bureau of Alcohol, Tobacco and Firearms continues to monitor the interstate transport of cigarettes because its regulatory powers have nothing to do with the product's health risks.

There are, of course, surprises. No one expected the Consumer Product Safety Commission under President Reagan to take a serious interest in the health risks of urea-formaldehyde, but it did, as Sanford Weiner reports. Apparently, the commission staff, suffering under criticism that it focused only on trivial matters, was looking for a technology-oriented issue when the hazards of urea-formaldehyde insulation came to its attention. A subsequent finding in an industry-sponsored study that formaldehyde may cause cancer brought the issue to center stage. Even some of the president's appointees on the commission recognized the specter of fear that the word *cancer* invokes among consumers, and voted for a ban on the use of the

Insulating material. Once the health risk was identified as cancer, the interests concerned with the preservation of a hard-line policy against human exposure to carcinogens were mobilized and all uses of formaldehyde, a major bonding and stiffening chemical, became targets.

Obviously, a ban is the most serious intervention government can consider. Ranked on the basis of their impact upon sales, there are five other categories of possible action. First, the government could restrict the distribution of products through such mechanisms as taxes, controls on sales, and advertising bans. Second, the government may issue consumer guidelines, publicly condemning the use of a product. Third, it may require package labels or inserts that identify the presence of ingredients previously implicated as harmful, or that note potential consequences of consumption or use. Fourth, the government could conduct an educational campaign to inform consumers of the benefits and risks of particular consumption patterns. And fifth, it could initiate research on the potential harms of a product.

Among the products we have examined in this volume, only urea-formaldehyde insulation and cyclamate-sweetened foods and drinks have been banned by the federal government. (In the case of urea-formaldehyde the ban was soon overturned in the courts.) The damning evidence in both instances was self-incriminating. The first studies reporting potential harm were reported by the producing industry's own laboratories. There are times, apparently, when industry scientists are to be believed.

As the artificial sweetener case indicates, effective bans occur only when the consumer has an alternative product available to fill immediately the precise needs met by a condemned product. According to Linda Cummings, the Food and Drug Administration's attempts to ban saccharin were frustrated by its own overly eager removal of cyclamate from the market. Banning saccharin would have left the diet industry without a viable substitute. Complaints by soft drink manufacturers and would-be dieters gained congressional support to protect saccharin even though the evidence against it was more incriminating than that against cyclamate. Cigarettes, although they have dedicated critics who wish their total elimination, lack a viable substitute for the committed smoker and thus, stand immune from a ban. Without a substitute, some continued production and sale of banned products is certain; witness the contraband traffic in alcohol during Prohibition.

Producers naturally wish to protect their sales as much as possible from impact by government. Thus, they prefer research initiatives over government-sponsored consumer education programs and these market interventions over product-labeling requirements, the issuance of consumer use guidelines, and distributional restrictions. When any such actions are proposed, they offer voluntary initiatives as alternatives. More and more firms sponsor nutrition education programs for consumers and provide nutrition information labeling on their products to head off potential actions by government. As reported in the cholesterol case, the strong reaction of ranchers to the so-called McGovern Guidelines, which had proposed reductions in the consumption of beef, indicates the great sensitivity of producers to an official suggestion that their products may be harmful.

Advocacy groups often are unaware of, and even uninterested in, the effects that particular governmental actions may have upon product sales. It seems symbolic victories are sufficient to satisfy their organizational maintenance needs. Consider the ban on radio and television advertisements for cigarettes and the warning label requirement for cigarette packages. The advertising ban reduced drastically the use of apparently effective counter advertisements warning of the dangers of cigarette smoking.[18] The warning label protects the manufacturers from product liability suits without having much impact upon consumption beyond deterring the casual smoker.[19]

Commodities: The Other Market

Agricultural lobbyists follow closely three of the health risk controversies examined here. Nearly all the tobacco leaf grown in the United States is used in the manufacture of cigarettes. Dairy farmers and cattle ranchers produce foods rich in cholesterol and saturated fat. The demand for domestic sugars is in part affected by the increased consumption of artificial sweeteners. Once farmers worried only about the weather and interest rates. Now they must worry about the vagaries of epidemiology as well.

What God and the bankers will not guarantee, the federal government attempts to do. The markets for most major agricultural commodities are government-managed to protect the income of farmers. Although the arrangements vary greatly in detail, the basic mechanisms are the same for each crop. The government sets a minimum market price through a formula acceptable to farmers and buys any production that remains unsold. Invariably, farmers find the price attractive and produce more of the commodity than can be cleared commercially. Acreage allotments, soil banks, and other programs imposed to curtail production never quite work. In determining agricultural productivity, the skills of geneticists, chemists, and soil engineers apparently exceed those of the regulators. The government ends up with jammed warehouses, including, we learn, several years supply of tobacco and more butter and cheese than anyone knows what to do with. Not all farmers are included in these schemes (ranchers and egg farmers must at least partially fend for themselves) and many, especially those working marginal land or small units, eke out a bare subsistence, but the cost to the taxpayer is impressive, exceeding $15 billion in 1985.[20]

The consumer also pays. The price of milk is much higher than it needs to be and the price of cigarettes and sugar is artificially raised as well.[21] It would seem that the government has stumbled upon an effective, if expensive, way to reduce consumer exposure to some risky products. Higher priced dairy foods and cigarettes inhibits consumption of these products. (So too for sugar but at least some teeth are saved even if more use of artificial sweeteners is encouraged.) In seeking to protect the income of farmers, agricultural price supports protect the consumer. At last, there is an unintentional policy consequence that can be said to be beneficial.

It would seem, then, that farmers need not be very concerned about the ultimate hazards caused by their harvests. What difference does it make to them that cigarettes are judged to be dangerous or that butter can kill if the government will purchase at favorable prices all the tobacco leaf and milk that fearful consumers shun? The consumption of at least certain risky products has declined without affecting agricultural commodity production.

Agricultural lobbyists worry about the future, though. The continued accumulation of unwanted stocks is considered threatening to farmers.[22] There can be no assurance that the government will long be permitted to subsidize the production of commodities that it warns consumers to avoid. Advocacy groups are already beginning to complain about the government's free distribution of nutritiously suspect commodities to the nation's poor and its promotion of tobacco purchases abroad.[23] It is not surprising therefore that commodity associations have strongly opposed attempts to have government designate agriculturally based products as health risks. Their political influence buttresses that of the product manufacturers and further inhibits the government's ability to identify the risks consumers face.

Marketing the Fear of Risks

The challenge of business is to make money in whatever economic environment prevails. The current environment may seem especially difficult for the producers of consumer goods. Consumers are sensitive to information that certain ingredients or products are health risks. Scientific studies revealing even the possibility of a product risk are quickly broadcast by the news media, which forces the issue of control onto agency and legislative agendas. As uncertain as a finding of potential risk might be, it can devastate the most carefully conceived product plan. And yet, some firms manage to make good news for themselves out of bad.

It is striking how often the outcome hinges upon the competitive initiative of one or more companies. Although the specific action varied, there is widespread commercial exploitation of consumer awareness of product risks. Governmental processes are usually lengthy and inconclusive, with the contending sides of a risk debate struggling for political advantage. At some point, a firm chooses to act, altering drastically and apparently permanently the market for an accused product.

Examples abound. In the salt case there was little need for legislative action after one company began to market salt-free baby foods because soon there was no salt in baby foods. Public awareness of the possible dangers, real or not, of a high-fat diet increased dramatically when Fleischmann began to use its "Mr. Cholesterol" television spots. Sales of tampons dropped sharply not only with the withdrawal from the market of the leading superabsorbent brand, Procter & Gamble's Rely, but also as Tampax initiated an advertising campaign heralding the return of its "original formula" tampons. Nearly every smoker now smokes a filtered cigarette, hoping for the best.

Federal regulation intended to preserve fair competition and wise legal counsel familiar with this regulation prevent firms from asserting that their brands are safer or healthier than a rival's when such claims cannot be precisely proven. But advertisements calling attention to the fact that a specific brand is free of or low in an ingredient that has been implicated as risky in news media reports of scientific studies or agency investigations convey a legally protected and very effective competitive message. Indeed, the mere labeling of a brand as being low in a particular ingredient implies that being high is somehow harmful and is likely to be enough to sway a cautious, though not necessarily well-informed, consumer.

Vague fears about product risks are prevalent among consumers, encouraged by continuing, if low level, news coverage of alarming discoveries. Firms, through repetitive advertisements, then amplify these fears for market advantage. It is these advertisements, rather than any specific news report about a scientific study or an agency inquiry, that probably provides the consumer with the health information that affects buying decisions. Simple slogans such as "Low in Salt" and "Cholesterol Free," repeated 10,000 times in attention-catching ways, surely have more impact upon consumers than a gray-jacketed government study once mentioned in a *New York Times* story and possibly available for perusal at the local library. And just to make sure, companies often reprint the *Times* headline or excerpts from the government study in advertisements for their low-sodium or cholesterol-free brands.

Firms that seize upon this strategy often are ones suffering market share declines or companies anxious to enter a new market dominated by a few established producers. The market leaders may attempt to resist through threats of suits, appeals to dealers, or heavy counteradvertising, but they reformulate their own brands or introduce new ones if consumers begin to defect in appreciable numbers. Moralizations about unethical tactics that undermine consumer confidence pass quickly when market shares erode.

Of course, firms whose products are accused of being health risks have other options. Through trade associations or individually, they may seek political redress, requesting retraction of unfavorable reports and recantations by offending officials. Or they may, directly or indirectly, marshal their own set of scientists to gather evidence that supports the product's wholesomeness while noting the flaws in contradictory work. Recall the cultivation by the manufacturers of salty foods of the "potassium hypothesis" as an explanation for hypertension.[24]

The sophistication of industry in meeting risk challenges advances. A common tactic now is to support public advocacy groups that are favorable to business, helping to create an intellectual environment opposed to regulation. For example, the American Council on Science and Health, which has a host of corporate sponsors, frequently criticizes the validity of risk claims; the American Enterprise Institute, also heavily supported by firms, reminds us of the dangers of government intervention in the marketplace. Some producers have launched major advertising campaigns to cultivate positive, healthy images for threatened products.[25] Meat, we are told, builds strength and milk helps fight osteoporosis. But the force of competition is so overwhelming that it may matter little how powerful the political connections, how correct the scientific argument, or how much counteradvertising is initiated once a rival has decided that consumer confidence in a product is vulnerable. In the case of product risks at least, reinforcing a suspicion is easier than removing one.

Promoting Prevention

Changes in diet and behavior are promoted as cost-effective policies to extend life. And yet, with the exception of cigarette smoking and perhaps the consumption of saturated fats, longevity has little to do with avoiding product risks as we know them. Life extension tables indicate that significant gains in life expectancy can occur only with a reduction in violent deaths, most especially motor vehicle accidents and homicides, which take a heavy toll of the young.[26] Heart disease and cancer are the curse of the elderly; their reduction at plausibly achievable rates would affect hundreds of thousands of people, but would not extend life greatly for very many. Your mother's advice as you left the house with the family car was correct: Don't drive fast or hang out with a rough crowd.[27]

Much broader life-style changes are advocated as part of a national preventive health strategy, perhaps because so little can be done abut violence in the society without doing violence to the values of the society. Incarcerating all teenagers might be an answer, but it is unoffered. Unafraid, the young do not heed risk advice. It is the not-so-young who wish most for the secrets of long life.

Among the major promoters of preventive health measures are health care providers, physicians, and hospital administrators, who are often asked to explain both why life is so short and why death is so expensive. Not surprisingly, they wish to identify with policies that promise more than just extending life expensively at the margin. But they have other motives as well. For some medical practitioners, prevention is a desirable alternative to what they believe is an overreliance on exotic technologies in the treatment of chronic disease. For others, it is a useful way to deflect consideration of policies that would restrict access to health care technologies either through government regulation or private initiative. And for still others, prevention is a potential new market for their services made redundant by increased competition.[28]

Politicians, too, find prevention an intriguing strategy, beset as they are by the need to control government expenditures for health care services.

Rather than face the unpleasant task of choosing between limiting access to care for government beneficiaries or restructuring the health care system and perhaps jeopardizing its ability to deliver high-quality care, they embrace the wonderfully reassuring vision of lower health care costs through life-style improvements. Apparently it matters not that those most dependent upon the government for the financing of their health care, primarily the elderly, are too decrepit to benefit from preventive measures even if these measures are as efficacious as claimed.

The life gains of prevention are very difficult to determine. Despite extensive effort, scientists still do not know how much one can achieve by reducing intake of red meat, going light on the salt, and drinking sugared as opposed to artificially sweetened drinks.[29] The benefits, if they can ever be identified, may be more psychological than life-extending.

The cost savings of prevention are not elusive, but illusionary. A thorough review of the economics of risk reduction programs shows that there is a tendency to overstate the cost-effectiveness of risk reduction because of a failure to calculate fully the costs of these programs relative to the cost of caring for unavoided disease.[30] More important, prevention proponents consistently ignore the extra societal costs incurred, especially the increased pension costs, for people who escape the snare of one life hazard before they are caught by another. Ironically, these costs are greatest for the behavior change that is statistically the most beneficial, quitting cigarette smoking.

Conclusions

Consumers surely are overwhelmed by advice on product risks. As Mark Segal points out, reports beget reports. Associations and agencies are constantly marking boundaries, asserting their independent role in particular policy domains by commenting on every developing issue. Let a potential risk be discovered and soon all possibly relevant professions, government departments, and trade groups will stake out public positions in order to protect established interests or to proclaim new ones. Add the news appeal of risk stories, the availability of advertising dollars to protect and promote products, and the ongoing flood of scientific data and there is no shortage of guidance for the concerned.

Unfortunately, most of the organizations (and the individuals) that offer advice on product risks seem driven to exaggeration. The competition for the attention of peers, donors, news editors, public officials, and customers is so intense that the irresistible temptation is to shout in order to be heard amidst the din. Careers are as much at risk in the controversies as is the public's health.

Because of the distortions that this competition produces, it is no surprise that consumers have difficulty in sorting product risks. The range of risks is likely to appear to be narrow because the importance of a single risk to most, if not all, of its champions stands independent of the potential health effects. For each of the participants in each of the disputes, including those who are supposedly defending the product, there are legitimate reasons to claim special priority for their perspective on risk. In the process, both big and small risks become larger in the minds of consumers, but not necessarily proportionately.

Behavior has changed. We smoke fewer cigarettes, consume less milk and eggs, and reach for the salt shaker less often than we once did. Per capita consumption of butter is down 37 percent since the 1960s and per capita vegetable oil consumption has nearly doubled during the same period.[31] We also worry a great deal about trivial hazards, wondering whether our preference for corn muffins or coffee is dangerous, for example. Seat belts go unbuckled while nuclear power plants are shunned. Some health gains have been made, although at the loss of much perspective.

How different Americans are because of all this. The British, for instance, want their food endorsed by the Queen and the richer the better. Not us. We want what we eat or drink to be sanctioned officially by the Surgeon General. The grammar (or the beverage for that matter) may not be the best, but a recent advertisement for RC 100 diet cola captures the current mood. It reads "RC 100 GOT NOTHING: NO SUGAR, NO CAFFEINE, NOTHING—BUT FLAVOR."

We are increasingly consumed by a fear of risks, one might argue, because we are ever more affluent and less religious. Per capita income has increased despite recessions. Attempts to buttress religion through politics notwithstanding, church participation continues to decline.[32] Prosperity gives more reason to cling to this life. Does heaven promise video cassette recorders and trips to the beach? The erosion of religious faith reduces the assurance that something else lies beyond. Although a substantial majority of Americans still claim to believe in an afterlife, few of us appear eager to test our faith.[33] Instead, we seek solace in medicine's technological advances and worry about what our daily products are doing to us.

Product liability laws protect us from obvious harms. Corporate lawyers preach caution to executives whenever they are tempted to ignore probable evidence that a firm's product maims or kills. Contingency fee arrangements ensure that even the poorest of all potential claimants receive representation. Juries increasingly offer victims or their survivors significant compensation for proven wrongs.

Administrative action can protect us from continuing harms. Federal and state agencies patrol markets with some effectiveness, seeking to identify and control the sale of unsafe products. The research investment to ferret out the dangerous is large. Despite the opposition of producers, we now have labels to read and warnings to heed. Some products are no longer available for sale; others have their use restricted.

But what can protect us against the exploitation of our fear of unknown or marginal harms? Only an awareness of the inclination of institutions to exploit our vulnerability, it would appear. We want responsive organizations and professions. Competition keeps these institutions responsive, but at a cost. Americans are traditionally distrustful of government. We need now to be as skeptical of the behavior of research institutions, public interest groups, the news media, and businesses as we are of governmental behavior.

Choice is what we cherish, the opportunity to select our companions, our politicians, our causes, our entertainment, our products. In the case of products, no less than in the others, the consequences of our choices can be disastrous. The information that we need in order to choose wisely surely is distorted, but not entirely absent. Amidst the competitive din there is guidance if we care to listen carefully. That we persist in ignoring safe pleasures or in reaching for dangerous ones is to be expected, for we cherish the institutions that always permit and, at times, even encourage such errors.

NOTES

Chapter 1

1. Susan Bartlett Foote, "Corporate Responsibility in a Changing Legal Environment," *California Management Review* 26 (Spring 1984): 217–26.

2. See, for example, Pascal James Imperato and Greg Mitchell, *Acceptable Risks* (New York: Viking, 1985); John Urquhart and Klaus Heilmann, *Risk Watch: The Odds of Life* (New York: Facts on File, 1984); "One Man's Acceptable Risk is Another Man's Accident," *Economist*, 19 January 1985, pp. 81–82; Charles Perrow, *Normal Accidents: Living with High Risk Technologies* (New York: Basic Books, 1984).

3. Committee on the Institutional Means for Assessment of Risks to Public Health, National Research Council, *Risk Assessment in the Federal Government: Managing the Process* (Washington, D.C.: National Academy Press, 1983); R. A. Albert, *Toward a More Uniform Federal Strategy for the Assessment and Regulation of Carcinogens* (Washington, D.C.: Office of Technology Assessment, 1980). Note also John D. Graham and James W. Vaupel, "Value of a Life: What Difference Does It Make?" *Risk Analysis* 1, no. 1 (1981): 89–95; William P. Ruckelshaus, "Risk, Science and Democracy," *Issues in Science and Technology* 1 (Spring 1985): 19–38; and Alvin M. Weinberg, "Science and its Limits," *Issues in Science and Technology* 2 (Fall 1985): 59–72.

4. Mary Douglas and Aaron Wildavsky, *Risk and Culture* (Berkeley: University of California Press, 1982).

5. Harvey M. Sapolsky, "Science, Voters, and the Fluoridation Controversy," *Science* 162 (October 1968): 427–33. Also Harvey M. Sapolsky, "Social Scientists' Views of a Controversy in Science," *American Journal of Clinical Nutrition* 22 (August 1969): 1397–1406.

6. Common misconceptions about life chances are discussed in Daniel S. Hamermesh and Frances W. Hamermesh, "Does Perception of Life Expectancy Reflect Knowledge?" *American Journal of Public Health* 73 (August 1983): 911–14.

7. The importance of these studies is discussed in Robert H. Miles, *Coffin Nails and Corporate Strategies* (Englewood Cliffs, N.J.: Prentice-Hall, 1982). The specific citation for the *Reader's Digest* article is L. M. Miller and J. J. Monahan, "The Facts Behind the Cigarette Controversy," *Reader's Digest* 65 (July 1954): 1–6.

8. Nicholas L. Petrakis, "Historical Milestones in Cancer Epidemiology," *Seminars in Oncology* 6 (December 1979): esp. pp. 436–37. See also Richard Doll, "The Smoking-Induced Epidemic," *Canadian Journal of Public Health* 72 (November–December 1981): 372–81; and Harvey M. Sapolsky, "Political Obstacles to the Control of Cigarette Smoking in the United States," *Journal of Health Politics, Policy and Law* 5 (Summer 1980): 277–90.

9. Aaron Wildavsky, "Doing Better and Feeling Worse: The Political Pathology of Health Policy," *Daedalus* 106 (Winter 1977): 105–23.

10. Anthony S. Wohl, *Endangered Lives: Public Health in Victorian Britain* (Cambridge, Mass.: Harvard University Press, 1983).

11. Reuel A. Stallones, "The Rise and Fall of Ischemic Heart Disease," *Scientific American* 243 (November 1980): 53–59; "Why the American Decline in Coronary Heart Disease?" Editorial, *Lancet* (26 January 1980): 183–84; Michael P. Stern, "The Recent Decline in Ischemic Heart Disease Mortality," *Annals of Internal Medicine* 91 (1979): 630–40; William B. Kannel, "The Meaning of the Downward Trend in Cardiovascular Mortality," *Journal of the American Medical Association* 247 (12 February 1982): 877–80; A. E. Harper, "Coronary Heart Disease—An Epidemic Related to Diet?" *American Journal of Clinical Nutrition* 37 (April 1983): 669–81;

Richard F. Gillum et al., "Decline in Coronary Heart Disease Mortality: Old Questions and New Facts," *American Journal of Medicine* 76 (June 1984): 1055–65; Lee Goldman and E. Francis Cook, "The Decline in Ischemic Heart Disease Mortality Rates," *Annals of Internal Medicine* 101 (December 1984): 825–36; Gina Kolata, "Heart Panel's Conclusions Questioned," *Science* 227 (4 January 1985): 40–42.

12. Devra Lee Davis et al., "Cancer Prevention: Assessing Causes, Exposures, and Recent Trends in Mortality for U.S. Males 1968–1978," *Teratogenesis, Carcinogenesis, and Mutagenesis* 2, no. 2 (1982): 105–35; D. M. Geddes et al., "Lung Cancer: Future Prospects" in W. Duncan, ed., *Lung Cancer: Recent Results in Cancer Research,* vol. 92 (Berlin: Springer-Verlag, 1984), 118–27; M. G. Marmot and M. J. Shipley, "Inequalities in Health—Specific Explanations of a General Pattern?" *Lancet* (5 May 1984): 1003–6; Edith Efron, *The Apocalyptics: Cancer and the Big Lie* (New York: Simon & Schuster, 1984).

13. E. C. Hammond, "Smoking in Relationship to the Death Rate of One Million Men and Women," *National Cancer Institute Monograph* 19 (1966): 127; Richard Doll and A. B. Hill, "Mortality in Relation to Smoking: Ten Years' Observations on Male British Doctors," *British Medical Journal,* no. 5395 (30 May 1964): 1399; Richard Doll and R. Peto, "Mortality in Relation to Smoking: Twenty Years' Observations," *British Medical Journal,* no. 6051 (December 1976): 1525–36; Richard Doll, "Smoking and Death Rates," *Journal of the American Medical Association* 251 (1 June 1984): 2854–57.

14. Philip M. Boffey, "After Years of Cancer Alarms, Progress and the Mistakes," *New York Times,* 20 March 1984, p. C1.

15. Stuart W. Leslie, *Boss Kettering: Wizard of General Motors* (New York: Columbia University Press, 1983), 149–80; Joseph Pratt, "Letting the Grandchildren Do It: Environmental Planning During the Ascent of Oil as a Major Source of Energy," *Public Historian* 2 (Summer 1980): 28–61; David Rosner and Gerald Markowitz, "A 'Gift of God'?: The Public Health Controversy over Leaded Gasoline During the 1920s," *American Journal of Public Health* 75 (April 1985): 344–53; and David Ozonoff, "One Man's Meat, Another Man's Poison: Two Chapters in the History of Public Health," *American Journal of Public Health* 75 (April 1985): 338–40.

16. Under recent Environmental Protection Agency regulation the lead content of regular (leaded) gasoline is to be reduced by 90 percent and leaded gasoline is to be totally banned by 1995, some think unwisely. Helen E. Kelly, "The Misdirected War Against Leaded Gasoline," *ACSH News & Views* (January–February 1985): 1ff. But note Lois Ember, "EPA Study Backs Cut in Lead Use in Gas," *Chemical and Engineering News* 62 (9 April 1984): 18; "EPA Calls Classic Lead Studies Flawed, But Researchers Stand Firm on Findings," *Medical World News* (12 March 1984): 59; Earl V. Anderson, "Phasing Lead Out of Gasoline: Hard Knocks for Lead Alkyls Producers," *Chemical and Engineering News* 56 (6 February 1978): 12–16.

17. Ward Worthy, "Federal Food Analysis Program Lowers Detection Limits," *Chemical and Engineering News* 61 (7 March 1983): 23–24.

18. Aaron Wildavsky, "Richer is Safer," *Public Interest* 60 (Summer 1980): 23–39.

19. Joseph A. Schumpeter, *Capitalism, Socialism and Democracy* (New York: Harper & Row, 1942).

20. Barry Bruce-Briggs, ed., *The New Class?* (New Brunswick, N.J.: Trans-Action Books, 1979).

21. Paul Slovic, Baruch Fischhoff, and Sarah Lichtenstein, "Informing People About Risk," in Louis A. Morris et al., eds., *Banbury Report 6: Product Labeling and Health Risks* (Cold Spring Harbor, N.Y.: Cold Spring Harbor Laboratory, 1980). Note also Baruch Fischhoff, "Managing Risk Perception," *Issues in Science and Technology* 2 (Fall 1985): 83–96.

22. Jack Walker, "Origins and Maintenance of Interest Groups in America," *American Political Science Review* 77 (June 1983): 390–406; "Mobilization of Political Interests," paper presented at 1983 meetings of the American Political Science Association, Chicago, Ill.

23. Mancur Olson, *The Logic of Collective Action: Public Goods and the Theory of Groups* (Cambridge, Mass.: Harvard University Press, 1965).

24. See Charles McCarry, *Citizen Nader* (New York: Saturday Review Press, 1972); Simon Lazarus, *The Genteel Populists* (New York: Holt, Rinehart & Winston, 1974); Richard C. Leone, "Public Interest Advocacy and the Regulatory Process," *Annals of the American Academy of Political and Social Sciences* 400 (March 1972): 46–58; William Symonds, "Washington in the Grip of the Green Giant," *Fortune* (4 October 1982): 137ff.

25. Peter H. Stone, "Not-So-Strange Bedfellows in Conservative Think Tanks," *Washington Post National Weekly Edition,* 17 June 1985, pp. 11–12.

26. Seymour Martin Lipset and William Schneider, *The Confidence Gap: Business, Labor, and Government in the Public Mind* (New York: Free Press, 1983); "Confidence in American Institutions," *The Gallup Report,* no. 217, October 1983. The erosion of confidence in societal institutions, Lipset has recently argued, stemmed largely from persistent economic stagnation. Ironically, the revival of the economy during Ronald Reagan's first administration has, according to polls, partially restored trust in government, and especially in the presidency, but not in business, which continues at a low ebb in confidence scores. Seymour Martin Lipset, "Feeling Better: Measuring the Nation's Confidence," *Public Opinion* 8 (April–May 1985): 6–9ff.

27. Lipset and Schneider, *Confidence Gap,* pp. 364–65.

Chapter 2

1. Susan Wagner, *Cigarette Country: Tobacco in American History and Politics* (New York: Praeger, 1971), 44–46.

2. The history of the Federal Cigarette Labeling and Advertising Act of 1965 is examined in A. Lee Fritschler, *Smoking and Politics: Policymaking and the Federal Bureaucracy* (New York: Appleton-Century-Crofts, 1969). Note also Elizabeth B. Drew, "The Quiet Victory of the Cigarette Lobby: How It Found the Best Filter Yet—Congress," *Atlantic Monthly* 216 (September 1965): 76–80; and Donald W. Garner, "The Cigarette Industry's Escape from Liability," *Business and Society Review* 33 (Spring 1980): 22–25.

3. See Kenneth Michael Friedman, *Public Policy and the Smoking-Health Controversy* (Lexington, Mass.: Lexington Books, 1975); James L. Hamilton, "The Demand for Cigarettes: Advertising, the Health Scare, and the Cigarette Advertising Ban," *Review of Economics and Statistics* (November 1972): 401–11; Kenneth E. Warner, "The Effects of the Anti-Smoking Campaign on Cigarette Consumption," *American Journal of Public Health* 617 (July 1977): 645–50.

4. The basic work on smoking demographics is by Jeffrey Harris. See his "Cigarette Smoking Among Successive Birth Cohorts of Men and Women in the United States During 1900–80," *Journal of the National Cancer Institute* 71 (September 1983): 473–79 and citations in note 8, below.

5. Kenneth E. Warner, "Cigarette Smoking in the 1970s: The Impact of the Anti-Smoking Campaign on Consumption," *Science* 211 (13 February 1981): 729–31. See also Kenneth E. Warner and Hillary A. Murt, "Premature Deaths Avoided by the Anti-Smoking Campaign," *American Journal of Public Health* 73 (June 1983): 672–78.

6. Estimates of the total number of smokers in 1980 range from 52.4 million offered by the federal government to the industry's 56 million.

7. G. M. Smith et al., "Licit and Illicit Substance Use by Adolescents," in *Analysis of Actual Versus Perceived Risks* (New York: Plenum, 1983), 183–201; Harry A. Lando, "Data Collection and Questionnaire Design: Smoking Cessation in Adults," in J. Grabowski and C. S. Bell, eds., *Measurement in the Analysis and Treatment of Smoking Behavior,* National Institute on Drug Abuse Research Monograph 48 (Rockville, Md.: Public Health Service, 1983), 74–89.

8. Jeffrey E. Harris, "Cigarette Smoking in the United States, 1950–1978," in *Smoking and Health,* Report of the Surgeon General, Washington, D.C.: U.S. Department of Health, Education, and Welfare, January 1979, pp. A1–A29; Jeffrey E. Harris, "Patterns of Cigarette Smoking," in *The Health Consequences of Smoking for Women,* Report of the Surgeon General, Washington, D.C.: U.S. Department of Health and Human Services, January 1980, pp. 15–42.

9. Judith D. Miller et al., *National Survey on Drug Abuse: Main Findings 1982* (Rockville, Md.: National Institute on Drug Abuse, 1983), table 58, p. 79; Ian Steele, "WHO Survey Reveals More Youths, Especially Girls, Are Smoking," *Tobacco International* 184 (6 August 1982): 6–8.

10. R. Masironi and L. Roy, "Smoking and Youth: A Special Report," *World Smoking and Health* 8 (Spring 1983): 27–31.

11. "Gallup Smoking Audit," *The Gallup Report,* no. 190, 30 August 1981.

12. Ibid.; note also Roper Organization, *A Study of Public Attitudes Toward Cigarette Smoking and the Tobacco Industry in 1978,* vol. 1, May 1978. Released by the Federal Trade Commission.

13. "Gallup Smoking Audit"; Warner and Murt, "Premature Deaths"; M. L. Meyers et al., *Staff Report on the Cigarette Advertising Investigation* (Washington, D.C., Federal Trade Commission, May 1981); Office of Population Censuses and Surveys, *Smoking Attitudes and Behavior* (London: Her Majesty's Stationery Office, 1983).

14. Paul Cameron and Judy Boehmer, "And Coffee Too," *International Journal of Addictions* 17, no. 3 (1982): 569–74.

15. Roper Organization, *Study of Public Attitudes Toward Cigarette Smoking;* "Survey: Smokers Agree to Support NonSmokers," *Baltimore Sun,* 12 October 1983, cited in *Infolog* (Tobacco Institute) 83 (7 November 1983).

16. "Projecting a Professional Image," *American Way* (August 1983): 10, citing data reported in *Cox Report on the American Corporation* (New York: Delacorte, 1983).

17. Tobacco Institute, "Tobacco Industry Profile 1985," Washington, D.C., n.d. Tobacco may actually be the seventh most important crop, but no one knows the precise production and sales figures for marijuana.

18. Kenneth E. Warner, "The Economics of Smoking: Dollars and Sense," *New York Journal of Medicine* 83 (December 1983): 1273.

19. Charles Kellogg Mann, *Tobacco: The Ants and the Elephants* (Salt Lake City: Olympus, 1975), 27–52; and Economic Research Service, *Potential Mechanization in the Flue-Cured Tobacco Industry,* Agricultural Economic Report no. 169 (Washington, D.C.: Department of Agriculture, n.d.).

20. See Agriculture Marketing Service, *Tobacco in the United States* (Washington, D.C.: Department of Agriculture, 1973); Robert H. Miller, "Tobacco Price Support Programs," *Tobacco Situation* (June 1975): 33–36.

21. A thorough discussion of the support program's origins, features, and problems is contained in part I of William R. Finger, ed., *The Tobacco Industry in Transition* (Lexington, Mass.: Heath, 1981).

22. Johnny D. Braden, "Tobacco Acreage and Yields—Trends and Prospects," *Tobacco Situation* TS-135 (USDA, March 1971): 32–37; Verner N. Grise, "Recent Trends in U.S. Tobacco Farming," *Tobacco Outlook and Situation Report* TS-192 (USDA, September 1985): 38–40.

23. Elizabeth Wehr, "Quota Costs, Tobacco Levies Growing," *Congressional Quarterly* (11 June 1983): 1161.

24. Charles Holden, "One Hand Lights Up While the Other Wags a Finger," *Science* (29 July 1977): 443; "Tobacco Under a Cloud," *Economist,* 6 August 1977, pp. 27–28.

25. Richard Hall, "U.S. Tobacco Program Changes Will Help Growers in the 1980s," *Tobacco International* (15 October 1982): 8–9; Roy B. Davis, Jr., "The Flue-Cured Tobacco Program, from a Producer's View," *Tobacco International* (18 February 1983): 7.

26. Hugh Kiger, "Sobering Elements in the Leaf Export Outlook," *World Tobacco* (October 1982): 85–89.

27. "Quality and Market Share Highlight U.S. Gatherings," *Tobacco Reporter* (May 1983): 60.

28. See table 29 in "Estimated Leaf Used for Cigarettes by Kind of Tobacco, 1950–82," *Tobacco Outlook and Situation* (September 1983): 24. The emphasis on low-tar cigarettes has caused a shift away from flue-cured tobacco toward burley, thus further weakening demand for flue-cured tobacco and depreciating the value of flue-cured stocks. In 1983, for the first time in U.S. history, tobacco imports exceeded exports in volume though the value of the exports remained higher than that of the imported crop.

29. Ibid.; note also Richard Hall, "Marketing: Keystone of the Future United States Tobacco Policy," *Tobacco International* (1 April 1983): 7–10; and Verner N. Grise, "U.S. Cigarette Consumption: Past, Present, and Future," *Tobacco International* (18 February 1983): 20.

30. The total market surplus exceeds three years' supply when trade stocks are counted. Elizabeth Wehr, " 'Tobacco Boys' Rally Troops to Repel Anticipated Attacks by Health, Price Support Foes," *Congressional Quarterly* (11 June 1983): 1158. See also Robert H. Miller, "Prospects for U.S. Flue-Cured Under the No Net Cost Program," *Tobacco International* (1 April 1983): 19–25; Keith Schneider, "Tobacco Industry Wilting," *Boston Globe,* 31 July 1983.

31. Elizabeth Wehr, "Complex Tobacco Measures May Face Delays," *Congressional Quarterly*

(9 July 1983): 1415; Elizabeth Wehr, "Bill to Cut Dairy Production Faces Possible Reagan Veto," *Congressional Quarterly* (26 November 1983): 2493.

32. Hugh Kiger, "The Dangers of Protectionism," *Tobacco Reporter* (April 1984): 52; "The Tobacco Lobby's Hot Potato," *Washington Post National Weekly Edition,* 4 June 1984, p. 18; "A Fork in Tobacco Road," *Economist,* 30 November 1985, pp. 25–29.

33. "Tobacco Price Props Come Under Criticism Even by the Growers," *Wall Street Journal,* 1 April 1985, p. 1.

34. "Deficit-Reduction Bill's Tortuous Journey Ends," *Congressional Quarterly* (5 April 1986): 764–66; Matt Wood, "New U.S. Program Approved," *Tobacco Reporter* (April 1986): 4; John Chivat, "Tobacco in Washington: An Interview with Congressman Charlie Rose," *Tobacco International* (1 April 1983): 50; "Some Frustrated Burley Farmers Question U.S. Price-Support System," *The (Louisville) Courier-Journal,* 27 November 1983; "Tobacco Farmers Glad to See Program Die," *Atlanta Journal and Constitution,* 20 November 1983, p. 6A; Timothy B. Clark, "Tax and Price Support Issues Causing Tobacco Interests' Solidarity to Crack," *National Journal,* 26 October 1985, pp. 2423–27.

35. The effects of an elimination of the price-support system are examined in Chris Bickers, "Tobacco Tomorrow: U.S. Leaf Production," *Tobacco Reporter* (April 1984): 46–50.

36. Richard B. Tennant, "The Cigarette Industry," in Walter Adams, ed., *The Structure of American Industry,* 4th ed. (New York: Macmillan, 1971), 216–55, esp. 220–23.

37. Gideon Doron, *The Smoking Paradox* (Cambridge, Mass.: Abt Books, 1979), chap. 2.

38. Tennant, "The Cigarette Industry," 223–27.

39. For more on the role advertising has played in the history of the industry, see Wagner, *Cigarette Country,* 59–62.

40. Joseph Cullman, "A Responsible Tobacco Industry Prevails," *United States Tobacco Journal* (22 June 1983): 11.

41. John Maxwell, Jr., "Top 20 World Cigarette Market Leaders," Lehman Brothers Kuhn Loeb Research, 16 November 1982; "Cigarette Makers Have Met the Bad News Head-on," *Business Week* (17 December 1984): 56–57; "Cigaret Sales Smolder Below 600 Billion," *Advertising Age* (18 November 1985): 61.

42. Arthur M. Louis, "The $150-Million Cigarette," *Fortune* 102 (17 November 1980): 121–25.

43. Stephen Taub, "The Hazards in Cigarette Stocks," *Financial World* (28 February 1983): 24–27; Michael C. Jensen, "Tobacco: A Coping Industry," *New York Times,* 19 February 1978, sec. 3, p. 1; Bradley Graham, "Tobacco Companies Fight Back," *Washington Post,* 5 November 1978, p. K-1; and "Philip Morris, The Hot Hands in Cigarettes," *Business Week* (6 December 1976): 60–64.

44. "Tobacco Industry," *Wall Street Transcript* (13 January 1983): 70, 204ff.

45. Gwen Kinkead, "Philip Morris Undiversifies," *Fortune* (29 June 1981): 62–65.

46. "China, Reynolds Preparing to Fire Up New Cigarette," *Asian Wall Street Journal Weekly,* 25 April 1983, p. 12. See also "Chinese Cigarettes by the 1,000,000,000," *World Tobacco* (March 1983): 67–71; D. Rizio, "RJR and China Enter into New Cooperation," *Tabak Journal International* (August 1984): 340, 342.

47. "Japan Expands its List of Tariffs to be Reduced," *Wall Street Journal,* 27 December 1982, p. 1; Louis Kraar, "Japan Blows Smoke About U.S. Cigarettes," *Fortune* (21 February 1983): 99–100ff. About half of the world's production of tobacco products is controlled by state monopolies. See T. Shien, "Japan: End of the Monopoly Already Bringing Far-Reaching Effects," *Tobacco International* (7 September 1984): 14–16ff.

48. "Future Retail Threat to Tobacco Goods Branding?" *World Tobacco* (October 1982): 57–60; "Liggett Group Goes Generic at Home and Abroad," *Tobacco International* (1 April 1983): 71–73; "R. J. Reynolds Plans 25–Cigarette Packs, Signalling a Possible Price-Cutting War," *Wall Street Journal,* 25 May 1983, p. 7; "Reynolds vs. Philip Morris: Dramatic Moves in Different Directions," *Business Week* (11 July 1983): 101–4.

49. "Barclay Back to Square 1," *Advertising Age* (18 April 1983): 1; "Liggett Defends B&W," *Advertising Age* (11 July 1983): 3; "B&W Loses Barclay 1 mg Claim," *Advertising Age* (17 October 1983): 1.

50. "The Ultra-low-tar Gimmick," *Consumer Reports* (January 1983): 25ff; William Bennett, "Where There's Smoke—The Lowdown on Low-Tar and Other Hazardous Hypes," *The Boston*

Phoenix, 28 December 1982, sec. 2, pp. 7–8; "Cigarette Report: Low Tar in Command," *Tobacco International* (1 April 1983): 68–70.

51. "Tobacco Tax Receipts Total $6.7 Billion in FY 82," *Tobacco Observer* (February 1983): 3; "Congress Approves Bill to Raise $98.3 Billion in Taxes," *New York Times,* 20 August 1982, p. 1; "The Long, Hot Summer of '83," *Tobacco Reporter* (November 1983): 58–63; "Cigarettes Produced $9.3 Billion in Tax Revenues in Fiscal 1984," *U.S. Tobacco and Candy Journal* (28 March/17 April 1985): 3.

52. "Cigarette-tax Extension Sought," *The (Louisville) Courier-Journal,* 26 October 1983, p. 1. "Cigarette Ad Ban and Tax Increase Urged," *Washington Post,* 13 November 1985, p. 6.

53. "Why the Cigarette Makers are so Nervous," *Business Week* (20 December 1982): 55.

54. Kenneth E. Warner, "The Federal Cigarette Excise Tax," March 1981, background paper for the National Conference on Smoking and Health, New York City, November 1981; Eugene M. Lewit, Douglas Coate, and Michael Grossman, "The Effects of Government Regulation on Teenage Smoking," *Journal of Law and Economics* 24 (December 1981): 545–69; Jeffrey E. Harris, "Increasing the Federal Excise Tax on Cigarettes," Editorial, *Journal of Health Economics* 1, no. 2 (1982): 117–20.

55. "Cigarette Contraband," *Economist,* 11 March 1978, p. 42; "Organized Crime is Linked to Cigarette Smuggling," *New York Times,* 22 October 1977, p. 8. See also Kenneth E. Warner, "Regional Differences in State Legislation on Cigarette Smoking," *Texas Business Review* 56 (January–February 1982): 27–29.

56. "Congress Votes Penalties for Cigarette Bootlegging," *Congressional Quarterly Weekly Report* (21 October 1978): 3057.

57. "Bootleg Cigarettes," Editorial, *Washington Post,* 17 October 1978; "Wants Proposed 80% Cut Restored to ATF's Budget," *U.S. Tobacco and Candy Journal* (30 May–15 June 1985): 9.

58. Bob Lee, "How Can Your Patients Quit?" *Medical World News,* (23 May 1983): 43–63. See also "A Cigarette Study the Industry Likes," *Business Week* 201 (8 August 1978): 33–34; and Jean L. Marx, "Health Officials Fire Up Over 'Tolerable' Cigarettes," *Science* (1 September 1978): 795–98.

59. The use of evidence in the political controversy surrounding smoking is examined in Stanley Joel Reiser, "Smoking and Health: The Congress and Causality," in S. A. Lakoff, ed., *Knowledge and Power* (New York: Free Press, 1966), 293–311. Note also Theodore D. Sterling, "The Statistician vis-à-vis Issues of Public Health," *American Statistician* 27 (December 1973): 212–17; and Richard Doll, "Smoking and Death Rates," *Journal of the American Medical Association* 251 (1 June 1984): 2854–57.

60. See P. R. J. Burch, "The Surgeon General's 'Epidemiologic Criteria for Causality': A Critique," *Journal of Chronic Diseases* 36, no. 12 (1983): 821–36.

61. See Michael C. Jensen, "Tobacco: A Potent Lobby," *New York Times,* 14 February 1978, sec. 3, p. 1; Bob Dart, "Tobacco Institute Fights for an Industry Under Fire," *Atlanta Journal and Constitution,* 11 September 1983; G. E. Markle and R. J. Troyer, "Smoke Gets in Your Eyes: Cigarette Smoking as Deviant Behavior," *Social Problems* 26 (1979): 611–25; "Altered Perspective," *Wall Street Journal,* 5 November 1982, p. 1.

62. James E. Roper, "The Man Behind the Ban on Cigarette Commercials," *Reader's Digest* (March 1971): 213–18.

63. The American Heart Association, the American Cancer Society, and the American Lung Association have formed a coalition to combat smoking. See Philip M. Boffey, "Health Groups Assail Cigarette Ads," *New York Times,* 17 February 1984, p. A17.

64. James Q. Wilson, *Political Organizations* (New York: Basic Books, 1973).

65. Television heroes may drink, but they almost never smoke. Warren Breed and James R. De Foe, "Drinking and Smoking on Television, 1950–1982," *Journal of Public Health Policy* 5 (June 1984): 257–70. But times may be changing. See Jon Cruz and Lawrence Wallack, "Trends in Tobacco Use on Television," *American Journal of Public Health* 76 (June 1986): 698–99.

66. The catalog of government antismoking programs is contained in "Smoking Control," *Public Health Reports* 98 (September–October 1983): 107–16.

67. C. E. Koop, Julia M. Jones Lecture delivered at annual meeting of the American Lung Association, Miami Beach, Fl., 20 May 1984. Note also Judith K. Ockene, "Toward a Smoke-Free Society," *American Journal of Public Health* 74 (November 1984): 1198–1200; "Voluntary

Agencies Working to Achieve Smoke-Free Society by the Year 2000," *Medical World News* (25 June 1984): 63.

68. R. J. Reynolds and Philip Morris are the nation's fourth and fifth largest advertisers. Their combined expenditures on tobacco advertisements exceeded $850 million in 1982. The total for all the major tobacco firms is approximately $1.2 billion; no other product group has reached the $1 billion mark. "100 Leaders Parry Recession with Heavy Spending," *Advertising Age* 54 (8 September 1983): sec. 1, p. 68.

69. Markle and Troyer, "Smoke Gets in Your Eyes". Note the acceptance of tobacco companies as corporate sponsors for public television. "RJR new PBS Underwriter," *Advertising Age* 54 (29 August 1983): sec. 1, p. 20.

70. According to one poll, 75 percent of the public thinks that side-stream smoke is harmful, "Poll Finds Public Assertive on Health," *New York Times,* 2 May 1985. The belief is so deeply held that some think there are two antitobacco movements, one against cigarettes and the other against smokers' pollution. Ronald E. Shor et al., "The Distinction Between the Antismoking and Nonsmoking Movements," *Journal of Psychology* 106 (1980): 129–46. Some of the evidence of the health effects of side-stream smoke is reviewed in Pelayo Correa et al., "Passive Smoking and Lung Cancer," *Lancet* (10 September 1983): 905–7; see also T. Hirayama, "Nonsmoking Wives of Heavy Smokers Have Higher Risk of Cancer: A Study in Japan," *British Medical Journal* 282 (1981): 183–85, and 283 (1981): 1466; and L. Garfinkel, "Time Trends in Lung Cancer Among Non-Smokers and a Note on Passive Smoking," *Journal of the National Cancer Institute* 66 (1981): 1061–66. Note also "The Murky Hazards of Secondhand Smoke," *Consumer Reports* (February 1985): 13–16; and "Passive Smoking Risk Overestimated?" *Medical World News* (11 November 1985): 68.

71. Christopher Cobey, "The Resurgence and Validity of Antismoking Legislation," *Davis Law Review* 7 (1974): 167–95; Warner, "Regional Differences in State Legislation on Cigarette Smoking"; David Bauman, "Smoking Bans Draw Support," *USA Today,* 24 April 1985.

72. Harvey M. Sapolsky, "The Political Obstacles to the Control of Cigarette Smoking in the United States," *Journal of Health Politics, Policy and Law* 5 (Summer 1980): 277–90; W. Lance Bennett, *Public Opinion in American Politics* (New York: Harcourt Brace Jovanovich, 1980), 20–23.

73. Steve Taravella, "Smoking Rule Doesn't Worry Employers in San Francisco," *Business Insurance* (13 June 1983): 2; see also Jonathan E. Fielding and Lester Breslow, "Health Promotion Programs Sponsored by California Employers," *American Journal of Public Health* 73 (May 1983): 538–42; Marvin M. Kristein, "How Much Can Business Expect to Profit from Smoking Cessation?" *Preventive Medicine* 12 (1983): 358–81; Thomas Stachnik and Bertram Stoffelmayer, "Worksite Smoking Cessation Programs: A Potential for National Impact," *American Journal of Public Health* 73 (December 1983): 1395–96. See also Diana Chapman Walsh, "Corporate Smoking Policies: A Review and an Analysis," Boston University Health Policy Institute, May 1983; and Carol Cain, "No Smoking: Employers Say Restrictions Can Cut Costs," *Business Insurance* (17 January 1983): 3ff. See also Marvin Kristein, "Wanted: Smoking Policies for the Workplace," *Business and Health* (November 1984): 14–17; Jonathan E. Fielding, "Health Promotion and Disease Prevention," *Annual Review of Public Health* 5 (1984): 237–65.

74. "Office Smokers Feel the Heat," *Business Week* (29 November 1983): 102. See also William L. Weis, "Giving Smokers Notice," *Management World* 13 (July 1984): 41, 44; and Milt Freudenheim, "Smoking Toll Spurring Curbs," *New York Times,* 1 October 1985, p. D2. Not surprisingly, smoking has also become grounds for divorce.

75. The American Lung Association sponsored a series of antismoking advertisements featuring Brooke Shields, the well-known teenage actress and jeans model, after they had been disclaimed by the federal Office of Smoking and Health because of tobacco industry criticism of the selection of Ms. Shields on grounds that her sensual jeans advertisements made her an inappropriate role model for teenagers. Recent Lung Association advertisements use a black teenager who is warned not to be a cigarette-smoking "Dragon Lady" if she values her social life.

76. James Repace, "Risks of Passive Smoking," Center for Philosophy and Public Policy Working Paper RC-4, College Park, Md., 1983; Shirley Hobbs Scheibla, "Where There's Smoke There's Certain to be a Lawsuit," *Barron's,* 5 January 1985; Constance Holden, "ADAMHA Funding Pressed," *Science* 227 (11 January 1985): 147–49; Ed Bean, "Cigarettes and Cancer: Lawyers Gear Up to Battle Tobacco Firms," *Wall Street Journal,* 29 April 1985; John

Crudele, "Market Place: Conflicting Tobacco Views," *New York Times,* 2 May 1985; Stephen Chapman, "Trying to Pass the Butt . . . Smokers and Liability," *Washington Times,* 16 May 1985; "Tobacco Companies Are In For The Fight Of Their Lives," *Business Week* (11 November 1985).

77. Kenneth E. Warner, "An Ounce of Prevention, a Pound of Promotion," *Medical Journal of Australia* 70th year, vol. 1, no. 5 (5 March 1983): 207–10; Ken Cummins, "The Cigarette Makers: How They Get Away With It," *Washington Monthly* 16 (April 1984): 14–24; Elizabeth M. Whelan, "When Newsweek and Time Filtered Cigarette Copy," *Wall Street Journal,* 1 November 1984; Kenneth E. Warner, "Cigarette Advertising and Media Coverage of Smoking and Health," *New England Journal of Medicine* 312 (7 February 1985): 384–88; "Federal Panel Would Ban All Cigarette Advertising," *Washington Post,* 24 February 1985; George Silver, "The Smoking Gun," Letter to the Editor, *Lancet* (7 March 1985): 509; D. Owen, "The Cigarette Companies: How They Get Away With Murder, Part II," *Washington Monthly* 17 (March 1985): 48–54; "Harvard Dean Seeks Curb on Tobacco Ads," *Boston Globe,* 27 April 1985.

78. "Anti-Smoking Pioneer Continues War on Tobacco as Leader of ASH," *New York Tribune,* 14 January 1985.

79. Nonprofit smoking cessation efforts are described in Office of Smoking and Health, *State and Local Programs on Smoking and Health* (Rockville, Md.: Department of Health and Human Services, n.d.); also see Lee, "How Can Your Patients Quit?" Terry F. Perchacek, "An Overview of Smoking Behavior and its Modification," in Norman A. Krasnegor, ed., *Behavioral Analysis and Treatment of Substance Abuse* (Rockville, Md.: Public Health Service, June 1979); "Modification of Smoking Behavior," in *Smoking and Health,* Report to the Surgeon General (Rockville, Md.: Department of Health, Education, and Welfare, Public Health Service, 1979), chap. 19; Simon Chapman, "Stop-Smoking Clinics: A Case for Their Abandonment," *Lancet* (20 April 1985): 918–20.

80. As an example of the interest in prevention see Sallie J. Drury, "Wellness Can Be the Solution to Rising Health Care Costs," *Business Insurance* (21 November 1983): 25–28; also note "FAH Backs Alcohol, Tobacco Taxes to Bail Out Medicare," *Modern Healthcare* (September 1983): 63; and "Advisers Back Alcohol, Tobacco Tax Boost," *Washington Post,* 5 November 1983, p. 1. For an excellent comprehensive review of the prevention strategy see Robert Evans, "A Retrospective on the 'New Perspective,' " *Journal of Health Politics, Policy and Law* 7 (Summer 1982): 325–44.

81. Dr. Elizabeth Whelan, the director of the American Council on Smoking and Health (ACSH), and industry-sponsored policy research group, often speaks out on the confusion caused by government claims about dietary, environmental, and smoking hazards. See her editorial "Uncle Sam, M.D.," *ACSH News & Views* 4, (January–February 1983): 4.

82. A description of the activities of one of the leading marketers of antismoking and smoker aid products is found in Pat Sloan, "Jeffrey Martin Wants More Brands to Promote," *Advertising Age* (5 September 1983): 4.

83. Jeff Franks, "No Smoke Gets in Your Eyes," *Venture* 7 (April 1985): 92.

84. The Southern Baptist Convention has condemned tobacco and the North Carolina Council of Churches is debating the issue. "Tobacco and Morality," *Atlanta Constitution,* 5 April 1984, p. 1.

85. "Time to Kick the Habit—Or the Tobacco Companies," *Economist,* 30 November 1985, p. 25.

Chapter 3

1. FNB, *Toward Healthful Diets* (Washington, D.C.: National Academy of Sciences, 1980).

2. Jane E. Brody, "Panel Reports Healthy Americans Need Not Cut Intake of Cholesterol: Nutrition Board Challenges Notion That Such Dietary Change Could Prevent Coronary Heart Disease," *New York Times,* 28 May 1980, p. 1; Editorial, "Cholesterol Does Count," *Washington Post,* 2 June 1980, p. 1; Editorial, "A Confusing Diet of Fact," *New York Times,* 3 June 1980, p. A18; Editorial, "The Scientific Method," *Wall Street Journal,* 4 June 1980, p. 24; Robert MacNeil, Dr. DeWitt Goodman, Jim Lehrer, Dr. Wayne Calloway, Dr. Robert Olson, "The Cholesterol Question," "The MacNeil/Lehrer Report," 28 May 1980; "National Academy of

Sciences Report on Healthful Diets," Hearings Before the Subcommittee on Domestic Marketing, Consumer Relations, and Nutrition of the Committee on Agriculture, House of Representatives, 96th Congress, 2d Session, 18 and 19 June 1980; "Dietary Guidelines for Americans," Senate Hearings Before the Subcommittee on Agriculture, Rural Development, and Related Agencies, Committee on Appropriations, 96th Congress, 2d Session; "The Nutritionist Who Prepared the Pro-Cholesterol Report Defends It Against Critics," *People* (16 June 1980): 58–64.

3. "Research Council Group Warns Against Diet Panaceas," *National Academy of Sciences Press Release* (distributed 27 May 1980 for release morning of Wednesday 28 May 1980); Brody, "Panel Reports."

4. "Chicago Heart Association Press Conference" (30 May 1980), edited transcript, p. 1.

5. For descriptive accounts of the reaction to the FNB report see "Food Board's Fat Report Hits Fire," *Science* 209 (11 July 1980): 248–50; "Academy on Griddle for Fat's-Okay Report," *Science and Government Report* 10 (15 June 1980): 1–2; "Academy President Assailed for Diet Report," *Science and Government Report* 10 (1 July 1980): 1–3. Professional and government reaction can be found in the Senate and House hearings cited in note 2, above.

6. "Food Biz Linked to Diet Report," *New York Daily News,* 1 June 1980, p. 1.

7. See Jean L. Marx and Gina Bari Kolata, *Combating the # 1 Killer: The Science Report on Heart Disease* (Washington, D.C.: American Association for the Advancement of Science, 1978) for a good nontechnical explanation of heart disease, causes, and research.

8. There are many reviews of the diet–heart disease link. A recent comprehensive review can be found in D. M. Berwick, S. Cretin, and E. B. Keeler, "Cholesterol, Heart Disease, and Policy," in *Cholesterol, Children and Heart Disease* (New York: Oxford University Press, 1980), chap. 2.

9. Letitia Brewster and Michael F. Jacobson, *The Changing American Diet* (Washington, D.C.: Center for Science in the Public Interest, 1978); USDA, Economic Research Service, *Food Consumption, Prices, and Expenditures 1960–1980* (Washington, D.C.: USDA Statistical Bulletin no. 672, 1981).

10. J. Bruce Bullock, "Consumer Preference Structure For Meats: Has It Shifted?" Journal Paper no. J3853, Oklahoma Agricultural Experiment Station, Stillwater, Okla.; Rueben C. Buse and Aliza Flieschner, "Trends in U.S. Food Consumption," *Economic Issues* no. 67, Department of Agricultural Economics, College of Agricultural and Life Sciences, University of Wisconsin-Madison, April 1982; David Smallwood, James Blaylock, and James Zellner, "Factors Influencing Food Choice," *National Food Review* (Washington, D.C.: USDA, Economics and Statistics Service, Spring 1981), 20.

11. Food and Drug Administration (FDA), Department of Health, Education, and Welfare (DHEW), *FDA Consumer Nutrition Knowledge Survey, Report I, 1973–74* (Washington, D.C.: FDA, DHEW Publication no. [FDA] 76-2058, 1976); FDA, DHEW, *FDA Consumer Nutrition Knowledge Survey, Report II, 1975* (Washington, D.C.: FDA, DHEW Publication no. [FDA] 76-2059, 1976); *A Summary Report on U.S. Consumers' Knowledge, Attitudes and Practices About Nutrition—1980, Issue: Fat/Cholesterol* (Minneapolis: General Mills, 1980), 16; Judy Lea Jones and Jon Weimer, "Perspective on Health-Related Food Choices," *1981 Agricultural Outlook Conference, Session 26* (Washington, D.C.: November 1980), 2; Judy Jones and Jon Weimer, "A Survey of Health-Related Food Choices," *National Food Review* (Washington, D.C.: USDA, Economics and Statistics Service, Fall 1980), 17; Judy Jones Putnam and Jon Weimer, "Nutrition Information—Consumers' Views," *National Food Review* (Washington, D.C.: USDA, Economics and Statistics Service, Spring 1981), 18–20.

12. A summary of the findings of those hearings can be found in DHEW-FDA, USDA-Food Safety and Quality Service, Federal Trade Commission-Bureau of Consumer Protection, "Food Labeling: Tentative Positions of Agencies," *Federal Register* 44 (21 December 1979), Proposed Rules, pp. 75990–76020.

13. Henry C. McGill, Jr., has written a review of the scientific evidence that includes a good historical account of the scientific developments: "The Relationship of Dietary Cholesterol to Serum Cholesterol Concentration and to Atherosclerosis in Man," in Symposium: Report of the Task Force on the Evidence Relating Six Dietary Factors to the Nation's Health, *American Journal of Clinical Nutrition* 32 (December 1979; suppl.): 2664–2703.

14. AHA, Central Committee for Medical and Community Program, "Dietary Fat and Its

Relation to Heart Attacks and Strokes" (New York: AHA, 1961). The AHA has continued its interest in diet and heart disease through a series of reports: AHA, Committee on Nutrition, Central Committee for Medical and Community Program, "Diet and Heart Disease" (New York: AHA, 1965). AHA, Committee on Nutrition, Central Committee for Medical and Community Program, "Diet and Coronary Heart Disease" (New York: AHA, 1973). AHA, Nutrition Committee of the Steering Committee for Medical and Community Program, "Diet and Coronary Heart Disease" (Dallas: AHA, 1978). AHA, Nutrition Committee, "Rationale of the Diet–Heart Statement of the American Heart Association" (Dallas: AHA, 1982).

15. P. D. White, H. B. Sprague, J. Stamler et al., "A Statement on Arteriosclerosis, Main Cause of 'Heart Attacks' and 'Strokes' " (New York: National Health Education Committee, 1959). This was preceded by a summary of the evidence relating fat to heart disease: I. H. Page, F. J. Stare, A. C. Corcoran et al., "Atherosclerosis and the Fat Content of the Diet," *Circulation* 16 (1957): 163–78.

16. *The American Heart Association Cookbook* (New York: David McKay, 1973, 1975, 1979).

17. AMA, Council on Foods and Nutrition, "The Regulation of Dietary Fat" (Chicago: AMA, 1962); AMA, Council on Foods and Nutrition, "Diet and the Possible Prevention of Coronary Atheroma" (Chicago: AMA, 1965); AMA, Council on Foods and Nutrition, "Diet and Coronary Heart Disease" (Chicago: AMA, 1972); FNB, National Research Council, and AMA, "Diet and Coronary Heart Disease," *Nutrition Reviews* 30 (October 1972): 223–25; AMA, Council on Scientific Affairs, "American Medical Association Concepts on Nutrition and Health" (Chicago: AMA, 1979).

18. FNB and AMA, "Diet and Coronary Heart Disease."

19. For an account of this activity see Philip L. White, "Statement of the American Medical Association to the U.S. Food and Drug Administration, Federal Trade Commission, U.S. Department of Agriculture Re: Food Labeling" (Chicago: AMA, 1980), 17–18.

20. A brief introduction to the FNB including a brief history and the current structure and participants is found in the annual pamphlet entitled "Food and Nutrition Board" (Washington, D.C.: National Academy of Sciences).

21. FNB, National Research Council, *Recommended Dietary Allowances,* 9th ed., rev. (Washington, D.C.: National Academy of Sciences, 1980).

22. Publications on the findings of the Framingham study are voluminous. For a succinct discussion of the major findings as well as a historical overview of the project see Thomas R. Dawber, *The Framingham Study: The Epidemiology of Atherosclerotic Disease* (Cambridge: Harvard University Press, 1980).

23. National Diet–Heart Disease Study Research Group, "The National Diet–Heart Study Final Report," *Circulation* 37, supp. I (1968); Diet–Heart Review Panel, Mass Field Trials of the Diet–Heart Question: Their Significance, Timeliness, Feasibility and Applicability (New York: AHA Monograph no. 28, 1969); Inter-Society Commission for Heart Disease Resources, Atherosclerosis Study Group and Epidemiology Study Group, "Primary Prevention of the Atherosclerotic Diseases," *Circulation* 42 (1970): A55.

24. Task Force on Arteriosclerosis of the National Heart and Lung Institute, *Arteriosclerosis,* vol. 1 (Washington, D.C.: DHEW, Public Health Service Publication no. [NIH]72-137, June 1971).

25. The final report of the MRFIT project was published in MRFIT Research Group, "Multiple Risk Factor Intervention Trial," *Journal of the American Medical Association* 282 (24 September 1982): 1465–77.

26. The Lipid Research Clinics Program, "The Coronary Primary Prevention Trial: Design and Implementation," *Journal of Chronic Diseases* 32 (1979): 609–31.

27. The National Heart, Blood Vessel, Lung, and Blood Act of 1972 (P.L. 92–423), 19 September 1972. This emphasis on prevention and dissemination was reaffirmed by Congress in August 1977 in the Biomedical Research Extension Act of 1977 (P.L. 95-83).

28. See Richard A. Rettig, *Cancer Crusade: The Story of the National Cancer Act of 1974* (Princeton, N.J.: Princeton University Press, 1977).

29. April 1967 hearings by the Senate Subcommittee on Employment, Manpower and Poverty held in Jackson, Miss. For a description of the development of interest in hunger and malnutrition in America see Kenneth Schlossberg, "Policy in the United States," in Beverly Winikoff, ed., *Nutrition and National Policy* (Cambridge: MIT Press, 1978), 326–59; Catherine E.

Woeteki and John B. Cordaro, "Nutrition Research Policy: U.S. Progress in the Past Decade," *Food Policy* 4 (November 1979): 285–94.

30. CBS television, "Hunger in America," May 1968; the Senate Select Committee was established by U.S. Congress, Senate Resolution 281, 90th Congress, 2d Session (30 July 1977).

31. For a description of SSC activities see Donna V. Porter, *Nutrition Policy Making in the United States Congress* (Ph.D. diss., Ohio State University, 1980), esp. chap. 4.

32. There is a voluminous literature describing the "iron triangle" in agriculture. This is a supportive relationship between a bureaucracy, its congressional overseers, and the regulated interest group. For example: Weldon Barton, "Coalition-Building in the U.S. House of Representatives: Agricultural Legislation in 1973," in James E. Anderson, ed., *Cases in Public Policy* (New York: Praeger, 1976), 141–62; Charles M. Hardin, "Agricultural Price Policy: The Political Role of Bureaucracy," in Don F. Hadwiger and William P. Browne, eds., *The New Politics of Food* (Lexington, Mass.: Lexington Books, 1978), 7–13; Laurellen Porter, "Congress and Agricultural Policy," in ibid., 15–22; Charles M. Hardin, *Presidential Power and Accountability* (Chicago: University of Chicago Press, 1974), chaps. 4–6; John P. Heinz, "The Political Impasse in Farm Support Legislation," *Yale Law Journal* 71 (April 1962): 952–78; Charles O. Jones, "Representation in Congress: The Case of the House Agriculture Committee," *American Political Science Review* 55 (June 1961): 358–72; Wayne D. Rasmussen and Gladys L. Baker, "Programs for Agriculture, 1933–1965," in Vernon Ruttan, Arley D. Waldo, and James P. Houck, eds., *Agricultural Policy in an Affluent Society* (New York: Norton, 1969), 69–88; Ivan Garth Youngsberg, "U.S. Agriculture in the 1970s: Policy and Prospects," in James E. Anderson, ed., *Economic Regulatory Policy* (Lexington, Mass.: Heath, 1975), 51–68.

33. 24 F.R. 9990 (10 December 1959).

34. See note 18, above; 30 F.R. 6984 (25 May 1965); 31 F.R. 3301 (2 March 1966). See Peter Barton Hutt, "Regulatory Implementation of Dietary Recommendations," *Food Drug Cosmetics Law Journal* (February 1981): 70–77; and Patricia Housman, *Jack Sprat's Legacy: The Science and Politics of Fat and Cholesterol* (New York: Richard Marek, 1981), 150–55.

35. *White House Conference on Food, Nutrition and Health: Final Report* (Washington, D.C.: Government Printing Office, 1970).

36. 21 CFR 101.25, promulgated in 38 F.R. 2132 (19 January 1973); 38 F.R. 20071 (27 July 1973).

37. A full description of these critiques and the portent of resulting changes can be found in Kenneth W. Clarkson and Timothy J. Muris, eds., *The Federal Trade Commission Since 1970: Economic Regulation and Bureaucratic Behavior* (Cambridge: Cambridge University Press, 1981). See Melvin J. Hinich and Richard Staelin, *Consumer Protection Legislation and the U.S. Food Industry* (New York: Pergamon, 1980); and Hutt, "Regulatory Implementation," 77–80 for descriptions of FTC food advertising activities.

38. Hinich and Staelin, *Consumer Protection Legislation,* 76–77.

39. A description of the legal restraints on margarine and the efforts by the margarine industry to combat them can be found in Siert F. Riepma, *The Story of Margarine* (Washington, D.C.: Public Affairs Press, 1970), esp. chaps. 6 and 7.

40. AHA, *Coronary Risk Handbook* (New York: American Heart Association, 1973).

41. For a description of the dairy price-support programs see James G. Vertrees, *Food and Agriculture Policy in the 1980s: Major Crops and Milk* (Washington, D.C.: Congressional Budget Office, 1981), chap. 4, "Dairy Price Support Alternatives," 33–43; James G. Vertrees and Peter M. Emerson, *Agricultural Price Support Programs: A Handbook* (Washington, D.C.: Congressional Budget Office, 1980), 18–19; James G. Vertrees and Peter M. Emerson, *Consequences of Dairy Price Support Policy: Budget Issue Paper for Fiscal Year 1980* (Washington, D.C.: Congressional Budget Office, 1979).

42. Interview with National Dairy Council Official, Chicago, August 1982.

43. See *Meat Board Reports* (8 December 1969, 8 July 1974, and 11 November 1974).

44. *Meat Board Reports* (8 December 1964).

45. FTC, *In the Matter of National Commission on Egg Nutrition, et al.,* Docket 8987 (Complaint 23 July 1974), 154.

46. "Eggs, Your Diet and Your Heart" (Park Ridge, Ill.: NCEN n.d.). Advertising text is found in FTC, *In the Matter of,* 91–94.

47. FTC, *In the Matter of National Commission on Egg Nutrition, et. al.* (Final Order, 24 November 1975).

48. The Egg Research and Consumer Information Act was approved in 1975.

49. For a list of National Nutrition Policy hearings and working papers, see Select Committee on Nutrition and Human Needs, Senate, *Index to Publications on Nutrition and Human Needs,* 93rd Congress, 94th Congress, 1st Session (March 1975), pp. VII–VIII.

50. Hearings before the Senate Select Committee on Nutrition and Human Needs, 94th Congress, 2d Session, 27 and 28 July 1976, *Diet Related to Killer Diseases* (Washington, D.C.: Government Printing Office, 1976).

51. Senate Select Committee on Nutrition and Human Needs, *Dietary Goals for the United States* (Washington, D.C.: Government Printing Office, February 1977).

52. Ibid., 13.

53. See "Victims of Reform: Nutrition Panel Nears End; Anti-Hunger Groups Worry Support Will Die, Too," *Congressional Quarterly Weekly Report* (26 November 1977): 2502–3.

54. Hearings before the Senate Select Committee on Nutrition and Human Needs, 95th Congress, 1st Session, 24 March 1977, *Diet Related to Killer Diseases III: Response to Dietary Goals of the United States Re Meat* (Washington, D.C.: Government Printing Office, 1977). Although additional hearings on eggs were also held, the impact of the egg lobby was less than that of the more powerful dairy lobby, or the more powerful and active meat lobby.

55. Select Committee on Nutrition and Human Needs, Senate, 95th Congress, 1st Session, *Dietary Goals for the United States, Second Edition* (Washington, D.C.: Government Printing Office, December 1977).

56. Ibid., 4.

57. Ibid.

58. Nick Mottern, "Dietary Goals," *Food Monitor* (March–April 1978); 8–10.

59. See Nancy K. Eskridge, "McGovern Chides NIH—Reordering Priorities—Emphasis on Nutrition," *BioScience* 28 (1978): 489–91; William J. Broad, "Jump in Funding Feeds Research on Nutrition," *Science* 208 (8 June 1979): 1060–64; William J. Broad, "NIH Deals Gingerly With Diet–Disease Link," *Science* 204 (15 June 1979): 1175–78; George Bray, "Nutrition in the Humphrey Tradition," *Journal of the American Dietetic Association* 75 (August 1979): 116–21; Daniel S. Greenberg, "NIH Says It's Moving On Nutrition Research," *Science and Government Report* 14 (15 October 1979): 1–3; William J. Broad, "New Strength in the Diet–Disease Link?" *Science* 206 (9 November 1979): 666–68.

60. "Symposium Report of the Task Force on the Evidence Relating Six Dietary Factors to the Nation's Health," *American Journal of Clinical Nutrition* 32 (December 1979; suppl.): 2621–2748.

61. *Nutrition and Your Health: Dietary Guidelines for Americans* (Washington, D.C.: USDA, DHHS, 4 February 1980).

62. U.S. Surgeon General, *Healthy People: The Surgeon General's Report on Health Promotion and Disease Prevention* (Washington, D.C.: DHEW, Public Health Service Publication no. 79-55071, 1979).

63. See note 61, above.

64. Ibid., 11.

65. Hearings before the House Subcommittee on Domestic Marketing, Consumer Relations, and Nutrition of the Committee on Agriculture, 96th Congress, 2d Session, 18 and 19 June 1980, *National Academy of Sciences Report on Healthful Diets* (Washington, D.C.: Government Printing Office, 1980).

66. Hearings before the Senate Subcommittee on Agriculture, Rural Development, and Related Agencies, Committee on Appropriations, 96th Congress, 2d Session (Washington, D.C.: Government Printing Office, 1980).

67. *Nutrition and Your Health: Dietary Guidelines for Americans,* 11–12.

68. *Ideas for Better Eating: Menus and Recipes to Make Use of the Dietary Guidelines,* Science and Education Administration, Human Nutrition, USDA (Washington, D.C.: Government Printing Office, January 1981).

69. *Boston Globe,* 9 January 1982.

70. William J. Broad, "Nutrition Research: End of an Empire," *Science* 213 (31 July 1981): 518–20.

71. "USDA Nutrition Information Policies Scored by Public Citizen," *Food Chemical News* (20 August 1984): 7–9.

72. See *Community Nutrition Institute Weekly Report* 12, no. 17 (29 April 1982): 1–2; 21, no. 22 (3 June 1982): 6; 12, no. 25 (24 June 1982): 6–7; 12, no. 33 (26 August 1982): 1–2; "Censored: USDA Suppresses Guide to Moderating Fat and Cholesterol: Food 2," *Nutrition Action* (July–August 1982): 9–11.

73. "USDA Appoints Review Panel for Dietary Guidelines," *Community Nutrition Institute Weekly Report* 12, no. 45 (18 November 1982): 1; "USDA Readies to Carve Up the Dietary Guidelines," *Nutrition Action* 10 (March 1983): 3–4.

74. See Mark Segal, chapter 4 of this volume.

75. "FDA Likely to Set Standards for Reduced Cholesterol Foods," *Food Chemical News* (8 July 1985): 30–31; "Options Being Considered on Cholesterol Labeling," *Food Chemical News* (12 August 1985): 36–37.

76. Lipid Research Clinics Program, "The Lipid Research Clinics Coronary Primary Prevention Trials Results: I. Reduction in Incidence of Coronary Heart Disease," *Journal of the American Medical Association* 251 (20 January 1984): 351–64; Lipid Research Clinics Program, "The Lipid Research Clinics Coronary Prevention Trial Results: II. The Relationship of Reduction in Incidence of Coronary Heart Disease to Cholesterol Lowering," *Journal of the American Medical Association* 251 (20 January 1984): 365–74.

77. National Institutes of Health Consensus Development Conference Statement, *Lowering Blood Cholesterol* (10–12 December 1984), Draft, 28 pages.

78. Committee on Diet, Nutrition and Cancer, Assembly of Life Sciences, National Research Council, *Diet, Nutrition and Cancer* (Washington, D.C.: National Academy Press, 1982).

79. Greg Moyer, "The Blitz Has Begun," *Nutrition Action* 10 (March 1983): 2; "CSPI to Mount Anti-Fat Campaign" *CNI Weekly Report* 12, no. 40 (14 October 1982): 6.

80. In the Dairy and Tobacco Adjustment Act of 1983; see also *Advertising Age* (2 July 1984); (12 July 1984): 35; (23 July 1984); (10 September 1984): 6; (15 November 1984): 3; (17 December 1984): 46; (7 January 1985); (31 January 1985).

81. Janet Meyers, "Food Growers Raising Bumper Ad Budgets," *Advertising Age* (16 September 1985): 98.

82. "Milking the Health Angle," *Public Relations Journal* (April 1985): 7–8.

83. Quoting Kathy McCharan, United Egg Producers, "Egg Industry Official Hits 'Prudent Diet for Everyone' Theory," *Food Chemical News* (4 February 1985): 27–28.

84. Quoting Thomas J. McDermott of the National Livestock and Meat Board, in "Surgeon General Planning 1986 Report on Diet and Health, AMI's Hoting says," *Food Chemical News* (1 October 1984): 7. See also "Cholesterol Reduction," *Food Chemical News* (23 January 1984): 2; "Meat Industry Diet/Health 'Principles' Stress 'Positive' Message," *Food Chemical News* (5 March 1984): 44–45; "Pork Group Officials Call for Meat Industry 'Statesmanship' on Diet-Health Issues," *Food Chemical News* (2 April 1984): 39; "High Blood Fats," *Food Chemical News* (28 May 1984): 2; Donna Leigh Yanish, "Meat Producers, Retailers Strive to Cut Sales Dip," *Advertising Age* (19 September 1985): 30–32.

85. The activities of Kellogg's, the FDA, and the FTC have been closely followed by *Food Chemical News* since October 1984. In addition see Janet Neiman, "All-Bran Ads May Inspire Health Trend," *Advertising Age* (29 October 1985): 2; Steven W. Colford, "MCs Move to Halt Kellogg Health Ads," *Advertising Age* (1 November 1984): 1; Steven W. Colford, "Advertisers Hunger for FDA word on Kellogg," *Advertising Age* (3 December 1984): 97; Steven W. Colford, "New All-Bran Ad Query," *Advertising Age* (18 February 1985): 82; Steven W. Colford, "FDA Hints Approval of Food Health Claims," *Advertising Age* (11 March 1985): 2; Steven W. Colford, "Food Marketers Let Health Claims Simmer," *Advertising Age* (18 March 1985): 12.

86. Richard L. Gordon, "Kill Food Rule: FTC Aide," *Advertising Age* (14 June 1982): 2; Marion Burros, "Panel to Vote Again on Rules to Limit Assertions on Foods," *New York Times*, 5 December 1982, p. 84; "FTC Tries Salvaging Food Ad Rule," *Advertising Age* (8 December 1982): 2; "Food Advertising Rule," *Food Chemical News* (20 December 1982): 2.

87. "Dietary Guidelines for Americans: No-Nonsense Advice for Healthy Eating," *FDA Consumer* (November 1985): 10–15.

88. " 'Know Your Count' Seen as Keynote of Cholesterol Education Program," *Food Chemical News* (25 November 1985): 12–13; see also "NIH Cholesterol Education Program Meeting

Set for November 15," *Food Chemical News* (28 October 1985): 26–27; "It's All-Out War on Fat and Cholesterol," *Medical World News* (9 December 1985): 81–82.

Chapter 4

1. High Blood Pressure Coordinating Committee, "New Hypertension Prevalence Data and Recommended Public Statements" (Washington, D.C.: Department of Health, Education and Welfare, 1978); Subcommittee on Definition and Prevalence of the 1984 Joint National Committee, "Hypertension Prevalence and the Status of Awareness, Treatment, and Control in the United States," *Hypertension* 7 (May–June 1985): 457–68. The Joint National Committee on Detection, Evaluation, and Treatment of High Blood Pressure is convened by the National Heart, Lung, and Blood Institute of the National Institutes of Health. However, some experts contend that this prevalence is overstated because the blood pressures of many of these individuals will regress to normal levels. See Norman Kaplan, "Hypertension: Prevalence, Risks, and Effects of Therapy," *Annals of Internal Medicine* 98, no. 5 (1983): part 2, 705.

2. Statement by Robert I. Levy, Director, National Heart, Lung, and Blood Institute, National Institutes of Health, Public Health Service, Department of Health and Human Services, presented on 13 April 1981 to the House Subcommittee on Investigations and Oversight of the Committee on Science and Technology. House Subcommittee on Investigations and Oversight of the Committee on Science and Technology, *Hearings on Sodium in Food and High Blood Pressure* (Washington, DC: Government Printing Office, 1981), p. 19.

3. For a discussion of the education program, see Robert I. Levy, "The NH,L,BI Overview," *Circulation* 198 (1982): 217–25.

4. Working Group on Risk and High Blood Pressure, "An Epidemiological Approach to Describing Risk Associated with Blood Pressure Levels," *Hypertension* 7 (July–August 1985): 641–51; Thomas R. Dawber, *The Framingham Study: The Epidemiology of Atherosclerotic Disease* (Cambridge: Harvard University Press, 1980).

5. Select Committee on GRAS (Generally Recognized As Safe) Substances, Life Sciences Research Office, Federation of American Societies for Experimental Biology, "SCOGS Report 102," 1979 (hereinafter referred to as SCOGS).

6. FNB, *Recommended Daily Allowances,* 9th ed., rev. (Washington, D.C.: National Academy of Sciences, 1980).

7. Marilyn S. Fregly and Melvin J. Fregly, "The Estimates of Sodium Intake in Man," in Melvin Fregly and Morley R. Kare, eds., *The Role of Salt in Cardiovascular Hypertension* (New York: Academic Press, 1982), 3–17.

8. Marketing Sciences Institute, "Determinants of Food Usage Behavior: A Market Segment Approach" (Cambridge: Marketing Sciences Institute, 1980); Gallup Organization, Inc., "Changing Food Preparation and Eating Habits" (Princeton, N.J.: Gallup, 1980). Both cited in *A Summary Report on U.S. Consumers' Knowledge, Attitudes, and Practices About Food* (Minneapolis: General Mills, 1980).

9. James T. Heimbach, "The Public Response to Labeling of the Sodium Content of Foods," (Washington, D.C.: FDA, 1983), table 12.

10. Robert P. Multhauf, *Neptune's Gift* (Baltimore: Johns Hopkins University Press, 1978), chap. 1.

11. Lewis K. Dahl, M. Heine, and L. Tassinari, "High Salt Content of Western Infant's Diet, Possible Relation to Hypertension in the Adult," *Nature* 198 (1963): 204; Lewis K. Dahl, "Salt in Processed Baby Foods," *American Journal of Clinical Nutrition* 21 (1968): 783; James Turner, *The Chemical Feast: The Ralph Nader Study Group Report on Food Protection and the Food and Drug Administration* (New York: Grossman, 1970), 87–92.

12. *White House Conference on Food, Nutrition and Health: Final Report* (Washington, D.C.: Government Printing Office, 1970), 44, 50.

13. Lloyd J. Filer, Jr., "Salt in Infant Foods," *Nutrition Reviews* 29 (1971): 27–28.

14. "Gerber Jumps on No-Salt Bandwagon," *Advertising Age* (6 June 1977): 4.

15. Data supplied by Gerber Products Company, Fremont, Michigan, 26 August 1982.

16. American Academy of Pediatrics, Council on Nutrition, "Salt Intake and Eating Patterns of Infants," *Pediatrics* 53 (1974):120.

17. Ibid., "Sodium Intake by Infants in the U.S.," *Pediatrics* 60 (1981): 444–45; Lloyd J. Filer, Jr., "Appropriate Consumption of Sodium and Potassium," in Philip L. White and Stephanie C. Crocco, eds., *Sodium and Potassium in Foods and Drugs* (Chicago: American Medical Association, 1980).

18. L. Ambard and E. Beaujard, "Causes de l'Hypertension Arterielle," *Archives of General Medicine* 1 (1904): 520–33.

19. W. Kempner, "Treatment of Hypertensive Vascular Disease with Rice Diet," *American Journal of Medicine* 4 (1948): 545–77.

20. Lewis K. Dahl, M. Heine, and L. Tassinari, "Effects of Chronic Salt Ingestion: Evidence that Genetic Factors Play an Important Role in Susceptibility to Experimental Hypertension," *Journal of Experimental Medicine* 115 (1962): 1173.

21. See Edward D. Freis, "Salt, Volume, and Hypertension," *Circulation* 53 (1976): 589–95; and Louis Tobian, "The Relationship of Salt to Hypertension," *American Journal of Clinical Nutrition* (suppl.) 32 (December 1979): 2739–48; Lot B. Page et al., "Blood Pressure of Qash'qai Pastoral Nomads in Iran in Relation to Culture, Diet, and Body Form," *American Journal of Clinical Nutrition* 34 (April 1981): 527–38.

22. Dawber, *Framingham Study.* The Framingham Study is a long-term, community-wide study of the risk factors associated with atherosclerotic disease.

23. J. D. Swales, "Dietary Salt and Hypertension," *Lancet* (31 May 1980): 1177–79. Also, F. O. Simpson, "Salt and Hypertension: A Skeptical Review of the Evidence," *Clinical Science* 57 (1979): 463s–80s. Trevor C. Beard et al., "Randomized Controlled Trial of a No-Added-Sodium Diet for Mild Hypertension," *Lancet* (28 August 1982): 455–58; Graham A. McGregor et al., "Double-Blind Randomized Crossover Trial of Moderate Sodium Restriction in Essential Hypertension," *Lancet* (13 February 1982): 351–55; Alan J. Silman et al., "Evaluation of the Effectiveness of a Low-Sodium Diet in the Treatment of Mild to Moderate Hypertension," *Lancet* (28 May 1983): 1179–82.

24. See for example, Louis Tobian, "Salt (NaCl) and Hypertension: Pathogenic Considerations," in Myron Winick, ed., *Nutrition and the Killer Diseases* (New York: Wiley, 1981); George R. Meneely and Harold D. Battarbee, "Sodium and Potassium," *Nutrition Reviews* 34 (1976): 225–35; Freis, "Salt, Volume, and Hypertension," 589–95.

25. Sir George Pickering, "Position Paper: Dietary Sodium and Human Hypertension," pp. 37–42, and John H. Laragh, "Frontiers in Hypertension Research: Past, Present, and Future," pp. 1–5, in John H. Laragh, ed., *Topics in Hypertension* (New York: Springer-Verlag, 1981).

26. Meneely and Battarbee, "Sodium and Potassium"; E. Reisin et al., "Effect of Weight Loss Without Salt Restriction on the Reduction of Blood Pressure in Overweight Hypertensive Patients," *New England Journal of Medicine* 298 (1978): 1–6; David A. McCarron, Cynthia D. Morris, and Clarice Cole, "Dietary Calcium in Human Hypertension," *Science* 217 (July 1982): 267–69; David A. McCarron, "Is Calcium More Important Than Sodium in the Pathogenesis of Essential Hypertension?" *Hypertension* 7 (July–August 1985): 607–27.

27. Levy statement, cited in note 3, above. Edward D. Freis, "Should Mild Hypertensives be Treated?" *New England Journal of Medicine* 307 (1982): 306–9. Mild and borderline hypertension is often defined as diastolic pressure between 90–104 mm mercury.

28. David Hyman and Norman Kaplan, "Treatment of Patients with Mild Hypertension," *Hypertension* 7 (March–April 1985): 165–70; *Statement on the Role of Dietary Management in Hypertension Control,* approved by the National High Blood Pressure Coordinating Committee, Department of Health, Education and Welfare, March 1979; Joint National Committee on Detection, Evaluation, and Treatment of High Blood Pressure, "The 1984 Report of the Joint National Committee on Detection, Evaluation, and Treatment of High Blood Pressure," *Archives of Internal Medicine* 144 (May 1984): 1045–57.

29. *White House Conference on Food and Nutrition.*

30. 21 CFR 101. Note that the FDA regulates virtually all processed foods; the Department of Agriculture's jurisdiction covers meats and poultry.

31. *Federal Register,* vol. 44 (21 December 1979): 76005.

32. Food, Drug, and Cosmetics Act [21 USC 321(g)].

33. SCOGS.

34. Sanford A. Miller, "The Implementation of Public Health Policy: Science and Reality," in Fregly and Kare, eds., *Role of Salt,* 443–51. Miller was the director of the Bureau of Foods, FDA, at the time he wrote this article.

35. Senate Select Committee on Nutrition and Human Needs, *Diet Related to Killer Diseases* (Washington, D.C.: Government Printing Office, 1977). See also chap. 3 of this book.

36. Senate Select Committee on Nutrition and Human Needs, *Dietary Goals for the United States* (Washington, D.C.: Government Printing Office, 1977, rev. 1977) (hereinafter referred to as the McGovern Report).

37. Senate Nutrition Subcommittee, *Hearings on Nutrition Labeling and Information* (Washington, D.C.: Government Printing Office, 1979), parts I–IV (hereinafter referred to as *Nutrition Labeling Hearings*).

38. S.1651, Department of Agriculture, Nutrition Labeling and Information Act of 1979; S.1652, Nutrition Labeling and Information Amendments to the Food, Drug, and Cosmetics Act.

39. U.S. Surgeon General, *Healthy People: The Surgeon General's Report on Health Promotion and Disease Prevention* (Washington, D.C.: Department of Health, Education and Welfare, 1979), 98, 131.

40. U.S. Department of Health, Education, and Welfare (DHEW), *Promoting Health/Preventing Disease* (Washington, D.C.: DHEW, 1980).

41. *Nutrition and Your Health: Dietary Guidelines for Americans* (Washington, D.C.: USDA, DHEW, 1980). In 1983, the *Guidelines* underwent review by a joint Department of Health and Human Services/USDA scientific committee. For a discussion of this process, and the often controversial issues involved, see Sanford A. Miller and Marylin Stephens, "Scientific and Public Health Rationale for the Dietary Guidelines for Americans," *American Journal of Clinical Nutrition* 42 (October 1985): 739–45. Because the second edition of *Guidelines,* released in 1985, followed the example of the first in omitting quantitative recommendations, it was attacked by some critics. Deborah Lee Wood, "Critics Chastise New Federal Guidelines for Maintaining a Proper Diet," *Chicago Tribune,* 7 November 1985, sec. 7, p. 9.

42. Kristen McNutt, "Dietary Advice to the Public: 1957–1980," *Nutrition Reviews* 38 (1980): 353–60, reviews the many public statements.

43. FNB, *Toward Healthful Diets* (Washington, D.C.: National Academy of Sciences, 1980).

44. FNB, *Research Needs for Establishing Dietary Goals for the U.S. Population* (Washington, D.C.: National Academy of Sciences, 1979).

45. Interview with Food and Drug Administration official, 26 October 1982.

46. H.R. 628 and 2169, 97th Congress, 1st Session; telephone interview with congressional staff member, Washington, D.C., 14 February 1982.

47. American Medical Association, Council on Scientific Affairs, "Sodium in Processed Foods" (Chicago: American Medical Association, 1982), 1.

48. See David R. Mayhew, *Congress: The Electoral Connection* (New Haven: Yale University Press, 1974) for a discussion of the electoral incentives that impel some members of Congress to seek visible issues.

49. House Subcommittee on Investigations and Oversight of the Committee on Science and Technology, *Hearings on Sodium in Food and High Blood Pressure* (Washington, D.C.: Government Printing Office, 1981). Hearings were held in April 1981 (Hereinafter referred to as Gore Hearings.) In the 98th Congress the bill was reintroduced as H.R. 17. It was reintroduced in the 99th Congress, 1st Session, by (now Senator) Gore and Congressman Smith.

50. See Turner, *Chemical Feast,* chap. 5. For a discussion of the controversies generated by the Reagan-era FDA's embrace of voluntarism, see Julie Kosterlitz, "Reagan Is Leaving His Mark on the Food and Drug Administration," *National Journal,* 6 July 1985, pp. 1568–72.

51. Interview with Food and Drug Administration official, 26 October 1982.

52. House Subcommittee on Health and the Environment, *Hearings on Sodium and Potassium Content Labeling—H.R. 4031* (Washington, D.C.: Government Printing Office, 1981), held 25 September 1981 (hereinafter referred to as Waxman Hearings).

53. See Andrew S. McFarland, *Public Interest Lobbies* (Washington, D.C.: American Enterprise Institute for Public Policy Research, 1976), 18–19.

54. CSPI testimony at Gore Hearings.

55. This issue is discussed in Michael S. Baram, *Alternatives to Regulation* (Lexington, Mass.: Lexington Books, 1982), 141–42.

56. See for example, Bonnie F. Liebman, Letter to the Editor, "Sodium Intake and Sodium Sensitivity," *Nutrition Reviews* 39 (1981): 350.

57. Phone conversation with CSPI staff member, 13 December 1982. CSPI letter to Congressman Thomas J. Bliley, Jr. (R., W. Va.), 5 April 1982. Author's files.

58. The discussion of staff and membership groups in this section is taken from McFarland, *Public Interest Lobbies*. See also James Q. Wilson, *Political Organizations* (New York: Basic Books, 1973), 321–25.

59. Telephone interview with public interest group representative, 7 October 1982.

60. AHA, "Rationale of the Diet–Heart Statement of the American Heart Association," *Circulation* 65 (1982): 839A–51A; McNutt, "Dietary Advice," 19.

61. AHA, "Rationale," 850A.

62. AHA, "Rationale."

63. Interviews with congressional staff members, 19 May 1982 and 6 June 1982; Paul Taylor, "On Sodium, Low-Key Lobbying Wins," *Washington Post,* 26 March 1982, pp. 12–13.

64. AMA comments on FDA Docket no. 80N-0314, 2 September 1982. AMA statement to the FDA, USDA, and FTC, 5 March 1980, reprinted in *Nutrition Labeling Hearings,* 174–76.

65. SCOGS.

66. "Hayes Urges Sodium Labeling Creativity," *Food Engineering* (April 1982): 22–30.

67. Gore Hearings, 174.

68. Office of Executive Communications, Minutes of Bureau of Foods Management Meeting, 17 March 1981. Food and Drug Administration, Bureau of Foods, 8 April 1981.

69. Karen De Witt, "New Phase in Dispute on Salt," *New York Times,* 1 July 1981. See FDA Status Report on sodium activities, January 1983, for a summary (Washington, D.C.: Food and Drug Administration, January 1983).

70. Waxman Hearings; Linda Demkovich, "The FDA's New Boss Finds Regulation 'Absolutely Essential'—Sometimes," *National Journal,* 29 August 1981, p. 1543.

71. Bureau of Foods Memorandum of Meeting, 20 August 1982.

72. *Federal Register* 47 (18 June 1982): 26580–95. Final regulations were not issued until 18 April 1984, with industry compliance due by 1 July 1985. In June 1985, the FDA acceded to industry requests, and delayed implementation until 1 July 1986. 21 CFR 101 and 105, *Federal Register* 49 (18 April 1984): 15510–35. "Sodium Labeling Rule is Postponed by FDA," *American Medical News* (14 June 1985): 22.

73. Interview with Food and Drug Administration official, 21 June 1982. Following a pattern typical of public interest groups, CSPI filed suit against FDA, charging that its petitions had been unlawfully denied. Particular attention was paid in the suit to the deferral of a decision on salt's GRAS status. Civil Action no. 83-0801, U.S. District Court for the District of Columbia, Center for Science in the Public Interest, and *Michael Jacobson* v. *Arthur Hull Hayes, Jr., and Margaret Heckler.*

74. FDA Status Report.

75. Ibid.; see also National High Blood Pressure Educations Program, *Infomemo,* Fall 1981.

76. "Dear Colleague," letter to U.S. physicians from Commissioner Hayes, 24 June 1982. Personal files.

77. Linda E. Demkovich, "Critics Fear the FDA Is Going Too Far in Cutting Industry's Regulatory Load," *National Journal,* 17 July 1982, pp. 1249–52. Kosterlitz, "Reagan Is Leaving His Mark."

78. SCOGS.

79. Marylin Chou and David Harmon, Jr., eds., *Critical Food Issues of the Eighties* (New York: Pergamon, 1979), 18–41, 151–59.

80. Department of the Interior, Bureau of Mines, *Minerals Yearbook 1981* (Washington, D.C.: Government Printing Office, 1981), chap. on salt, p. 1.

81. The Salt Institute has twelve U.S. members. A number of U.S. salt producers, particularly the smaller ones, are not members of the Salt Institute. For this reason, as well as different data collection policies, Bureau of Mines data and Salt Institute data are not comparable. However, almost all of the U.S. salt producers who produce food-grade salt are members of the Salt Institute. Hence, its data (which include aggregated sales data, unlike that of the Bureau of Mines) are useful in gaining an understanding of the role food-grade salt plays in the salt industry. One further caveat is in order; it is not possible to know how much salt categorized as food-grade salt ended up in other uses, such as parking lot de-icing, nor how much salt originally categorized in a nonfood category was used in food processing.

However, because we are not interested in using these data to establish actual consumption, and because we are interested in trends, where it is assumed that much of this uncertainty will tend to wash out, these data problems are not terribly significant.

82. See note 80, above; data kindly supplied by the Salt Institute.

83. Morton-Norwich Products Inc., *Annual Report,* 1981.

84. "Morton-Norwich: Pouring Cash into Chemicals and Household Goods," *Business Week* (3 May 1982): 56–57.

85. Diamond Crystal Salt, *Annual Report,* 1981; Akzona, Inc., *Annual Report,* 1981.

86. "Salt: A New Villain?" *Time* (15 March 1982): 64–71.

87. Morton Lite Salt label and advertising copy.

88. "Morton Asks Lite Salt Order Review," *Advertising Age* (9 August 1982): 54. "Morton Lite Salt Ad May Contain Hypertension Statement, FTC Rules," *Food Chemical News* (21 March 1983): 33.

89. Robert C. Terry, Jr., *Road Salt, Drinking Water, and Safety* (Cambridge: Ballinger, 1974).

90. Marietta Whittlesey, *Killer Salt* (New York: Avon, 1977); "Salt: A New Villain?" *Time* (15 March 1982).

91. Chou and Harmon, *Critical Food Issues.*

92. William E. Dickinson, "The Sodium Issue: A Need for Fairness," *Food Processing* (May 1982): 196.

93. Statement of W. Dickinson, president, Salt Institute, at Waxman Hearings, 209. See *Nutrition Labeling Hearings,* pp. 167–68.

94. Dickinson, at Waxman Hearings, 209.

95. Ibid.; Dickinson, "Sodium Issue."

96. Intracompany correspondence, General Mills, Inc., Minneapolis, 14 September 1980.

97. Interview at General Foods, White Plains, New York, 4 October 1982.

98. FDA Status Report on Sodium Activities, January 1983. Also, personal communication, F. Edward Scarbrough, Center for Food Safety and Applied Nutrition (formerly Bureau of Foods), FDA, 9 February 1985. Note that the new sodium labeling regulations, 21 CFR 101 and 105, *Federal Register* 49 (18 April 1984): 15510–35, require that all foods that have nutritional information labeling add sodium labeling. In early 1983, approximately 55 percent of foods under FDA jurisdiction bore nutrition labeling. Hence, as this new rule takes effect, there will be a marked increase in the volume of sodium labels. Roger W. Miller, "Food Labels to Tell More About Sodium," *FDA Consumer* (July-August 1984): 30–31.

99. 21 CFR 105.69.

100. Thomas Horst, *At Home Abroad: A Study of the Domestic and Foreign Operations of the American Food-Processing Industry* (Cambridge: Ballinger, 1974); Robert A. Buzzel and E. M. Nourse, *Product Innovation in the Food Processing Industry* (Boston: Division of Research, Graduate School of Business Administration, Harvard University, 1967).

101. FDA Status Report.

102. Janet Neiman, "Salt-less Foods: A Market About to Happen," *Advertising Age* (1 November 1982): 3.

103. Ibid.

104. Ibid.

105. Advertisement for Riopan antacid in *New England Journal of Medicine* 307 (1982).

106. Tom Bayer, "Frito-Lay Sees Nutrition Drive as Long-Term Asset," *Advertising Age* (15 March 1982): 14.

107. The symposium was held in 1980, and entitled "The Salt Talks."

108. FDA Status Report.

109. Mr. Pepper is sold by Tone Bros. of Des Moines, Iowa.

110. "Morton-Norwich," *Business Week* (3 May 1982).

111. N. R. Kleinfeld, "Revlon: Cosmetics Show Their Age," *New York Times,* 31 May 1984, pp. 27, 30. Reflecting on what the reporter characterized as one of Revlon's "marketing disasters," an industry analyst states that *NoSalt* ". . . tasted like hell. . . . Everyone bought it the first time, but no one bought it the second time."

112. "NAB Turns Down Meat Group's Complaint About Ad for Salt Substitute," *Food Chemical News* (14 March 1983): 28–29.

113. For a discussion of this point see, Charles E. Morris, "The Food Industry's Role in Diet and Health," *Food Engineering* (June 1982): 57–66.

114. Marian Burros, "Tuna with Less Salt," *New York Times,* 29 September 1982, p. C7.

115. FDA regulation 21 CFR 101.9(i)(1); Morris, "The Food Industry's Role." As a result of concerns involving such issues as sodium-related health claims, and more recently, a dispute with the FTC and Kellogg's over the cereal manufacturer's use of claims on the package of its All-Bran cereal that eating high-fiber cereals could prevent cancer, the FDA planned to issue a policy statement on public health messages on food labels. The FDA was concerned that Kellogg's was making unsubstantiated claims. "Cereal Ad Sparks Regulatory Dispute," *American Medical News* (22 March 1985): 3. Also "FDA Issuing Statement on Label Controversy," *American Medical News* (21 June 1985): 32.

116. James T. Heimbach, "The Public Response to Labeling of the Sodium Content of Foods," (Washington, D.C.: Food and Drug Administration, 1983).

117. Campbell Moses, ed., *Sodium in Medicine and Health* (Baltimore: Reese Press, 1980).

118. Theodore Van Itallie, "Symposium on Current Perspectives in Hypertension," *Hypertension* 4 (1982 supplement III): 177–183; "Nutrition and Blood Pressure Control: Current Status of Dietary Factors and Hypertension, 13–15 September 1982," *Annals of Internal Medicine* 5 (1983): part 2.

119. International Life Sciences Institute (ILSI) brochure; interview with ILSI official, Washington, D.C., 15 September 1982. In 1985, ILSI merged with the Nutrition Foundation.

120. Potato Chip Information Bureau, "Potato Chip Information Booklet" (San Francisco: Potato Chip Information Bureau, n.d.).

121. Salt Institute, *Straight Talk About Salt* (Alexandria, Va.: Salt Institute, 1982). Information provided by the Salt Institute.

122. Gina Kolata, "Value of Low-Sodium Diets Questioned," *Science* 216 (2 April 1982): 38–39.

123. Phillip M. Boffey, "Experts Challenge Low-Sodium Diet," *New York Times*, 14 September 1982, p. C1; "Is Salt Really That Bad?" *Newsweek* (27 September 1982): 86. The favorable press response to these conferences can be contrasted with the skeptical reaction to the Gerber press conference in 1971.

124. Artemis P. Simopoulos, "The Nutritional Aspects of Hypertension," *American Journal of Clinical Nutrition* 42 (November 1985): 909–12. Also, Michael J. Horan, Mordecai P. Blaustein, John B. Dunbar et al., "NIH Report on Research Challenges in Nutrition and Hypertension," *Hypertension* 7 (September–October 1985): 818–23.

125. McCarron, "Is Calcium More Important?"; and Graham A. MacGregor, "Sodium Is More Important Than Calcium in Essential Hypertension," *Hypertension* 7 (July-August 1985): 628–37. The more recent research by McCarron led to Matt Clark, "Salt: Should I or Shouldn't I," *Newsweek* (2 July 1984): 67. On the continuing controversy that McCarron's findings created in the scientific community, see Beverly Merz, "Filling in the Blanks of the Hypertension Puzzle," *Medical World News* (27 August 1984): 38–46.

126. For public opinion data on the saltiness of various foods, see Roper Organization, *Roper Reports*, 81–9, Y, Question 46, September 1981.

Chapter 5

1. National Research Council (NRC)/National Academy of Sciences (NAS), *Saccharin: Technical Assessment of Risks and Benefits, Report No. 1* of the Committee for a Study on Food Safety Policy (Washington, D.C.: NAS, November 1978), ES–2.

2. Chris W. Lecos, "Sweetness Minus Calories," *FDA Consumer* (February 1985): 18.

3. NRC/NAS, *Saccharin*, ES–2.

4. Gerald Walker, "The Great American Dieting Neurosis," *New York Times Magazine*, 23 August 1959, p. 12.

5. *Beverage Industry* (March 1985): 17.

6. Senate Committee on Agriculture, Nutrition, and Forestry, "One Hundred Years of Food Protection," *Food Safety: Where Are We?* (Washington, D.C.: Government Printing Office, July 1979), chap. 1.

7. Marshall S. Shapo, *A Nation of Guinea Pigs* (New York: Free Press, 1979).

8. American Cancer Society, "Guidelines for Advice to the Public on Human Carcinogens," Position Paper, New York City, February 1982.

9. Interview, National Cancer Institute, National Institutes of Health, Bethesda, Maryland, April 1983.

10. Office of Technology Assessment, *Cancer Testing Technology and Saccharin* (Washington, D.C.: Government Printing Office, 1977).

11. R. W. Morgan and O. Wong, "A Review of Epidemiological Studies on Artificial Sweeteners," *Food and Chemical Toxicology* 23, no. 4–5 (1985): 529.

12. Office of Technology Assessment, *Cancer Testing,* 3–4.

13. Robert Hoover and Patricia Hartge, "Non-Nutritive Sweeteners and Bladder Cancer," *American Journal of Public Health* 72, no. 4 (1982): 382.

14. Alexander M. Walker et al., "An Independent Analysis of the National Cancer Institute Study on Non-Nutritive Sweeteners and Bladder Cancer," *American Journal of Public Health* (1982): 376–77.

15. Clifford Grobstein, "Saccharin: A Scientist's View," in Robert Crandall and Lester Lave, eds., *The Scientific Basis of Health and Safety Regulation* (Washington, D.C.: Brookings Institution, 1981), 121.

16. Comptroller General of the United States, *Regulation of Cancer-Causing Food Additives—Time for a Change?* (Washington, DC: General Accounting Office, 11 December 1981), 3.

17. Phyllis Lehmann, "More Than You Ever Thought You Would Know About Food Additives," *FDA Consumer* (April 1979): 53.

18. James Turner, *The Chemical Feast: Report on the Food and Drug Administration* (New York: Grossman, 1970), 6. A Ralph Nader study group report.

19. Ralph Westfall and Harper W. Boyd, Jr., "Abbott Laboratories," in Conrad Berenson, ed., *The Chemical Industry* (New York: Wiley, 1963).

20. James Fallows, "Picking up the TAB," *Washington Monthly* 4 (November 1972): 20–28.

21. Turner, *The Chemical Feast,* 9.

22. "How Calorie Growth Boosts Soft Drink Sales," *Beverage Industry 1983 Annual Manual* (Philadelphia: Beverage Industry, 1983), 36; and Gail Bronson, "The Soda Wars—A Report from the Battlefront," *U.S. News and World Report* (8 July 1985): 58.

23. "Diet Cola Makers Fatten Up Ad Budgets for a Head-On Fight," *Printer's Ink* (31 May 1963): 8.

24. Turner, *The Chemical Feast,* 9.

25. Wayne L. Pines, "The Cyclamate Story," *FDA Consumer* (December 1974–January 1975): 20.

26. Ibid.

27. *Printer's Ink* (17 May 1964): 3; and (14 August 1964): 7.

28. NAS, *Sweeteners: Issues and Uncertainties* (Washington, D.C.: National Academy of Sciences, 1975), 177–81.

29. Pines, "The Cyclamate Story," 20.

30. Ibid., 26.

31. "Panel Launches New Study of Cyclamates," *San Diego Evening Tribune,* 12 July 1975.

32. *Abbott Laboratories* v. *Patricia Harris, secretary of HEW, and Sherwin Gardner, acting commissioner of the FDA, Complaint for Declatory Relief and Injunction* (U.S. District Court: Northern District of Illinois, Eastern Division, 10 September 1979), 10.

33. NAS, *Sweeteners,* 4.

34. Ellen Speiden Parham, "Comparison of Responses to Bans on Cyclamate (1969) and Saccharin (1977)," *Journal of the American Dietetic Association* 72 (January 1978): 59–62.

35. J. C. Louis and Harvey Z. Yazijian, *The Cola Wars* (New York: Everest House, 1980), 107.

36. *Abbott Laboratories* v. *Harris and Gardner;* Marjorie Sun, "Cyclamate's Safety Still Unresolved," *Science* 28 (28 June 1985): 1514–15; "Cyclamate Revisited," *FDA Consumer* (June 1985): 40; National Research Council, *Evaluation of Cyclamate for Carcinogenicity* (Washington, D.C.: National Academy Press, 1985).

37. Dan J. Forrestal, *Faith, Hope and $5000: The Story of Monsanto* (New York: Simon & Schuster, 1977), chap. 1; "Korean Saccharin Is Subject to Duty Charge Next Quarter," *Chemical Marketing Reporter* (22 February 1982): 19; and "Saccharin Prices May Increase as Korea's GSP is Eliminated," *Chemical Marketing Reporter* (26 April 1982): 23.

38. Forrestal, *Faith, Hope, and $5000,* 16.

39. NRC/NAS, *Saccharin,* 1–5.

40. Robert M. Sandri, "Making Good Sugar-free Drinks," *Food Engineering* 25 (May 1953): 79.

41. NRC/NAS, *Saccharin*, 1–7.

42. Ibid., ES–8.

43. NRC/NAS, *Food Safety Policy: Scientific and Societal Considerations, Report No. 2* (Washington, D.C.: NAS, November 1978).

44. "Saccharin and its Salts," *Federal Register* vol. 42 (15 April 1977), 19996–20010.

45. NRC/NAS, *Saccharin*, 1–8.

46. NAS, *Sweeteners*, 151; and NAS/NRC, *Saccharin*, 1–9.

47. John H. Weisburger, "Safety Assessment of Saccharin," *American Health Foundation (AHF) Reports*, paper presented at AHF's Food and Nutrition Committee winter meeting, 5 December 1979; and Robert Hoover, "Saccharin—Bitter Aftertaste?" *New England Journal of Medicine* 302, no. 10 (1980): 574.

48. Morgan and Wong, *A Review*, 529.

49. William Havender, "Ruminations on a Rat: Saccharin and Human Risk," *Regulation* (March–April 1979): 17.

50. NRC/NAS, *Saccharin*, ES–3–ES–6.

51. Food, Drug and Cosmetic Act, Sec. 409(C)(3)(A), 1958; and *Congressional Quarterly* (26 March 1977): 539–41.

52. Linda E. Demkovich, "Saccharin's Dead Dieters are Blue, What is Congress Going to Do?" *National Journal* (31 October 1981): 1950.

53. Center for Science in the Public Interest, "Food Safety Legislation," Washington, D.C., September 1981, p. 1.

54. Interview at Juvenile Diabetes Foundation, New York City, August 1983.

55. American Cancer Society, "Position on Saccharin," New York City, November 1980.

56. Richard D. Lyons, "Depth and Finesse of Lobbying Against Saccharin Ban Expected to Result in an 18-Month Postponement," *New York Times*, 8 October 1977.

57. James Turner, "The Saccharin Ban Raises Phony Issues," *Community Nutrition Institute Newsletter* 7 (24 March 1977): 4–6.

58. Terrence Smith, "Saccharin," Report for the American Council on Science and Health, New York City, February 1979, pp. 11–12.

59. Gene Bylinsky, "The Battle for America's Sweet Tooth," *Fortune* (26 July 1982): 30.

60. R. Jeffrey Smith, "Aspartame Approved Despite Risks," *Science* 213 (28 August 1981): 986.

61. "FDA Approves Aspartame Use in Soft Drinks," *Advertising Age* (4 July 1983): 1.

62. Chris W. Lecos, "Aspartame," *FDA Consumer* (February 1985): 23.

63. Dan Quayle, "Bitter Price Support for Sugar," *New York Times*, 28 July 1982. Also Department of Agriculture, *Provisions of the Agriculture and Food Act of 1981*, Agricultural Economic Report no. 483 (Washington, D.C.: Government Printing Office, March 1982); "Sugar Bill Called Aid to Fructose," *New York Times*, 2 November 1981; Stanley W. Angust, "Commodities: Sugar Now!" *Forbes* (28 January 1985): 128; "Sugar Sickens Free Traders," *Economist*, 2 March 1985, p. 65; "Sugar Could Bury Reagan's Caribbean Policy," *Business Week* (23 September 1985): 36.

64. Pamela G. Hollie, "Aspartame Builds a Market," *New York Times*, 3 September 1983, pp. 29–30.

65. Peter Petre, "Searle's Big Pitch for a Tiny Ingredient," *Fortune* (3 September 1984): 73; Christopher Lorenz, "Sweetening the Consumer," *Financial Times*, 14 February 1985, p. 29; "NutraSweet's Elimination of the Middleman Paying Off," *Boston Globe*, 21 April 1985, p. 96; Fran Brock, "Midwest Marketer of Year: G. D. Searle," *Adweek* (May 1985): 17–18.

66. "Why Monsanto is Bucking the Odds," *Business Week* (5 August 1985): 75–76.

67. Steven Flax, "It's Sugar, All Right But It's Not Fattening," *Fortune* (9 December 1985): 117. See also Kathleen A. Meister, "Low-Calorie Sweeteners," Report of the American Council on Science and Health, New York City, July 1984, p. 42.

68. "FDA Doesn't Savor a New Chance to Ban Saccharin," *Medical World News* (6 July 1981): 71–72; "Senate Panel OKs Continued Saccharin Use," *Congressional Quarterly* (20 April 1985): 730; "Filling the FDA Sweetener Bowl," *Medical World News* (24 June 1985): 65–66.

69. "Critics Say Cyclamate Not So Sweet," *Medical World News* (22 July 1985): 34.

Chapter 6

1. Lisa Belkin, "Fears of Toxic Shock Syndrome Alter Buying Habits," *New York Times,* 4 March 1985.

2. James Todd et al., "Toxic-Shock Syndrome Associated with Phage-Group-I Staphylococci," *Lancet* (25 November 1978): 1116–18.

3. Michael T. Osterholm et al., "Toxic-Shock Syndrome in Minnesota: Results of an Active-Passive Surveillance System," *Journal of Infectious Diseases* 145 (April 1982): 458–64; Jeffrey P. Davis et al., "The Effect of Publicity on the Reporting of Toxic-Shock Syndrome in Wisconsin," *Journal of Infectious Diseases* 145 (1982): 449–57.

4. Centers for Disease Control, "Toxic-Shock Syndrome—United States," *Morbidity and Mortality Weekly Report* 29 (23 May 1980): 229–30.

5. Centers for Disease Control, "Follow-up on Toxic-Shock Syndrome—United States," *Morbidity and Mortality Weekly Report* 29 (27 June 1980): 297–99.

6. Centers for Disease Control, "Follow-up on Toxic-Shock Syndrome—United States," *Morbidity and Mortality Weekly Report* 29 (19 September 1980): 441–45.

7. Walter F. Schlech III et al., "Risk Factors for Development of Toxic Shock Syndrome," *Journal of the American Medical Association* 248, no. 7 (1982): 835–39.

8. Mary Harvey et al., "Toxic Shock and Tampons: Evaluation of the Epidemiologic Evidence," *Journal of the American Medical Association* 248, no. 7 (1982): 840–46.

9. Kathryn N. Shands et al., "Toxic Shock Syndrome: Case-Control Studies at the Centers for Disease Control," *Annals of Internal Medicine* 96, no. 8 (1982): part 2, 895–98.

10. Bill Rados, "Tampons, TSS and Medical Device Law," *FDA Consumer* (February 1981): 7–9.

11. Marjorie Sun, "FDA Caffeine Decision Too Early, Some Say," *Science* 209 (1980): 1500.

12. House of Representatives, Committee on Energy and Commerce, Subcommittee on Oversight, *Medical Devices Regulation: FDA's Neglected Child,* Committee Print 98-F (Washington, D.C.: Government Printing Office, 1983).

13. Confidential interviews with FDA staff members.

14. Confidential interview with senior FDA official.

15. Dean Rotbart et al., "Taking Rely Off Market Cost Procter & Gamble a Week of Agonizing," *Wall Street Journal,* 3 November 1980.

16. Dean Rotbart, "Rely Counterattack: P&G Is Going All Out To Track Toxic Shock and Exonerate Itself," *Wall Street Journal,* 26 June 1981.

17. Rotbart et al., "Taking Rely Off Market." Pines later wrote that his intent was to maximize pubilc information, not necessarily to pressure P&G, but widespread pubilcity automatically created pressure on the company.

18. Ibid.

19. Confidential interview with FDA legal staff member.

20. Rotbart et al., "Taking Rely Off Market."

21. Pamela Sherrid, "Tampons After the Shock Wave," *Fortune* (10 August 1981): 114–29. In 1984 Tampax became Tambrands, Inc.

22. "New Activity Hits Hygiene Field," *Advertising Age* (28 January 1980): 3, 73.

23. "Tampax Faces Life," *Forbes* (29 May 1978): 61.

24. Peter Vanderwicken, "P&G's Secret Ingredient," *Fortune* (July 1974): 75–79, 164–65; Paul Gibson, "Procter & Gamble: It's Got a Little List," *Forbes* (20 March 1978): 33–34.

25. Larry Edwards, "P&G Finally Expands Rely Test After Rivals Played Their Hands," *Advertising Age* (7 August 1977): 1.

26. Dean Rotbart et al., "Procter & Gamble Isn't Ready to Give Up," *Wall Street Journal,* 5 November 1980.

27. Rotbart et al., "Taking Rely Off Market."

28. Centers for Disease Control, "Toxic-Shock Syndrome—Utah," *Morbidity and Mortality Weekly Report* 29 (17 October 1980): 495–96.

29. Rotbart et al., "Taking Rely Off Market."

30. Ibid.

31. There have been over 400 suits; P&G has lost a few cases, and settled some out of court, but most are still pending.

32. "P&G Ads Say Don't Use Rely," *Chemical Week* (15 October 1980): 22.
33. Rotbart et al., "Taking Rely Off Market."
34. James K. Todd, "Toxic Shock Syndrome—Scientific Uncertainty and the Public Media," *Pediatrics* 67, no. 6 (1981): 921–23.
35. Susan Okie, " 'Toxic-Shock Syndrome' Disease Is Striking Young Women," *Washington Post,* 30 May 1980.
36. "Disease Linked to Tampons Is Still Elusive," *New York Times,* 30 August 1980.
37. Leon Sigal, *Reporters and Officials* (Lexington, Mass.: Heath, 1973); and Sharon Dunwoody, "The Science Writing Inner Club," *Science, Technology and Human Values* 5 (Winter 1980): 14–22.
38. Unpublished transcript of newscast, KCRA (Sacramento), 15 August 1980. In the files of the National Academy of Sciences, Committee on Toxic-Shock Syndrome, Washington, D.C.
39. Sherrid, "Tampons After the Shock Wave," 116.
40. When the FDA was unable to persuade Tampax to comply, Johnson & Johnson and Playtex eventually dropped their labels as well. Mandatory labeling finally took effect in December 1982.
41. Sherrid, "Tampons After the Shock Wave."
42. M. T. Osterholm et al., "Tri-State Toxic-Shock Syndrome Study," *Journal of Infectious Diseases* 145 (April 1982): 431–40.
43. About 15 percent of the new cases were not related to tampons. Most were after surgery or childbirth or similar situations in which staph bacteria might gain entry into the body. Osterholm et al., "Toxic-Shock Syndrome in Minnesota."
44. Confidential interviews with senior FDA officials.
45. J. T. Mills et al., "Control of Production of Toxic-Shock Syndrome Toxin by Magnesium Ion," *Journal of Infectious Diseases* 151 (June 1985): 1158–61.
46. Nan Robertson, "Toxic Shock," *New York Times Magazine,* 19 September 1982, p. 117.
47. Confidential interview with senior scientist working on toxic shock studies.

Chapter 7

1. *Gulf South Insulation* v. *Consumer Product Safety Commission* (CPSC), 701, Federal Reports, 2d series, 1147 (Fifth Circuit Court, 1983).
2. D. J. Hanson, "Effects of Foam Insulation Ban Far Reaching," *Chemical and Engineering News* (29 March 1982): 34–37.
3. Cited in Maggie Lawson, "How to Destroy a Business," *National Review* (7 August 1981): 896.
4. Kay Dally et al., "Formaldehyde Exposure in Nonoccupational Environments," *Archives of Environmental Health* 36 (1981): 277–84.
5. Ann Crittenden, "Built-In Fumes Plague Homes," *New York Times,* 7 May 1978, sec. 3, p. 1.
6. Diane Burton Robb, "Our House Was Endangering Our Health," *Redbook* (October 1982): 82–89.
7. National Academy of Sciences, *Indoor Pollutants* (Washington, D.C.: National Academy Press, 1981), 46.
8. *Gulf South* v. *CPSC,* 1137.
9. For a review of the health effects see A. G. Ulsamer et al., "Overview of Health Effects of Formaldehyde," in J. Saxsena, ed., *Hazard Assessment of Chemicals—Current Developments* (New York: Academic Press, 1984), 337–400.
10. Problems in current research and the needs for more studies are discussed in National Research Council, Committee on Aldehydes, *Formaldehyde and Other Aldehydes* (Washington, D.C.: National Academy Press, 1981).
11. K. L. Geisling et al., "A New Passive Monitor for Determining Formaldehyde in Indoor Air," paper presented at International Symposium on Indoor Air Pollution, Health and Energy Conservation, Amherst, Mass., 13–16 October 1981.
12. D. Smith, M. Bolyard, and E. Kennedy, "Instability of Formaldehyde Air Samples Collected on Solid Sorbent," *American Industrial Hygiene Association Journal* 44 (1983): 97–99.

13. Thad Godish, "Interpretation of Formaldehyde Sampling Results," Ball State University, Natural Resource Note no. 4, Muncie, Indiana, 1982.

14. L. P. Hanrahan et al., "Formaldehyde Vapor in Mobile Homes," *American Journal of Public Health* 74 (September 1984): 1025–26.

15. "Fumes: Washington is Confused," *New York Times,* 7 May 1978, sec. 3, p. 9.

16. Richard I. Kirkland, Jr., "Product-Safety Czars," *Fortune* (15 June 1981): 128–34.

17. Confidential interview with CPSC senior staff member.

18. Confidential interview with CPSC senior staff member.

19. The results are reported in J. A. Swenberg et al., "Induction of Squamous Cell Carcinomas of the Rat Nasal Cavity by Inhalation Exposure to Formaldehyde Vapor," *Cancer Research* 40 (1980): 3398–3402; and W. D. Kerns et al., "Carcinogenicity of Formaldehyde in Rats and Mice after Long Term Inhalation Exposure," *Cancer Research* 43 (1983): 4382–92.

20. Quoted in Phil McCombs, "Home Insulation Sales Off," *Washington Post,* 17 December 1978.

21. Confidential interview with CPSC staff member.

22. T. B. Clark, "At Last, a Battle Plan for the Regulatory War on Cancer," *National Journal,* 27 October 1979, pp. 1808–11.

23. "Report of the Federal Panel on Formaldehyde," *Environmental Health Perspectives* 43 (1982): 139–68.

24. Marjorie Sun, "Study Shows Formaldehyde is Carcinogenic," *Science* 213 (11 September 1981): 1232; R. E. Albert et al., "Nasal Cancer in the Rat Induced by Gaseous Formaldehyde and Hydrogen Chloride," *Journal of the National Cancer Institute* 68 (1982): 597–603.

25. Confidential interview with senior CPSC staff member.

26. House of Representatives, Committee on Science and Technology, Subcommittee on Investigations, "Formaldehyde: Review of Scientific Basis of EPA's Risk Assessment," (Washington, D.C.: Government Printing Office, 20 May 1982), 81.

27. Reprinted in ibid., 122.

28. Michael deCourcy Hinds, "Insulation Group Criticizes Agency," *New York Times,* 21 January 1982, p. C5.

29. Kirkland, "Product-Safety Czars."

30. Cited in Karen DeWitt, "Industry Group Against Foam Insulation Ban," *New York Times,* 6 December 1980, p. 8.

31. Michael deCourcy Hinds, "Working Profile: Nancy Harvey Steorts," *New York Times,* 13 May 1982.

32. *Chemical Marketing Reporter* (9 February 1981).

33. R. Daley testimony in House Committee cited above in note 26, 157–70.

34. Marjorie Sun, "OSHA's New Thoughts on Cancer Policy," *Science* 217 (2 July 1982): 35.

35. Marjorie Sun, "EPA May be Redefining Toxic Substances," *Science* 214 (30 October 1981): 525.

36. N. A. Ashford et al., "A Hard Look at Federal Regulation of Formaldehyde," *Harvard Environmental Law Review* 7 (1983): 297–370.

37. The epidemiology is exhaustively reviewed in "Report of the Consensus Workshop on Formaldehyde," *Environmental Health Perspectives* 58 (1984): 323–81; and Environmental Protection Agency, Office of Toxic Substances, "Preliminary Assessment of Health Risks to Garment Workers and Certain Home Residents from Exposure to Formaldehyde," unpublished draft, May 1985.

38. L. Green, A. Boggs, and S. Wolf, "Formaldehyde: Evidence and Issues," unpublished paper, Harvard School of Public Health, March 1984.

39. E. P. Acheson et al., "Formaldehyde in the British Chemical Industry," *Lancet* (17 March 1984): 611–16.

40. W. E. Halperin et al., "Nasal Cancer in a Worker Exposed to Formaldehyde," *Journal of the American Medical Association* 249 (1983): 510–12.

41. R. J. Levine et al., "The Mortality of Ontario Undertakers," *Journal of Occupational Medicine* 26 (1984): 740–46.

42. See E. P. Acheson et al., "Formaldehyde Process Workers and Lung Cancer," *Lancet* (12

May 1984): 1066; and the discussion in OSHA, "Occupational Exposure to Formaldehyde: Proposed Rule and Notice of Hearing," *Federal Register* 50 (10 December 1985): 50441–42.

43. "Report of Consensus Workshop," 339.

44. J. H. Olsen et al., "Occupational Formaldehyde Exposure and Increased Nasal Cancer Risk in Man," *International Journal of Cancer* 34 (1984): 639–44.

45. R. B. Hayes et al., "Tumors of the Nose and Nasal Sinuses: A Case Control Study," paper presented at the Twenty-first Congress on Occupational Health, Dublin, Ireland, September 1984.

46. Marjorie Sun, "Formaldehyde Ban is Overturned," *Science* 220 (13 May 1983): 699.

47. *Gulf South* v. *CPSC,* 1146.

48. Cited in Marjorie Sun, "A Firing over Formaldehyde," *Science* 213 (7 August 1981): 630.

49. *International Union, UAW* v. *Donovan,* 756, Federal Reports 2d series, 164–65 (D.C. Circuit Court, 1985).

50. Cited in K. B. Noble, "U.S. to Offer Pair of Choices for New Formaldehyde Rule," *New York Times,* 28 November 1985.

51. OSHA, "Occupational Exposure."

52. Confidential interview with public interest group lawyer.

53. Dally et al., "Formaldehyde Exposure: Nonoccupational Environments," *Archives of Environmental Health* 36 (November–December 1981): 277–84.

54. House of Representatives, Committee on Government Operations Subcommittee on Consumer Affairs, "Federal Response to Health Risks of Formaldehyde" (Washington, D.C.: Government Printing Office, 18–19 May 1982).

55. Tamar Levin, "Insulation Lawsuits Abound," *New York Times,* 25 May 1982, p. D1.

56. Frederica Perera et al., "Formaldehyde: A Question of Cancer Policy?" *Science* 216 (18 June 1982): 1285–91.

57. M. Kraft and N. Vig, "Environment Policy in the Reagan Presidency," *Political Science Quarterly* 99 (Fall 1984): 415–40.

Chapter 8

1. The classic work is by Fischhoff and associates who compare expert and public attitudes toward risk. See Baruch Fischhoff et al., "How Safe is Safe Enough? A Psychometric Study of Attitudes Toward Technological Risks and Benefits," *Policy Sciences* 9 (1978): 127–52; Paul Slovic, Baruch Fischhoff, and Sarah Lichtenstein, "Rating the Risks," *Environment* 21 (April 1979): 14–39. A similar comparison of expert and public ranking of risks appears in Prevention Research Center, *The Prevention Index: A Report Card on the Nation's Health* (Emmaus, Penn.: Rodale Press, 1984).

2. There are many wonderful analyses of the distinctive features of the American political system. My favorite is James Q. Wilson, *American Government: Institutions and Politics,* 2d ed. (Lexington, Mass.: Heath, 1983).

3. See K. Malcolm Maclure and Brian MacMahon, "An Epidemiologic Perspective of Environmental Carcinogenesis," *Epidemiologic Review* 2 (1980): 19–48; J. N. Morris, "Epidemiology and Prevention," *Health and Society* 60 (Winter 1982): 1–16.

4. Jan Winsten, "Science and the Media: The Boundaries of Truth," *Health Affairs* 4 (Spring 1985): 5–23.

5. The studies are effectively discussed in Joseph R. Gusfield, *The Culture of Public Problems: Drinking-Driving and the Symbolic Order* (Chicago: University of Chicago Press, 1981), esp. chaps. 3 and 4.

6. William Havender, "Does Business Cause Cancer?" *Fortune* (23 July 1984): 127. For the scientific debate see Ernst L. Wynder and Gio B. Gori, "Contribution of the Environment to Cancer Incidence: An Epidemiologic Exercise," *Journal of the National Cancer Institute* 58 (April 1977): 825–32; Richard Peto, "Distorting the Epidemiology of Cancer: The Need for a More Balanced Overview," *Nature* 284 (27 March 1980): 297–300; Samuel S. Epstein and Joel B. Swartz, "Fallacies of Lifestyle Cancer Theories," *Nature* 289 (15 January 1981): 127–30. Note also John T. Edsall, "Two Aspects of Scientific Responsibility," *Science* 212 (3 April 1981): 14.

7. See letters to the editor by Alvin M. Weinberg, Samuel S. Epstein, Joel B. Swartz, and Bruce N. Ames, "Cancer and Diet," *Science* 224 (18 May 1984): 656ff., commenting on Bruce N. Ames, "Dietary Carcinogens and Anticarcinogens," *Science* 221 (23 September 1983): 1256–64.

8. Baruch Fischhoff, "Managing Risk Perceptions," *Issues in Science and Technology* 8 (Fall 1985): 83–96 discusses the full range of distortions affecting public perceptions of risk.

9. S. Robert Lichter and Stanley Rothman, "What Interests the Public and What Interests the Public Interests," *Public Opinion* 6 (April–May 1983): 44–48.

10. See the discussion of the decision by the American Red Cross to establish a blood banking program in Alvin W. Drake, Stan N. Finkelstein, and Harvey M. Sapolsky, *The American Blood Supply* (Cambridge, Mass.: MIT Press, 1982), chap. 5.

11. Or perhaps the appeal is just to the public interest leaders themselves who are upper-middle-class liberals and graduates of elite universities. Lichter and Rothman, "What Interests the Public and What Interests the Public Interests."

12. S. Robert Lichter and Stanley Rothman, "Media and Business Elites," *Public Opinion* (November 1981): 42–60; Stanley Rothman and S. Robert Lichter, "The Nuclear Energy Debate: Scientists, the Media, and the Public," *Public Opinion* 5 (August–September 1982): 47–52.

13. "American Cancer Society Critics Praise Recent Stance on Issues," *Medical World News* 25 (12 March 1984): 65–66.

14. News coverage of a product risk can be overwhelming. Johnson & Johnson's clipping service turned up more than 140,000 newspaper stories on the Tylenol disaster during the year following the first poisoning death in 1982. Company officials gave over 50 television interviews and logged 2,500 media contacts within the first three months of the crisis. David R. Clare, "The Tylenol Story," in *Cross Currents in Corporate Communications* 12 (1984): 42.

15. The convention may be passing. The *Washington Post,* and perhaps some other newspapers as well, now list a cause of death for each passing, a policy that is certain to tempt the amateur epidemiologists in us all to seek the path to long life through diligent reading of obituaries.

16. Reinhard Bendix, *Max Weber: An Intellectual Portrait* (Berkeley: University of California Press, 1978).

17. Margaret M. Heckler, "In Aid of AIDS Research," *New York Times,* 27 July 1983; Judith Randal, "Too Little Aid for AIDS," *Technology Review* 87 (August-September 1984): 10ff. Whatever the priority, some are not satisfied. Note the *Boston Sunday Globe* editorial, "Taking AIDS Seriously," 20 January 1985, p. A22, which calls for a "unified federal battle plan, . . ." more research and treatment funds, and ". . . a massive public education campaign on AIDS." While the secretary of the Department of Health and Human Services worried about AIDS, the Surgeon General worried about video games. "Surgeon General Sees Danger in Video Games," *New York Times,* 10 November 1982.

18. Kenneth E. Warner, "The Effects of the Anti-Smoking Campaign on Cigarette Consumption," *American Journal of Public Health* 67 (July 1977): 645–50; Kenneth E. Warner, "Cigarette Smoking in the 1970s: Impact of the Anti-Smoking Campaign on Consumption," *Science* 211 (13 February 1981): 729–31.

19. See G. Doron, *The Smoking Paradox: Public Regulation of the Cigarette Industry* (Cambridge, Mass.: Abt Books, 1979); and A. Lee Fritschler, *Smoking and Politics,* 3d ed. (New York: Prentice-Hall, 1983), esp. 4.

20. Jonathan Rauch, "Writing a Blank Check," *National Journal,* 23 March 1985, p. 625; note also James Bovard, "Stop Coddling Farmers," *New York Times,* 16 January 1985, p. A23; Ford S. Worthy, "Getting Uncle Sam Off the Farm," *Fortune* (18 March 1985): 128–32.

21. The sugar price support regime alone costs consumers $2–3 billion according to a recent report by the General Accounting Office, *U.S. Sweetener/Sugar Issues and Concerns* (Washington, D.C.: General Accounting Office, 1984).

22. Bruce Stokes, "A Divided Farm Lobby," *National Journal,* 23 March 1985, pp. 632–38; "The Sour Ploy of the Sugar Lobby," Editorial, *New York Times,* 9 December 1985. The effort to hold onto price supports has gotten some lobbyists and politicians into deep trouble. See Michael McMenamin and Walter McNamara, *Milking the Public* (Chicago: Nelson-Hall, 1980), which describes the scandals associated with the dairy industry lobby.

23. See for example, Steve Mufson, "Cigarette Companies Develop Third World as a Growth Market," *Wall Street Journal,* 5 July 1985, p. 1.

24. The use of experts by companies to counteract expert testimony against their products represents a new twist to the continuing battle between experts that is so much a part of our political life. The more common pattern is for advocacy groups to seek expert assistance in challenging the technical claims made by firms and agencies in support of new ventures such as the construction of power plants and transportation facilities. See Dorothy Nelkin, "The Political Impact of Technical Expertise," *Social Studies of Science* 5, no. 1 (1975): 35–54, for an analysis of the conflict among experts.

25. Tom Post, "Preserving Endangered Products," *Fortune* 109 (5 March 1984): 70–71.

26. See Robert M. Kaplan, "Behavioral Epidemiology, Health Promotion, and Health Services," *Medical Care* 23 (May 1985): 564–83, esp. table 1, p. 566; Leon S. Robertson, *Injuries: Causes, Control Strategies, and the Public* (Lexington, Mass.: Lexington Books, 1983); Susan P. Baker et al., *The Injury Fact Book* (Lexington, Mass.: Lexington Books, 1984). If the very recent gains in mortality reduction can be extended for several generations, an unlikely prospect, then the toll taken by heart disease would nearly disappear and a significant increase in life expectancy would occur. See John M. Owen and James W. Vaupel, "An Exercise in Life Expectancy," *American Demographics* 7 (November 1985): 36–69.

27. With apologies to Aaron Wildavsky, "Doing Better and Feeling Worse: The Political Pathology of Health Policy," *Daedalus* 106 (Winter 1977): 105–24, still the best health policy article ever written.

28. Robert Evans, "A Retrospective on the 'New Perspective,' " *Journal of Health Politics, Policy and Law* 7 (1982): 325–44.

29. Robert M. Kaplan, "The Connection Between Clinical Health Promotion and Health Status: A Critical Overview," *American Psychologist* 39 (July 1984): 755–65.

30. Louise B. Russell, "The Economics of Prevention," *Health Policy* 4 (Winter 1984): 85–100.

31. Karen Bunch, "U.S. Food Consumption on the Rise," *National Food Review* 29 (Winter/Spring 1985): table 1, p. 1 and table 2, p. 3.

32. George Gallup, Jr., "50 Years of Gallup Surveys of Religion," *Gallup Report* (May 1985): 3–5 and 40–41. But some feel the decline has been reversed. See Peter Francese, "Population Trends Spell Change for Churches," *Advertising Age* (25 April 1985): 37.

33. "Heavenly Possibilities," *Washington Post National Weekly Edition,* 14 January 1985, p. 39. For a confirming observation see James S. McCormick and Peter Skrabanek, "Holy Dread," *Lancet* (24 December 1984): 1455–56.

INDEX